A Treasury of

FAVORITE
SERMONS

BY LEADING AMERICAN RABBIS

A Treasury of
FAVORITE
SERMONS
BY LEADING AMERICAN RABBIS

EDITED BY
SIDNEY GREENBERG

JASON ARONSON INC.
Northvale, New Jersey
Jerusalem

This book was set in 11 pt. Garamond by Hightech Data Inc. and printed and bound by Book-mark Press, Inc. of North Bergen, NJ.

Library of Congress Cataloging-in-Publication Data

A treasury of favorite sermons by leading American rabbis / compiled
    and edited by Sidney Greenberg.
        p.   cm.
    Includes index.
    ISBN 0-7657-6061-4
    1. Jewish sermons, American. I. Greenberg, Sidney, 1917–
BM735.T74   1999
296.4'7—dc21   98–40645
                                                                    CIP

Printed in the United States of America on acid-free paper. For information and catalog write to Jason Aronson Inc., 230 Livingston Street, Northvale, NJ 07647-1726, or visit our website: www.aronson.com

Acknowledgments

The editor acknowledges with warmest appreciation the rabbis who were kind enough to grant permission to include their sermons in this volume. His gratitude is also extended to the following who granted permission to include the sermons of others:

Block Publishing Company for "The View From a Hospital Window" by Jacob Rudin

Mrs. Kallia Bokser for "We Belong to One Another" by Ben Zion Bokser

Rabbi Ezra M. Finkelstein for "What Is Conservative Judaism?" by Louis Finkelstein

Mrs. Hulda J. Gittleson for "The Purest Democracy" by Roland B. Gittleson

Dr. Avram Goldstein for "Kol Nidre Summons" by Israel Goldstein

Dr. David M. Gordis for "Leave a Little to God" by Robert Gordis

Dr. Moshe Greenberg for "The Birthright" by Simon Greenberg

Rabbi Erwin Groner for "Sources of Strength in Sorrow" by Morris Adler

Harper Collins Publishers for "Pro Vita Sua" by Solomon Goldman

Rabbinical Council of America for "The Grace of Tolerance" reprinted from the *Rabbinical Council of America Sermon Manual*

Mrs. Edith Silverstein for "God's Prayers" by Baruch Silverstein

Mrs. Edythe Steinberg for "To Hold With Open Arms" by Milton Steinberg

"Yesterday's Faith for Tomorrow" by Joseph H. Lookstein is used by permission of the author.

Preface

The sermons in this anthology represent rabbis of all denominations. It is a kind of who's who among the preachers in the American rabbinate of the last half century. What all the preachers have in common is a high regard for the sermon as a vehicle of enlightenment, inspiration, and enrichment. They bring to the sermon a sense of high purpose and uncompromising integrity. Pulpit aspirants can find in this book most valuable guidance in the choice of subjects and in the art of sermon construction. The serious Jewish reader will encounter messages that come from the deepest recesses of the hearts of the preachers and are therefore most likely to find lodging in the hearts of the readers.

Time has not been kind to the sermon. At a time of the fifteen second TV commercial, people have forgotten how to listen to a sustained presentation by a single speaker. The contemporary rabbis, harried and harassed by the multiple demands of time and energy the rabbinate makes of the pulpit rabbi, have sought and found alternate less taxing forms of teaching. Hence the emergence of the *D'var Torah*, the dialogue, the open discussion, in place of the exacting requirements and discipline of the sermon. But the absence of the sermon leaves a gaping void in the Sabbath and holiday services.

In an article in "Conservative Judaism" (Spring, 1996) Robert Kirschner wrote some sobering words on the subject: "Is There Still a Place for the Sermon?" A few sentences of his argument will indicate why he answers this question with a resounding affirmative. "Defending a religious tradition that compels moral conduct, that bears divine witness, what is the rabbinic role if not to speak out? As it is, rabbis find themselves on the margins of the secular, like channel 100 on a 99 channel receiver. How will they be heard? How will they get through to the Jewish people, let alone to society at large if not from the pulpits of their own synagogues?"

These compelling words underscore the significance of the sermon and help to explain in large measure the motivation of the editor in compiling this "treasury."

Contents

CONTENTS

CONTENTS

HARRY ESSRIG

Introduction

Many have announced the demise of the sermon; yet it has a peculiar kind of immortality. It has been linked with the spiritual and liturgical fortunes of our people. Absent though the people may be on an ordinary Sabbath, they would rise up in arms if the preacher would dare change the format of the service by omitting the weekly discourse. (Or is this a preacher's illusion?) When rating the competence of a pulpit candidate, the selection committee invariably gives preaching a very high score in the hierarchy of *ma'alot* (virtues) expected of the candidate.

Rabbi Harry Essrig has been editor and publisher of the "American Rabbi," Executive Vice-President Emeritus of the Board of Rabbis of Southern California, rabbi of Temple Emanuel, in Grand Rapids, Michigan, and Air Force Chaplain during World War II. Rabbi Essrig received his Ph.D. from the University of Michigan. He is a licensed marriage and family therapist.

The highlight of each High Holy Day service is the sermon (another presumptuous prejudice). The preacher exerts considerable effort and displays severe anxiety in the weeks of preparation required for the command performance. The people, once again impressed by the oratory, wisdom, and wit of their spiritual mentor, leave the sanctuary with the benign feeling that during the rest of the year the Lord's work is being attended to, though for the most part in their *absentia*. The Sabbaths immediately following Simchat Torah usher in a subtle depressive mood that afflicts the now-jilted performers, suddenly bereft of large and enthusiastic audiences, but the crowded and hectic schedule leaves no time for self-pity. The faxed services give a lift to the waning spirit and the cycle is resumed. The battle against apathy is joined once again though the robed warriors may often wonder: *Lemi ani amayl* (The salary is good but who needs the frustration?)?

In moments of discouragement, we turn to the stellar preachers contemporaneous with us or those already gone to their eternal rewards. Our religious life has always been punctuated by the brilliance with which past and present colleagues have woven tapestries of meaning around the words of the Torah and the Midrash or made the human condition with all its anomalies and paradoxes a bit more transparent. Who has not been thrilled when coming across a classical sermon that shines a new light on a clichéd theme? No wonder that Marc Saperstein's *Jewish Preaching 1200–1800: An Anthology* excited the rabbinical and scholarly worlds alike! This monumental work affirmed the centrality and relevance of the sermon to the constant and required revitalization of the Jewish spirit in all ages.

True that many of us are too harried the week long to pause in our hectic rounds and withdraw to our study to hone out a meaningful discourse. Yet I can attest from personal experience as editor and publisher of "The American Rabbi" for twenty-eight years that the homiletical juices are still flowing in our veins. This anthology is proof positive the homiletical harvest is still reaped and the twentieth century need not take a back seat in terms of pulpit excellence. Here is a record worth preserving for our own edification or as source material for a future historian. Hopefully this volume will reignite the languishing embers of an institution first established by the Jewish genius. (Need preachers be reminded of the trite and still powerful symbol of the burning bush.)

Of course the delivered sermon is at best ephemeral. The parishioner is uplifted for thirty minutes or so. (As the late Israel Bettan reminded our Homiletics class: If you can't strike oil in twenty minutes, quit boring.) The message is registered in our minds and impressed on the heart, but the impact is fleeting. Thin wisps of the spoken word loiter in the listener's quaint memory. Naturally the sermon's effect is enhanced by the style of delivery, the gestures, the cadence, the caliber of the voice, the sweep of emotions, etc. The experience is a concentrated one, heightened by an appeal to many senses (especially to overcome the threat of drowsiness). Hence a good number of us prefer to depend on the extemporaneous mode as the best way of engagement. This could well be the primrose path or a most thorny one.

On the other hand, there are those who like to fashion the sermon in the forge of the study. Missing of course is the eye contact with the worshippers and the reciprocal effect of shared emotions. The spoken word must be ancillary to the written word. Proof of this is the fact that most of us bring a manuscript to the pulpit on the High Holy Days. Preaching is an honorable and sacred art, to be ennobled by care and diligence. The process of writing imposes on us a discipline and a corrective to an otherwise perfunctory assignment.

The sermons presented in this anthology open windows (a phrase now popular with computer-wise preachers) to the landscape of preachers who assigned the highest priority to their pulpit stint. In the new technological assault upon the conventional forms of communication, who knows how the pulpit will fare, be perhaps transformed? Open forums, dialogues with the congregation, faxed sermons and Torah commentaries, pabulum of all varieties and innovative seductions based on TV models—what a plethora of challenges to the trite spectacle of a man or woman addressing a group of people "chained" to their seats and at the mercy of one voice! Some are already excited by the venture into space-age pulpiteering. I hope that the majority will cleave to what has passed muster for centuries. Here then is a nostalgic glimpse at what selected rabbis thought worthwhile to share with us. You will note, the very excellence of their writing is proof positive that the demise of the sermon has been slightly overexaggerated. As Ezekiel said: "Bedamayich chayee . . ." or to give this phrase an homiletical twist: By the blood, sweat, and tears of our labors, we will guarantee the survival of the sermon.

MORRIS ADLER

Sources of
Strength in Sorrow

The heterogeneity of human life is an easily recognized fact. Innumerable distinctions and divergences separate men, one from the other. Language, social custom, religion, race, and political affiliation are important areas in which people differ. Yet there are universal similarities which link all conditions of men into one global brotherhood. There are patterns that occur in the life of each and transcending difference gives to human life a common base. Else we would not understand one another and society would be a Babel in which people would be incapable of intercommunication. Nor would we be able to study human behavior and derive from our study general laws that prevail throughout the human family.

All men are born of woman and in travail come into being. All reach out for love and acceptance and all need association with their fellowmen for their fulfillment. All are daily moving forward to a fate

Rabbi Morris Adler was considered by many to be the leading spokesman of the Detroit Jewish community. He devoted himself to the field of adult Jewish education, on which he lectured and wrote extensively. He wrote *Great Passages from the Torah* (1947) for adult Jewish study, and *World of the Talmud* (1958).

that none may escape. A not insignificant bond is found in the pathos that hangs over all human existence. We are all kindred in mortality; we are all brothers and sisters in sorrow.

Who among us has not at one time or another known the sharp pain of grief, the poignant hurt of loss? Who has been able to insulate himself against the slings and arrows of outrageous fortune or escape the disappointment and melancholy to which human flesh is heir? Is there any one here to whom sadness is strange or anguish alien? Is there an individual from whom life has not wrung tears or whose lips have never uttered a sigh? The words of the Bible apply to all: "But man is born unto trouble, as the sparks fly upward."

For life frequently fails to spare us as with seeming, unconcerned impartiality it compels the good and the wicked, the righteous and the evil, the rich and the poor, the learned and the simple, to drink of the cup of bitterness and pain.

We harbored a hope, tenderly nurtured it through the years, only to have it dashed one day before our eyes. We once enjoyed health, but are now ailing. Once we were well known and rejoiced in the friendship of many, but time has passed over us like a merciless storm and left us bent, weary, and forgotten. Children who were to bring fullness to our life failed us. Who has not yearned only to be denied; dreamed only to be mocked? Every hospital bed reveals our weakness and every tombstone declares our mortality. Each of us has escorted a dear one to his or her final resting place, feeling that a part of us had passed away with our beloved. Every mortal has a date with adversity, loss, and death. Nor are the young free of sorrows. There are frustrations that youth alone experiences with unique intensity until wisdom teaches resignation. It seems inevitable that anticipation exceed achievement and hope run beyond realization.

If there is one experience that is common to all men, then it is sorrow. An old and familiar story illustrates the universality of sadness. A patient came to a physician in the city of Naples. He complained of melancholia. He could not rid himself of a deep feeling of sadness. The physician said, "I advise you to visit the theater where the incomparable Carlini is appearing. This great comedian daily convulses large crowds with laughter. By all means go to see Carlini. His amusing antics will drive away your melancholy."

At these words, the patient burst into tears and sobbed, "But, doctor, I am Carlini."

2

One of the perennial problems of human life is how can we face sorrow, seeing that we cannot evade it. How can man live with the adversity he is powerless to overcome? How can one reconcile oneself to loss, frustration, and grief? These are questions that loom larger in the lives of most people than the eternal problems about which philosophers endlessly wrangle and are more insistent than the issues that statesmen and diplomats are wont to deal with.

There is a mystery that hovers over the great problem of human suffering. Job wrestled with the gnawing question of the triumph of the wicked and the sorrows of the righteous. We who are contemporaries to the slaughter of innocent millions can ask questions with a poignancy and pathos unequalled in the past. Though centuries intervene between Job and ourselves, we are no nearer to an answer. We are confronted by a dark, insoluble enigma beyond our mortal comprehension. The *why* quivering on the lips of a mother whose child has been taken; the *wherefore* that rises in the heart of one whose beloved was struck down in the noon-brightness of life; the challenges hurled at us by those who are racked with pain cannot be fully answered. No human mind has the key that will unlock this eternal riddle. One trifles with the sorrows of others, who in such cases presumes to attempt explanations adequate to their grief.

Yet, though no full answer is available to illumine this dark area, we must still, somehow, learn to live with anguish and misfortune. Are there any guideposts on the lonely road of sadness, which can lead our feet back to paths of light? Have the experience and wisdom of the past any counsel and guidance for us, so that we may bravely endure the dark?

I have already alluded to one significant fact about sorrow that we should early learn, its universality. Have we the right to expect exemption? We live, why we know not, in a world in which sadness accompanies life and none may lead a charmed existence. When sorrow overtakes us, it is not because a special malignant fate has singled us out, though at the first moment it may so appear to us. As the seasons embrace both winter and summer, so does the climate of life include the wintry chills of age as well as the springtime of love, the autumn with its yellow sere, and the summer sun. This awareness that sorrow is our common lot will not restore a lost one or heal an ailment. It should, however, save us from an outpouring of that self-pity to which we would succumb were we to feel that none has ever suffered as we.

3

Sorrow is the obverse side of love. To ask for immunity from sorrow is to ask for more than a special dispensation granted no other. It is to ask that we love not, gain no friends, or devotedly serve any cause. To enter into any relationship of deep meaning is to run the risk of sorrow. When we become parents or link our life to another's or find a friend who is closer than a brother, we inevitably expose ourselves to the pangs of separation or the grief of injury or illness or death. But let us for a moment consider the alternative. One meets people whom life has wounded deeply. Fate dealt them a harsh blow. A dear one died, or a friend betrayed a trust. A hope failed of fulfillment or a kindness was repaid with ingratitude. They decide never again to give hostages to life. Life is not going to find an exposed flank in their case. They will not open their hearts in trust; they will not permit acquaintance to ripen into friendship; they are prepared to forego love, family, children. They are resolved that no human being will become so dear to them that his passing will bring grief. They protect themselves against sorrow. But they also shut out the possibilities of joy, companionship, the richest and most vital satisfactions of life. Charles Dickens' *Great Expectations* tells of a woman whose groom disappeared on their wedding day. She wears her wedding gown through the years and compels her life to stop still and deathlike at the hour of her great sorrow.

Such surrender does not necessarily indicate deepest feeling. There are people whose self-pity is greater than their grief and who in mourning replace the object of their sorrow with their own hurt.

We shall be helped in maintaining our balance during life's trials if we remember that sadness is the universal heritage of mankind. The contingency of pain is the only condition on which love, friendship, and happiness are ever offered to us. This recognition is the hallmark of maturity.

Nor should we forget even in grief, when we are crushed by a sense of overwhelming loss and deprivation, that much remains. Much remains in the sense that Lord Tennyson meant when he wrote on the occasion of the death of a dear friend:

> I hold it true, whate'er befall
> I feel it when I sorrow most
> 'Tis better to have loved and lost
> Than never to have loved at all.

4

Even as we pine that a dear one has died, let us be grateful that he has lived. The fact of life once lived is never utterly cancelled out by death. Love has come into our life and its impress cannot be erased. The poet suggests that if part of us dies when a close one is taken from us, part of the loved one survives in us.

> Your gift of charity and young heart's ease
> And the dear honor of your amity
> For these once mine, my life is rich with these,
> And I scarce know which part may greater be
> What I keep of you, or you rob of me.

The essence of a loved one is not to be found in mortal frame and perishable body. The qualities of mind and heart have entered the stream of our life and live in a hundred places within us. We are never fully bereaved. We live on to the unseen accompaniment of one no longer visible. The riches of feeling love gave remain. The deepened character, the sensitized response, the greater unselfishness, these abide.

Our sorrow can bring understanding as well as pain, breadth as well as the contraction that comes with pain. Out of love and sorrow can come a compassion that endures. The needs of others hitherto unnoticed, the anxieties of neighbors never before realized now come into the ken of our experience, for our sorrow has opened our life to the needs of others. A bereavement that brings us into the lives of our fellowmen writes a fitting epilogue to a love that had taught us kindliness and forbearance and had given us so much joy.

Sorrow can enlarge the domain of our life, so that we may now understand the triviality of the things many pursue. We have in our hands a noble and refined measure for judging the events and objects we daily see. What is important is not luxury but love, not wealth but wisdom, not gold but goodness.

Our sorrow may so clear our vision that we may, more brightly see the God of Whom it was said, "The Lord is nigh unto them, that are of a broken heart." Beyond the hurry and turmoil of life rises the Eternal. There is God in a world in which love like ours could bloom. There is God in a world in which human beings could experience tenderness. There is God in a world in which two lives can be bound together by a tie stronger than death.

Out of that vision will come a sense of obligation. A duty, solemn, sacred, and significant rests upon us: To spread the love we have known to others, to share the joy which has been ours, to ease the pains which man's thoughtlessness or malice inflicts. We have a task to perform. There is work to be done and in work there is consolation.

Out of love may come sorrow. But out of sorrow can come light for others who dwell in darkness. And out of the light we bring to others will come light for ourselves—the light of solace, of strength, of transfiguring and consecrating purpose.

LEILA GAL BERNER

Whatever Happened to Isaac?

Today we once again revisit the terrifying tale of father and son, a mountain, an altar, a sacrificial fire, a knife. Today we once again recall that dreadful moment when Abraham, guided by divine Voice, led his son Isaac like a sheep to the slaughter. It is a story fraught with drama and tension.

As we read this frightful and disturbing tale, we are reminded that Torah's stories are about the first branches of our own family tree. These first Israelites—Abraham, Isaac, and Sarah—are our kindred, the progenitors of our people, the Jewish people. So it is not difficult to personalize the stories of the Bible, for in them we learn about ourselves.

In years past when I considered this tale, I wondered about father Abraham and why he listened to the voice of God telling him to de-

Rabbi Leila Gal Berner received her B.A. from the Hebrew University of Jerusalem and her M.A. and Ph.D. from the University of California at Los Angeles. She was ordained at the Reconstructionist Rabbinical College. Rabbi Berner has edited *OrChadash Siddur of Puai or Religious Fellowship.* She presently serves as spiritual leader of Congregation Bet Haverin in Atlanta, Georgia, and teaches in the Department of Religion at Emory University.

stroy his beloved son. I have also wondered about mother Sarah, and why she is so absent from the biblical account. Where was she anyway while her husband took the child of her old age, the child of her laughter away to be slaughtered? I've wondered about Isaac's acquiescence, Abraham's God-intoxication, God's own command, the angel, the ram. And today, I wonder: Whatever happened to Isaac after that terrible moment on the mountain top? What happened to the boy after the knife his father held so close to his neck was lifted and the two went home?

Torah gives us some biographical information. Shortly after the incident on the mountain, we learn that Sarah died. We can only imagine how shaken Isaac, just having survived a near-sacrifice, must have felt. He had lost his innocence on the mountain, and upon his return, he had also lost his tender protector, mother Sarah. Midrash tells us that Isaac mourned for three years and that he could find no solace until he met Rebecca who became his wife.

Rebecca was known as a strong woman, somewhat older than the average bride, and a kind of mother figure for Isaac. Midrash further tells us that she was able to comfort Isaac over Sarah's death because she was the counterpart of Sarah in person and in spirit. Thus, Isaac loses a mother and gains a "mother-wife," and somewhat later Isaac sires twin sons, Jacob and Esau.

These are the skeletal details of Isaac's life. But beyond the "facts," we long for details—what was Isaac's life like *after* the *Akedah*? With the exception of the sacrifice itself, for what may Isaac be known? What distinguished his life other than the sacrifice? What did he achieve? Was he an adventurer like his father Abraham, or a "God-wrestler" like his son Jacob?

Isaac was apparently not a man of great deeds. After his brush with death, Torah recounts the prosaic, ordinary details of his life, but we never read of Isaac achieving greatness. No adventurer was he; he never set out on a great journey that gave birth to a people. He never wrestled with an angel or became the father of the twelve tribes of Israel. In fact, Isaac never did much with his life after the moment on the mountain. He seemed to have lived a somewhat muted, passive existence, a life in some way replicating his moment on the altar. There he lay, mute and passive as terror descended upon him. Life acted upon Isaac; he never molded life itself.

8

We learn from the Torah narrative that Isaac actually lived an unhappy life. Even before their births, Isaac and Rebecca's twin sons struggled in Rebecca's womb. Wracked with pain, Rebecca asks God why she must suffer like this. God replies, "Two nations are in your womb. Two separate peoples shall issue from your body. One people shall be mightier than the other and the older shall serve the younger" (Genesis 25:23).

From the moment of their births, Isaac's sons were in conflict. As they grew older, Isaac's judgment about them was flawed—because he was blind, he could not recognize one son from the other and he mistakenly bequeathed his estate to Jacob, the younger of the twins, rather than to Esau, the rightful heir. And his mistake occurred because his own son, Jacob, deceived him.

Yes, Isaac was afflicted with blindness. Another midrash tells us that as he lay bound to the altar, as his father's hand stretched forth with a glistening knife to slaughter him, the angels in heaven cried, and their tears fell onto Isaac's eyes, searing them, ultimately causing his blindness. The same midrash also reports "the tears of the angels also fell upon the knife, so that it could not cut Isaac's throat, but from terror his [Isaac's] soul escaped him." Though we're not quite sure what is meant by "his soul escaped him," two interpretations are possible. One is that Isaac fainted from the sheer terror of the moment. This is suggested by the fact that the midrash tells us that Isaac was eventually revived by the angel's voice telling Abraham to stop the sacrifice.

A second interpretation of this phrase is much more disturbing: perhaps Isaac experienced such profound fear that "his soul" literally left him, he became traumatized forever, his soul would never be the same. In either case, it is clear that Isaac was a victim from beginning to end; an innocent lamb brought to slaughter, an innocent victim of a blindness caused, the rabbis tell us, by trauma and sadness, by the tragedy of that awful moment.

Yet another midrash tells us that Isaac grew old before his time, prematurely growing frail and wizened. Clearly the effects of that moment on the mountain, that knife shining above his neck were profound. Though Isaac's neck was never actually cut—the wounds, the scars of that experience were very deep.

I see an important teaching for our own lives in this story. If we indeed see our ancestors Abraham, Sarah, and Isaac as a real family, as human beings in relationship with one another, their story (this central story in our tradition) may serve as a paradigm—either positive or negative—for our own family relationships. So let us move from the specific story to some more general conclusions.

Abraham's act, however well-intentioned, however expressive of his faith in his God, left his son with lifelong emotional wounds, scars which radically limited Isaac's ability to lead a happy and fulfilling life. A pattern had been set into motion, a pattern of trauma and consequence, pain and tragedy from generation to generation.

Chaim Guri, one of Israel's greatest contemporary poets, wrote about Isaac after his experience on the mountain:

> . . . Isaac, it is told, was not sacrificed.
> He had a long life . . .
> until his eyes went dark.
> But that hour he bequeathed to his descendants
> still to be born
> a knife
> in the heart.

So, too, we may bequeath through our own actions a knife in the hearts of those we love most: our spouses, our children, our siblings. Our actions have a profound effect, far beyond the moment of their commission. We must be conscious of our deeds, understanding that they sometimes leave indelible impressions on the minds, hearts, and souls of those who are affected by them.

Now, certainly Abraham's binding of Isaac was no minor deed— it was an extreme of an extreme. But our acts need not be that extreme to leave their mark. When we ignore or mistreat our children, or our parents, or our spouses, or our friends, when we are insensitive to others' needs, when we are unkind, when we are cruel, when we are indifferent, we leave behind us pain and hurt and often these deeds, however small or big, have long-lasting effects. I am sure that each of us, if we delve deep into the recesses of our own memories, has a particularly painful recollection, a moment when we were profoundly hurt, a moment we will never forget, a moment that may have affected our patterns of behavior or our emotional responses ever since. Some of us were abused as children: emotionally, physically, or sexually. Some of us have suffered in psychologically unbalanced or dysfunctional families. Some of us are estranged from parents or siblings. Some of us have

10

been deeply, deeply wounded by those we loved the most; many of us have been traumatized, many of us are heirs to that "knife in the heart."

William Shakespeare wrote in his play *Julius Caesar*, "the evil that men do lives after them; the good is oft interred with their bones." Though I am not as sure about the second part of that statement, I do know that the first part is certainly true, "the evil that men do lives after them." Just as the "evil" of the binding of Isaac had its effects long after Abraham's death, so do our own deeds. It is essential to remember that we don't live alone in the universe, that our human relationships—with those we love and those we like and even with those we dislike—must be treated with care. Our present deeds, however apparently small, *will* leave their mark.

In the Bible, we are told "the deeds of the parents are a sign for the children" and "the sins of the parents are visited upon the children." Our acts so often committed selfishly or irresponsibly or indifferently are sins, the effects of which may only be felt in the next generation or the next or the next. What we do now will affect the future.

Lest it seem as if I think only of the "evil that men do," let me also stress that the good that we do in the world is equally important, and that it, too, leaves profound impressions. An act of kindness, a moment of sensitivity, of forgiveness, or apology, an acknowledgment of responsibility, an explanation, a pause to think about what we're doing—all of these are very, very important. An example, a seemingly minor incident that had a profound effect on one man's life:

A colleague once told me about a time when he led a Shabbat service in a small town in the Midwest. Knowing that there was among the group a middle-aged man who had been recently widowed and who missed his wife terribly, especially on Shabbat when she had lit the candles during all the years of their marriage, he invited the man to light candles with him and sing the blessing.

After his wife's death, there had been no more Shabbat candles in his home, for it never occurred to him that he could light the candles. He had never seen a man do so. But now, in that Shabbat service, after having been given this honor, the man realized that he could indeed take on this beloved ritual act as a way of honoring his beloved wife. From that week on, every Shabbat, candles once again shone in his home. His life was changed by his encounter with my colleague. Now, every Shabbat, he experiences the joyful memory of his wife whom he loved so dearly. In the flickering of the candles, he feels her presence with him on Shabbos, he feels her warmth, he can almost smell the soup simmering on the stove. He feels less alone. Joy had come to dwell once more in his home. My colleague's act of kindness was a small deed, but it had big results—important results.

Let me return to Isaac for a moment. In all the hundreds of *midrashim* about the sacrifice, I have never found one in which Abraham explains to Isaac the reasons for his act. I have found nothing to tell me if Abraham ever tried to ask Isaac's forgiveness, or if he ever tried to help his son understand the need for the sacrifice. Isaac, it seems, lived his life out never quite understanding, at least not from his father, why he had almost been killed. There was no moment at which Abraham tried to help Isaac to heal. What a pity! Perhaps if Abraham had sought to share his own feelings with his son, some of the pain, a bit of the lifelong sting that Isaac suffered might have been alleviated. Perhaps healing might have begun.

If we glean any personal lesson at all from his paradigmatic story, perhaps it is that when we fail to communicate with those we love, we prolong the pain and impede healing. It is a pity that so few of us have the courage to talk with one another about that which is most deeply painful to us. If we could take the risk, maybe, just maybe, the wound would sting less, the ache would dim.

Our High Holy Days offer us an opportunity to begin the healing process with those we have hurt and those who have hurt us. It is traditional at this time of year to get in touch with those from whom we have become estranged, to begin mending the emotional fences, to begin tearing down the walls of pain and bitterness. This is what this season is all about: reconciliation, apology, acknowledgment of responsibility, repentance, forgiveness.

A few years ago, when I needed to "do *teshuva,*" to reconcile with someone very dear to me, I was almost paralyzed at the prospect of making the first move. It just seemed too scary. A rather practical friend of mine, in whom I had confided, brusquely but wisely said to me: "Well, Leila, there's nothing to it but to do it!" Easier said than done, I thought. But she was right. There was no better time than the present. So I took a long, deep breath, said a silent prayer for understanding, and picked up the phone. "There's nothing to it but to do it." No wiser words had ever been spoken.

Now is the time to sincerely begin the work of *teshuva,* our inward turning, so that healing may begin.

Now is the time to "turn around" to a more conscious and conscientious way of living, ever mindful of the power and consequences of our actions.

Now is the time for reconciliation.

Now is the time to acknowledge our responsibilities.

Now is the time to communicate honestly with our loved ones and our friends.

Now is the time to apologize to those we have hurt and to heal.

Now is the time to forgive and to be forgiven, if that is possible. If it is not possible, to acknowledge the work that still needs to be done.

Now is the time to repent in the best sense of that word: not mindless breast-beating and self-abnegation, but mindful and resolute self-evaluation.

Now is the time for *tikkun ha-neshama*, "repair of our souls."

There are many "Isaacs" among us. Now is the time to be gentle. Now is the time to be resolved to heal our Isaacs' wounds so that there will be fewer raw places, fewer scars, fewer lives and futures damaged or even destroyed.

To rephrase Shakespeare just slightly, but significantly: "The evil that people do lives long after them, but the good need *not* be interred with their bones."

BEN ZION BOKSER

We Belong to One Another

It is written in the Book of Genesis: And God said: "Let us make a man in our own image and after our own likeness; and let them have dominion over the fishes of the sea, the birds of the air, the cattle, and over all the earth, and all the creeping things that creep upon the earth." The drama of creation was moving to its final climax. Chaos had been made submissive to the discipline of God's creative will. Heaven and earth had been formed with varied creatures to inhabit them. And now God proceeded to create a man, in whom He would breathe of His immortal spirit, to preside over the work of creation, to dominate it, and to govern it.

Many moments in the unfolding story of creation hold our minds with the grandeur of their conception. For our purpose this morning,

Rabbi Ben Zion Bokser was born in Lubomb, Poland in 1907 and came to the United States in 1920. He received his A.B. at CCNY, his Ph.D. at Columbia University, and was ordained at the Jewish Theological Seminary. During his career, he served as rabbi of the Forest Hills Jewish Center, faculty member of the Jewish Theological Seminary, editor of the radio program "The Eternal Light," and co-founding director of the Center for the Study of Ethics at Queens College.

15

let us contemplate the verse, "And God said: Let us make a man . . . and let them have dominion." From the very beginning, God sought not a lone person, but a multitude of persons as is clearly implied in the plural *Veyirdu,* and let them dominate. But the verse also emphasizes that all the multitude of persons began with a single man. The rabbis found this verse highly suggestive, and they drew many a fine homily from it. One of these homilies proclaims what is one of the basic doctrines of Judaism, the doctrine of human equality. What inference, the rabbis ask, are we to draw from the fact that all mankind derives from it a lesson in human friendship and peace. We are to infer from it the doctrine that the families of mankind must not vie with one another claiming, "My ancestry is more distinguished than yours."

This is the interpretation one rabbi gives to the phrase "like yourself" which occurs in the golden rule in Leviticus: "Thou shalt love thy neighbor as thyself." We usually take this phrase to describe the quality of love we are to show our neighbor. But is not this an impossible demand? How can one person achieve so total a transcendence of self and so total an identification with another person? It is therefore suggested that the phrase "as yourself" is an explanation of the call to love our neighbor. He is like yourself, as precious as you are, a creation of the same God, a descendant of the same ancestor. We are asked to love one another with whatever degree of love we can attain because everyone of us is as honorable as the rest of us.

Judaism does not teach us that people are the same. No two creatures of God are the same. Even flakes of snow under the microscope reveal uniqueness of design. Indeed, if two people were the same, then life could not be precious, because there would be so many duplicates among the people of the world. The rabbis of the Talmud put it this way, "A man strikes many coins from one die and they are all alike. The Holy One, praised be He, however, strikes every person from the die of the first man, but no one resembles another." It is the fact that each person is an original creation, a unique combination of assets for the purposes of life, that makes life precious. It is precious because it is irreplaceable. When Anne Frank died in the Nazi death camp, a light was extinguished that would have shone for all mankind. Of her light we were able to catch a glimpse, but there is some irreplaceable light in all people, and whoever hurts any of God's children hurts all of them. As the rabbis express it, "He who destroys one person has dealt a blow at the entire universe and similarly, he who sustains a single person, it is as though he had sustained the whole universe."

16

Speaking of his own people, the prophet Isaiah on one occasion said to them in the name of God, "They are plants of My planting, the work of My hands in whom I may be glorified." The world is like a garden, and God is the eternal gardener cultivating plants. Every person He has made is a flower in the garden of the universe. It would be a monotonous garden if all flowers were alike, if there were an unbroken sameness everywhere. It is in the uniqueness contributed by each piece of foliage that the beauty of the garden is established. When each person is allowed to flower to the fullness of his potentialities then he becomes a unique plant, precious by its very uniqueness, in the divine garden of life, and by his being brings glory to the Author of life.

The metaphor of a flower is illuminating of our problem in an even deeper sense. For the tragic fact is that not all flowers grow to their fullest excellence. A gardener casts many seeds upon the earth, but some will not take and some will begin the adventure of growing and become stunted on the way. The same applies to people. There is only this difference. A flower can be stunted only by outside environmental conditions. It has no free discretion as to what it will make of itself. A person may be crushed by outer circumstances; but he has something else—a free mind. By his spirit he can rise above outer circumstances. He can defy the outer pressures working to thwart him. He can also yield to his own lower self and by an act of his own will grow into a weed in the garden of life. But the possibilities of going astray apply to all people, in every human family. The roster of names of those who have made the world better because they have been in it includes representatives from every race and every nation and creed. The roster of those who have been delinquents of mankind are likewise from no one human community; we have all contributed to it. By virtue of the divine spirit in him, every man is summoned to greatness; and by virtue of his limitations as a finite creature, who must by his own discretion choose between right and wrong, every man is capable of losing his course and being diverted from his destiny.

Judaism has translated this principle into more specific meanings which are of the very ground of the moral concern in our time. One is the call for true religious universalism. As one rabbi in the Talmud phrased it, "Heaven and earth I call to witness, whether it be an Israelite or a pagan, man or woman, slave or maidservant, according to the work of every human being doth the Holy spirit rest upon him." Any person who leads a moral life and is sincere in believing in a universal

God, no matter what his formal religious affiliation, another rabbi once declared, is as precious in the sight of God as a High Priest in Israel. Why do some people claim that they alone possess the full truth about God, and all others are lost in darkness? If I respect another man, I must respect his perspectives in seeing life, though they differ from mine. I must respect them as vehicles of truth, because I believe that God who formed all life has scattered the seeds of His revelation among all of them. If I did not believe this I would be guilty of the arrogant claim, "I am better than you are."

Our principle has also spelled out the call to intellectual freedom. If I respect another man, I must respect his mind. His ideas in economics or politics may be different from mine. But by those very differences he may represent an emphasis that I perhaps ignored. He may have caught a dimension of the truth which escaped me. As Rabbi Judah Loew of Prague said, "As the multiplicity of creatures derives from God, so does the multiplicity of ideas . . . and although the ideas appear to negate one another they nevertheless each have a sphere of legitimate meaning." If a certain body of ideas appears to me exaggerations and distortions of the truth, I have at my disposal the weapons of reason to argue against them. Why do some people try to coerce men with unconventional ideas to conform or to be silent? To cite Rabbi Judah once more: "It is improper to suppress the views of an opponent, but it is more fitting to encourage them and to ponder their meaning . . . . Thus will a person attain a fuller truth." Anyone who claims that the truth is his private possession and that all others yield to him is guilty of the arrogant claim, "I am better than you are."

Our principle also carried the demand for racial equality. The rabbis tell of one of their colleagues who once, while on a journey, saw what seemed to him an ugly-looking man. "What an ugly creature!" he exclaimed. The man heard him and said, "Why don't you complain to the creator that He did not do a good job?" At once he realized the depth of his sin and he craved forgiveness. Is it not the depth of sin to segregate people on grounds of race, to say to a man, "Because the pigment of your skin is darker than mine, you have to go to a special school, travel in a special part of the bus, eat in a special restaurant, live in a special neighborhood!" In the garden of God's universe there is room for a variety of color. Any man who says, "My color alone is desirable, and all others are of inferior worth" is guilty of the sin of arrogance, of claiming before another family of mankind, "My ancestry is more distinguished than yours."

Adam was not a Jew. He was not a Christian. He was not a Democrat or a Republican, a Conservative or a Liberal. He was not a white man or a colored man. He was simply a man, and he was our common ancestor. All of us who walk this earth are his children. We belong to one another. Let us reach our hands across whatever frontiers may divide us and grasp them warmly, for we are by virtue of the way that God has fashioned us, brothers all. Let not the families of mankind vie one with the other claiming, "My ancestry is more distinguished than yours."

DOV PERETZ ELKINS

Words: The Curse and the Blessing

I. INTRODUCTION

Kol Nidre is about words. Words in promises we didn't keep. Words in dreams we wish we had kept. A word is like a diamond. It can cut the thickest glass and destroy it. It can shine with the most perfect beauty.

Let's think together for a few moments about the awesome power of words. Our words, and the words of others which we read and hear. The words we say and wish we didn't. The words we didn't say and wish we did.

Words can be a curse, and they can be a blessing. A word is a sword with two edges; one for good, one for evil. On Kol Nidre eve we are called to use our words wisely.

Rabbi Dov Peretz Elkins is a nationally known lecturer, educator, author, and book critic. He is the spiritual leader of Princeton Jewish Center in Princeton, NJ. Rabbi Elkins has written for Jewish and general press and is the author of twenty books, including *Humanizing Jewish Life: Judaism and the Human Potential Movement* and *My Seventy-Two Friends: Encounters with Refuseniks in the U.S.S.R.*, as well as a series of handbooks for Jewish group leaders.

Professor Heschel once said that we should choose our words as we write a check. Each additional zero makes a huge difference. We take great care with each number that falls from our pen onto a check. So should we take the same care in forming the vowels and the consonants which fall from our lips.

Words are a paradox. They are a curse and a blessing. The Talmud tells of Tobi the servant of the famous sage, Rabban Gamliel. Rabban Gamliel told Tobi to go to the marketplace and buy the best piece of meat he could find, and Tobi brought back a piece of tongue. The next day Tobi received the opposite instructions: to bring back the worst piece of meat he could find. Tobi brought back a piece of tongue. Rabban Gamliel was confused. When I asked you to bring back the best piece of meat, you brought a piece of tongue. When I asked you to bring back the worst piece of meat, you brought back a tongue. Please explain your logic! Answered Tobi: There is nothing better than a good tongue, and nothing worse than a bad tongue!

II WORDS AS CURSES

1) Words can be curses. We know about the danger and the potential curses in words from the *Al Chet* which we recite on Yom Kippur. Eleven of the 44 in the *Al Chet* are about sins of speech, Rabbi Sidney Greenberg calls evil speech "moral leprosy."

As the Presidential campaign of 1996 gets under way this year, we will all be subject to the dangers of campaign rhetoric. The last several presidential campaigns have turned uglier and uglier. The words are dirtier and dirtier. The worse you can smear your opponent, the better your chances are of winning. A lawyer told me once that in his first year of law school, an experienced attorney told him: When you have the facts you pound the facts; when you have the law, you pound the law; when you have neither you pound the table.

A lot of our political campaigns are just exercises in pounding the table. Those who have no issues; have no visions; have no solutions; all that's left is either to shout dirty words, or pound the table and make a lot of noise.

Malcolm Hoenlein, executive Vice President of Conference of Presidents of Major American Jewish Organizations, says that name calling in politics "obfuscates legitimate debate. If you engage in name-calling, you can't get to the real issues."

The abortion debate is consuming our country, and dividing America. A lot of heat, little light. Recent advertisement in *New York Times* (1-5-95): "Words Kill. Words are like bullets—they can be used to kill." "Words of hate helped pull the trigger last Friday in Massachusetts. Two innocent women are dead today because leaders of the extreme religious right are heedlessly using a war of words to inspire killing. They call abortion providers "baby killers." They call hard working, law-abiding citizens "murderers and sinners." They trivialize the Holocaust by equating it to abortion. In speech after speech, sermon after sermon, on endless placards paraded at endless protests, they encourage their followers to hate their neighbors. They urge them to shout vile names at young women who have done nothing wrong . . . . Worst of all, they inspire their followers to kill and label the killing of abortion providers "justifiable homicide."

Professor Mary Ann Glendon of Harvard University Law School wrote (Op-ed, *New York Times* 1-10-95): "Consider how brutal regimes of chattel slavery and apartheid were legitimized by the notion that blacks weren't fully human. The Supreme Court endorsed that view in 1857 when Dred Scott came before the Court as a man, only to be dismissed as a piece of property."

What all these people are talking about, and we Jews have been a prime target of it, is the language of dehumanization, which diminishes compassion and increases violence, plants seeds of hatred and destruction. When people are *untermenschen* (subhuman) what difference does it make if you gas and burn six million of them in the ovens of Auschwitz?

The rhetoric, the words, of the pro-life movement have promoted a coarsening of the spirit, a deadening of conscience, and a disregard for the humanity of one's opponents. If they are not "persons," why do we need to treat them with respect?

It is surely legitimate to be pro-life and antiabortion. Those who take that position would do better to build respect for women and mothers, children and families, and to build a culture that is respectful of both sexes, and supportive of child-raising families, and protective of the weak and the vulnerable, rather than tear down their opponents with words that can lead to murder.

Our enemies have characterized us as Deicides, bloodsuckers, cosmopolitans, and parasites. The Nazis called us Communists, and the

Communists called us Nazis. It started with Pharaoh who called Hebrew woman *Chayot*—animals (commentaries on Exodus 1:19), so he could treat them like slaves. Two of his subjects, Shifra and Puah, disobeyed, and denied his characterization, as did his own daughter, who took Moses into the palace.

Historian Paul Johnson, in his *History of the Jews* wrote: "One of the principal lessons of Jewish history has been that repeated verbal slanders are sooner or later followed by violent physical deeds. Time and again over the centuries, anti-Semitic writings created their own fearful momentum, which climaxed in an effusion of Jewish blood."

Maybe that's why we were so sensitive when Michael Jackson made a new album that talked about "kikes" and "sue me, Jew me." Because we knew that millions of people around the world would be hearing these nasty words of the King of Pop, and we are aware of what has happened to us before when nasty words were spoken about us. Ironically it was Steven Spielberg who had the most influence on getting Jackson to change the objectionable words, because Spielberg had just finished *Schindler's List* and it was fresh in his mind what words like "kike" and "untermensch" could cause in human casualties. Perhaps if we had the strength to object to all the vicious canards thrown against us before and during the Holocaust, we might have been spared the horrors that followed those deadly words.

We forced Michael Jackson to change the album and that nasty song because of observations like that of Frank Outlaw, a man with an unfortunate name and good heart, who wrote:

"Watch your thoughts; they become words. Watch your words, they become actions. Watch your actions, they become habits. Watch your habits, they become character. Watch your character, it becomes your destiny."

In an insightful passage in the Zohar we read that one of the causes of our slavery in Egypt was that "speech" (*dibbur*) was in exile along with the Israelites. The language of the slaves reflected the language of their oppressors, so they could not even conceive of the possibility of liberty. They were robbed not only of their freedom, but more fundamentally of the linguistic and conceptual tools necessary to envision liberty.

Rabbi Nehemiah Polen of the Hebrew College of Boston points out that: "It is curious that in a century which has repeatedly seen language usurped as a tool of political enslavement, and in a society which is now so sensitive to subtle modes of bias embedded in language, Jews have barely awakened to the ways in which the English language frequently opposes our most central cultural and religious affirmations.

"When we use the term 'Wailing Wall' instead of 'Western Wall' we propagate the notion, rooted in a hostile theology and culture, that the proper vocation of Jews is to "wail." When Jews employ the phrase "Old Testament," we unwittingly support the view that the Torah is at best incomplete, having been superseded in a new dispensation. We ought to know that Judea and Samaria are not the same as "the West Bank" and that "Arab Jerusalem"—a new form of verbal aggression currently seeking a foothold—does not designate the "Old City." (The Boston Jewish Advocate, 4-4-85).

Rabbi Polen also points out that Jerome Brunner, writing on the power of mathematical symbols, once said that good representation is a release from intellectual bondage . . . We must learn to express the world in the words of the Torah rather than those of the nightly news. Redeeming our language from exile would truly give us something to celebrate."

Yaffa Eliach tells the story about being at Auschwitz with members of President Carter's Holocaust Commission in 1979, and then going to the synagogue in Cracow to have services for Tisha B'Av. Suddenly a survivor stepped up to the bema and demanded to conduct a trial of God, a *Din Torah*. He asked Yaffa to be a witness. She answered: "I decline. No, not I. I have no quarrel with God, only with men! I, too, want a trial, but not at a synagogue nor at Nuremberg . . . . I would put on trial each Western university and library for harboring millions of malicious words written against an ancient people, words like murderous daggers hiding beneath the cloak of science and truth - the propaganda of conceited little men. I want to bring to trial the pulpits of countless churches where hate was burning like eternal lights. I want to try the music of Bach and Beethoven for allowing itself to be played while my brethren were led to their deaths. I want to try the botanist for cultivating flowers under the Auschwitz sun, the train conductors with their little red flags for conducting traffic as usual. I want to bring to trial the doctors with their white coats who killed so casually, who exchanged with such great ease the Hippocratic Oath for sheer hypocrisy.

"I want to bring to trial a civilization for whom [a human being]

25

was such a worthless being. But to bring God to trial? On what charges? For giving [humans] the ability to choose between good and evil?"

After the Oklahoma City bombing, President Clinton gave an important speech in which he blamed the mass destruction of life partly on the rhetoric of violence in our society, in our world. "We hear so many loud and angry voices today . . . They spread hate . . . . Bitter words can have consequences . . . . They leave the impression that violence is acceptable. When they talk of violence, we must stand up against them . . . ."

Anthony Lewis, with whom I mostly disagree, especially about the Middle East, made an excellent point after the Oklahoma bombing when he said that certain fanatic segments of American society have so demonized their opponents as un-American, treasonous, peculiar, that it isn't any wonder that violence ensues. The tact, says Lewis, was invented by Richard Nixon and Joseph McCarthy. A recent example was Newt Gingrich's statement before the Fall 1994 elections when he said that the Democrats are "the enemy of normal Americans."

"The drumbeat of right-wing rhetoric in the last few years has been Washington as the enemy, the inhuman monster. Has that no connection with the rise of groups that claim federal agents are about to descend on them in black helicopters . . . . Pat Robertson, leader of the Christian Coalition, is very like the country's most effective demagogue. He tells his followers that a satanic conspiracy started centuries ago by European bankers (with Jewish names) was behind Lincoln's assassination and is now trying to crush Americans under a "new world order." Do those words have consequences?

Rush Limbaugh thinks it is cute to refer to people with whose views he disagrees as "feminazis." In a climate of calculated hate for The Other, how can you expect to have the civil discourse that is the mechanism of Madisonian democracy? . . .

Says Anthony Lewis: "We cherish freedom of speech. But we can defend that freedom and still hold accountable leaders who play on fear and hatred. Words matter."

Some accuse today's right-wing fanatics, including Pat Robertson, of "throwing gasoline on the psychotic fires of the untethered militias running around this country." (Frank Rich, *New York Times* 4-27-95) Reasonable Republicans must stand up to the crazies in their party, and, as Barry Goldwater and Arlen Spector have said, stop them from "taking the Republican Party away from the Republican Party." Oklahoma

City was a wake up call to this country, and I fear that the call will have to come as often as the shofar does on Rosh Hashanah, 100 times a day, before many of the sane people wake up to the danger of words. The ubiquitous militia training manuals, anti-American tracts, computer programs which teach how to build bombs and wage wars of terrorism against democracy, and other propaganda materials are coming not only from rewritten Nazi materials, but new ones today from extremist groups of Nebraska, California and other places right here in our own country.

After the Oklahoma bombing a German authority on right-wing extremism wrote about his liberation from a militia group in his native country, and how he was sucked into the fanatic atmosphere. Ingo Hasselbach wrote: "Of course lots of people in the movement may have been horrified by the sight of burned children in the Oklahoma bombing, but my experience as a neo-Nazi taught me that enough militant ideology and conspiracy thinking can destroy even the most basic human sympathy." (*New York Times* Op-Ed 4-26-95).

Our African American brothers and sisters continue to suffer the consequences of ugly words. Whenever a Jew calls someone a *schvartze*, it can lead to a act of demeaning, diminishing, and discrimination. Or when we call someone a *"Shegetz"* or a *"Shiksa"*—two of the ugliest words in the Yiddish language—we prevent all possibility of dealing sensibly and rationally with our children who bring home mates of whom we do not approve.

Three years before he became president, Abraham Lincoln gave a speech in which he said that "When you have succeeded in dehumanizing the Negro, when you have put him down and made it possible for him to be but as the beasts of the field, when you have extinguished his soul in this world and placed him where the ray of hope is blown out as in the darkness of the damned, are you quite sure the demon you have roused will not turn and rend you?"

I think if more people would be careful with the words they use about the "other" race, or the "other" religion, or the "other" ethnic group, we might look a bit differently toward the plans of affirmative action with which our government has for decades successfully tried to undo the terror of our language against those who are not White Anglo-Saxon Protestants.

Rabbi Harold Schulweis, one of America's leading Jewish thinkers and teachers, has wisely pointed out that the words we have become accustomed to use to describe the rooms in our home have a powerful impact on our daily lives.

"Once upon a time there was a parlor in our home. The word came from the root 'parler' which means to speak. It was the place where family and friends gathered to speak to each other. Once there was a library and once upon a time there was a study. But today there is a television room. Once the family would gather around the radio. Once there was radio to listen to Jack Benny on Sunday night. Today the home is transferred and transformed into a television cineplex. The home has become privatized. There are two or three television sets in our home, one for each taste.

"In this sense the synagogue study group, or a *havurah*, is revolutionary. For it pulls you off the television couch into a society with three dimensional figures who speak, who ask, and can be answered. On TV, if you don't like Jay Leno, you can turn to David Letterman. If you don't like either one of them, you can surf around and turn to Donahue, and if you don't like Donahue, you can turn to Oprah. If you don't like Oprah, you can turn to Sally. If you don't like Sally, you can turn to Geraldo. You can turn people on and off at will. But [in a *havurah*] we are in one living room, with human beings who speak, who listen, who question, who ask, and the medium of exchange is talk.

"Speech makes us human. Speech keeps us human. Speech defines us. And speech is what we have in common. A synagogue study group, or *havurah*, depends upon speech, upon words. What do I say to you and how do I say it? In Hebrew the word for words is *devarim*, which also means things. Words are real. Words are weapons. Words are instruments. In our tradition we have a great respect for the word. Remember that God created the whole universe with a word. And we create a group with words, with words between us. The Book of Proverbs says (18:21) that death and life are in the power of the tongue, and they that love it shall eat the fruit thereof. A brother offended is harder to be won than a strong city. And their disputes are like bars of a castle.

"Words are important. Our relationship depends upon it. A *havurah* group lives and thrives upon words. The Bible and Talmud are filled with concern about the use of words, for words can be abused, words can elevate, lift, inspire, exalt; and they can also denigrate, debase, destroy. There is talebearing and profanity, blasphemy and inform-

28

ing, cursing and false flattery, mockery and lying." Beware of the power of words!

I want to provide two examples of the importance of words that touch on Israel and the Middle East. The first is Mr. Arafat. I am strongly in favor of the peace process, not because I trust Arafat, but because I don't trust him. I have no allusions that he has been overcome by a strong dose of philo-Judaism, or has become a born-again Zionist. He still talks about *jihad* and no explanations in the world will mean anything to me other than the fact that he wants to push Israel into the sea. But I think he has become a realist, along with being an incorrigible anti-Semite, and that he has no choice but to try to make peace with Israel in order to survive politically. But I will still fight the use of that pernicious word *jihad* and hope the leadership of Israel, the U.S., and world governments will not permit him to get away with saying it with impunity. It is a dangerous word, as dangerous as other vicious and inflammatory words we have referred to today.

The second issue regarding Israel is that the right-wing has co-opted the concept of security. It's another example of how a word has been taken by one side of an argument to mean what they want it to mean, and to use it as a scare tactic.

James Besser, Washington correspondent for a number of anglo-Jewish weeklies, says that "In the public policy wars, language can be kind of superweapon, a lesson antiabortion activists have put to effective use in recent years . . . ."

It's the same issue—in which language becomes a weapon. To the right wing, territorial concessions have been turned into an issue of jeopardizing Israel's security. As if reversing the Peace Process would assure Israel's security, or that a return to the Intifada would be the panacea for Israel's relationship with the Palestinians.

In my view the right wing has no clear vision of how to solve the problem, and they have co-opted a catchy phrase to push their ideology. To me signing a peace treaty and putting walled borders between us and the Palestinians is the very best method of creating long-term security for the State of Israel.

We have spent most of our words this evening on the words that bring curses, and alas there is little time, unfortunately, to talk about all the *wonderful* things which words can do.

The *midrash* points out that the Hebrew for words is *devarim*, and it has the same consonants as the word for wasps, *devorim*. While words can tear at us like wasps, and sting at our flesh, we must remember that they can also console us, flatter us, uplift us, and inspire us.

The words we say in our liturgy on these Days of Awe are words which can change our lives for the better. The *Mahzor* is filled with uplifting concepts, noble visions, inspiring thoughts, and poetically-crafted words that clean our slate and write and seal us in the collection of words we refer to as the Book of Life; as we pray to be inscribed and sealed for a year of goodness, love and peace.

We must all remember the positive power of words, the blessing of words, when we speak to our spouse, our children, our loved ones, our employees, our colleagues, and our friends. Doctors, lawyers, salespeople, teachers, waiters, customers, clients and neighbors, can all bless the people in their lives with words of cheer, words of warmth, words of support, healing and soothing words. An anonymous poet once wrote:

> If any little word of mine May make a life brighter,
> If any little song of mine May make the heart lighter,
> God help me speak the little word
> And take my bit of singing,
> And drop it in some lovely vale,
> To set the echoes ringing.

The prophet Hosea had this in mind when he said: "*Ke-chu eemachem devarim, ve-shuvu el Adonai Elohekha*" (14:3) — "Take words with you and return to the Lord."

For us Jews there are Hebrew and Yiddish words which are untranslatable, and yet tell us all we need to know about ourselves. Such words are those in the anonymous poem "All I Got Was Words."

All I Got Was Words—Anonymous

> When I was young and fancy free,
> My folks had no fine clothes for me
> All I got was words:

> > *Gott tzu danken*
> > *Gott vet geben*
> > *Zoln mir leben un zein gezunt*

When I was wont to travel far,
They didn't provide for me a car
All I got was words:

> *Geh gezunt*
> *Geh pamelech*
> *Hub a glickliche rayze*

I wanted to increase my knowledge
But they couldn't send me to college
All I got was words:

> *Hub saychel*
> *Zei nischt kein narr*
> *Torah iz di beste schorah*

The years have flown—the world has turned,
Things I've gotten, things I've learned,
Yet I remember:

> *Zog dem emes*
> *Gib tzedokah*
> *Hub rachmonas*
> *Zei a mensch!*

All I got was words.

HARRY ESSRIG

Making a Life or Making a Living

There is a world of difference between making a living and making a life. And sometimes the truth dawns on us when it is too late to do anything about it. Thus one of the epitaphs in the famous *Spoon River Anthology* of Edgar Lee Masters reads as follows:

> I bought every kind of machine that's known—
> Grinders, shellers, planters, mowers,
> Mills and rakes and plows and threshers—
> And all of them stood in the rain and sun,
> Getting rusted, warped, and battered,
> For I had no sheds to store them in,
> And no use for most of them.

Rabbi Harry Essrig has been editor and publisher of the "American Rabbi," Executive Vice-President Emeritus of the Board of Rabbis of Southern California, rabbi of Temple Emanuel, in Grand Rapids, Michigan, and Air Force Chaplain during World War II. Rabbi Essrig received his Ph.D. from the University of Michigan. He is a licensed marriage and family therapist.

And toward the last, when I thought it over,
There by my window, growing clearer
About myself, as my pulse slowed down,
And looked at one of the mills I bought—
Which I didn't have the slightest need of,
As things turned out, and I never ran—
A fine machine, once brightly varnished,
And eager to do its work,
Now with its paint washed off—
I saw myself as a good machine
That life had never used.

"A good machine that life had never used, a fine machine, once brightly varnished and eager to do its work." Too many lives alas have an air of waste about them, a sense of futility. Too many people are tormented by the feeling that they're getting nowhere, that there has been too little meaning in their striving and hoping. Especially do we start wondering about ourselves as we age. It is then that we ask: Where have all the years gone? To what purpose? What have we accomplished? What have we gotten out of life? And we are often overcome by a great disquiet, by the horrible thought that we have been a good machine that life had never put to its best use.

Could it be that we have confused the satisfaction of making a life with the necessity for making a living? Have we concentrated on achieving the latter to the utter neglect of the former? Do we understand some of the basic differences involved in these two approaches towards our purpose on this earth?

For essentially different values operate in each of the two instances. Both are essential for human happiness but each operates under somewhat contradictory conditions. One involves economics and the other is a matter of philosophy. And that's where the trouble begins!

When making a living our competitive instincts are stimulated. That is how we have been conditioned by the present social order. In our striving for material possessions, we become terribly acquisitive. We want to accumulate as much as we can, "I bought every kind of machine that's known—and all of them stood in the rain and sun, getting rusted, warped, and battered, for I had no sheds to store them in, and no use for most of them." In the field of economics, it is largely a question of grabbing as much as you can, of taking whatever is accessible to one's grasp, of reaching for what is often the impossible or even the undesirable. Our hunger is insatiable, though the rabbis have reminded us that man comes into the world with his fists clenched and departs with his fingers straight and limp. We arrive upon the mortal scene as if saying the whole world is mine, I shall adopt it and we leave as if saying, I adopted nothing from this world. "As he came forth of his mother's womb, naked shall he go back as he came, and shall take nothing for his labor, which he may carry away in his hand." This is the way Ecclesiastes, the gentle cynic, passed judgment on the acquisitive instinct. But in our mad pursuit for the treasures of this world, we are never mindful of the final stocktaking . . . and so we are ready to sacrifice a great deal of what really matters most to us for the sake of the so-called making a living.

We forget that building a life is the more crucial undertaking. For here we bring into play the social, the cooperative, the self-fulfilling instincts. In this regard, we are no longer man alone, isolated from and at war with his fellow beings, clawing his way through the jungle of materialist enterprise. Here the gregarious instead of the egocentric "I" emerges . . . the measure of our happiness and security becomes not what we take from others but what we give of ourselves.

The difference between making a living and building a life is so fundamental and yet few are able to distinguish the two. There stand in vivid contrast to each other two distinct realms of thought and behavior. For the material and spiritual values, the selfish versus the selfless goals, the greedy versus the generous motive. How can they be reconciled? This is the tragedy of our civilization that the pursuit of money and the possession of things becomes the standard and the measuring rod for human happiness and not the way in which we enjoy all the avenues of human expression that are open to us. No, this is not the way! Buying toys for our children or grown-up toys for ourselves is no substitute for love and security. Riches and mansions and yachts have never been the mark of a truly healthy and adjusted personality. But we call this a bromide, a rationalization, a sour-grapes philosophy of life. We do not learn from the experiences of other people and seem eager to find out the sad truth by ourselves and then it is too late to do anything but wonder over the futility of life. It is indeed heartbreaking to see so many people strain after the material things, pant after the second car in the garage, the mink coat, the clipping of more coupons, because so very often they are not able to enjoy the attainment of such possessions since their neighbors have already moved another rung up the ladder of social emulation. What a dizzy round of conspicuous consumption and vicarious enjoyment life becomes for many of us because we have never realized that a life like a house requires an architect and blueprints and good construction . . . and solid walls against the contingencies of life.

I am sure that many would prefer it to be otherwise. Yet what in the world happens to us, to our dreams, to our hopes? I am reminded of Heywood Broun, the great columnist of the depression era, who once received an invitation to attend a college class reunion. He decided not to go. "The reason I'm not going," he said, "is that I don't like to eat with dead men." Twenty years before, a class of college boys had faced the future, "strong in the will to strive, to seek, to find, and not to yield." But in many instances the bright will and the bright dream had lacked the vitality to live. They had quietly died and in their place had come earthbound complacency. Heywood Broun knew what happened. He could not make merry at the banquet table where he would have to look at lives that were "the graveyards of high expectations."

The graveyards of high expectations. When this happens, our lives become tinged with cynicism, warped by complacency, destroyed by egocentricity! For all of living is essentially a compromise with ideals and a scaling down of high expectations. No one can escape the corruption of our innocence, the shattering of some of our youthful visions, the defeat of our most sacred hopes. Sometimes we must surrender to the stern taskmaster that reality is what we may have cherished most at some stage of our lives. No, we cannot avoid some tarnishing of the golden dream. The question is: how much can we afford to sacrifice of our better selves? The answer is that too many give up much, too much, even more than is deemed necessary.

We do not build up our lives. What we do is tear down our dreams. When it is too late, we discover that the task of making a living has been substituted for the very process of living. We eat and talk and dream business! We neglect our family, our children because of business! We do not develop other interests, do not seek out other outlets and avocations for fear it will interfere with our business. Then "towards the last, when I thought it over, there by my window, growing clearer about myself, as my pulse slowed down"—then each man has a chance to ponder over the accumulation of things, "which I didn't have

36

the slightest need of," and the wastage of the most precious years. This is the tragedy of modern living, the roots of our discontent, the source of our disenchantment. Our lives have become graveyards of high expectations and there is no second chance, not ever!

For what is the essence of living? Matthew Arnold spelled it out in a very simple and precise sentence. "Life is not a having and a getting but a being and becoming." Life is not expansion in wealth alone but growth in the personal sense. It is not the accumulation of things or the piling on of possessions but the flowering of the spirit within. It is not to impress others with what we have but to reveal to them what we are. Of what value is it to stand on top of the pyramid of financial success when our souls have shrunk to a pygmy height? Why embrace the horizons and set out to conquer other worlds when we are yet slaves to our own folly and greed? Should we find it necessary to fill the emptiness of our hearts with the clatter of new toys, new acquisitions? Is it really essential to hide our deeper sense of worthlessness behind a facade of material possessions. What is life? A having and a getting? A chasing and a hunting? A hoarding and a keeping? Or a being and becoming? A chance to release his divine kernel within us that hungers so much for the true, the good, and the beautiful? Why do we kill this divine need? Why do we choke off this flower of our yearning for the better things in life with the weeds of avarice, envy, and discontent with our lot!

Let us not concentrate so much on making a living. Too often does this involve us in the false and superficial, the mediocre and second-rate. It is basically a matter of compulsion. We must obtain in some way the means of our existence and often we cannot stop to ask at what price this is done. But while making a living, let us also meditate on the necessity for making a life. For here we build on our strongest assets. Here we confront the true and the genuine in ourselves. Here we have our freedom of choice. We make a life not because we have to, but because we want to, because we want to be a good machine that can be of some use in this world.

This morning we have withdrawn from the hurry-burly world. We are alone with our thoughts and our better selves. We reach out for some bit of communion with whatever infinite sources of spiritual renewal there be available to each one of us. This is the time indeed to take a good look at ourselves and to understand what Edwin Markham had in mind when he wrote: "We are all blind, until we see that in the human plan nothing is worth the making if it does not make the man. Why build these cities glorious if man unbuilded goes? In vain we build the work, unless the builder also grows."

I would echo: In vain we make a living, unless we also build a life!

LOUIS FINKELSTEIN

What is Conservative Judaism?

A few weeks ago a rabbinical magazine, *Hapardes*, told the story of how
some seventy years ago, in the later years of the nineteenth century,
when the great synagogues of Eastern Europe were flourishing, a man
whom we know affectionately in rabbinic circles as Rabbi Yitzhak
Peterburger, or more formally by his name, Rabbi Yitzhak Blaser, came
to his Yeshiva, looked over the young students who were gathered, and
repeated the verse (Psalms 71:9): praying to God "He might not cast
me away in the later years of my life, and that as my strength wanes
He should not leave me." As he repeated the words, tears welled in his
eyes. "It is clear that my years are coming to an end, and it is a great
comfort to a person who is approaching the final years of his life to
see young people to carry on where he is about to leave off." So it is a
great comfort to me in these later years of my life to look about and

Rabbi Louis Finkelstein received his B.A. from CCNY, his Ph.D. from Columbia University, and was ordained at the Jewish Theological Seminary. This Talmudist
author and editor was Chancellor of the Jewish Theological Seminary and an executive council member of the United Synagogues of America.

see not only so many disciples in the Seminary, but throughout the Movement so many people young, and even those not young in years, young in strength and vigor, able and willing to carry on the work which Solomon Schechter so well began. I would like to paraphrase the words said eighteen hundred years ago by Rabbi Joshua ben Hananya:

> "Would that I knew how to uncover the dust from your eyes so that you who were so dedicated might see the disciples of your disciples carrying on in your teachings."

Rabbi Joshua believed that his teacher was alive, as I believe that Solomon Schechter is alive, and I repeat, "Would that I could uncover the dust of your eyes, Solomon Schechter, that you could see the disciples of your disciples carrying on so nobly."

I would like to speak to you tonight about Conservative Judaism. What is Conservative Judaism? In discussing this I shall be mentioning names which I am afraid are strange to all of you except the rabbis present, but that is the glory of these men. They were great men and became famous as scholars and not in other circles.

In the early years of this century there lived in Yorkville a man called Jacob David of Slutzk, or as we called him in Yiddish, Reb Yaakov Dovid Slutsker. He was a great scholar who wrote a commentary on the Yerushalmi, and I had the good fortune to hear him speak about 1908 or 1909. He once told this story, which was repeated to me a few months ago: When he was young, in about 1880, he happened to find himself in Vilna, and being a great scholar, he had on his mind even when he went to bed a difficult passage of the Talmud, a passage which he found difficult to reconcile with Maimonides. He could not see how such a thing could happen, and it was impossible for him to forget it. He lay tossing half the night thinking of how it could happen that Maimonides should differ from the Talmud. About 2:30 in the morning he recalled another passage which seemed to explain the matter. He got dressed and went to the synagogue to make sure his new interpretation was right. Everything was all right. There was the copy of Maimonides in the synagogue, there was the Talmud, but there was no place to put the books. The synagogue was almost as large as this hall, but it was so crowded with students, there was no free space. This happened about 1880. Well, we have moved a little from that time, and I imagine there isn't a synagogue where you could not find place for Maimonides and the whole Torah at 2:30 in the morning, or 10 o'clock at night, or even at 8.

There have also been other changes in these seventy-seven years. The people of Vilna were very poor. They lived in squalor and sordidness and perhaps also in filth. It was unpleasant to live in Vilna, and, thank God, it is quite pleasant in the Concord Hotel and in our homes. We have done very well materially, and, of course, I do not wish either you or myself to go back to the filth and squalor of Vilna. But if we had to make a choice, if we had to give up the Torah for the wealth which has come to us in America, then I say it was a change for the worse. We have given up more than we have gained, because while the Jews of Vilna did not have what we have, I am afraid we lack something they had. And if I were asked which had the better quality of life, if I had to choose one life or the other for myself or my children, I would choose Vilna.

This fact can be documented. Those Jews of Vilna produced us. They produced the grandchildren who contributed to the American wealth, became atomic scientists, and built our synagogues. But what kind of grandchildren will we produce? Will we transmit to our grandchildren the strength, the spiritual energy, the ability to do great things which our poor ancestors in Vilna were able to give us? There are a number of things that make us feel that perhaps we are doing a great deal—Camp Ramah, the United Synagogue. There are also a number of things which make one doubt whether we are doing very much; for the moral fiber of our children like that of American children generally, gives one great concern.

I suppose the *New Yorker* for October 26 has been read by many of you. It should be required reading of every American Jew and every American citizen. There is an article about the soldiers in Korea. It is quite a long article, but I read it through. The boys it talks about are our own children, the young citizens of this country. The author, having spoken to many generals, tells us that two hundred Turks were taken prisoner by the North Koreans, some of them wounded, and every single one came back alive. Seven thousand two hundred American soldiers were taken—more than one third of these captives died. Of course, they were treated harshly, but so were the prisoners of the Japanese in World War II, and those of the British in the Revolution. Yet those came back in large numbers. The general giving the terrible statistics said the pity is that these prisoners did not have to die. They could have come back alive. But our soldiers, our youth, were not brought up to face the problems of destitution and primitive life. They have been softened, and so the things they had to do for themselves, they could not do. The Turkish prisoners recognized one leader chosen from their ranks. When he was incapacitated someone else took his place, but among our soldiers there was chaos, and many even took the part of the enemy and collaborated. Remember that this was a general speaking, and referring to the army, he said: "We can't train character; character has to be trained in the home when the child is an infant. We can't do that job when the man comes to us; you must do it for us."

I am not interested simply in the army situation. I hope that there will not be another war of that or any other kind. But I am concerned when I think that we need generals to tell us our duty to our children. Let us approach the matter in another way. We all have heard, I suppose, that the Russians have launched a couple of satellites. I cannot vouch for the truth of what I am going to repeat—I am only repeating what I hear—it may be wrong, but if it is, then the mere fact that it is being said gives one concern. It is said that America was not able to launch a satellite because of service rivalry. It is widely believed by many Americans that at this time of peril to our nation when our very lives are at stake, patriotic citizens at the head of the Army, Navy, and Air Force are more concerned about the prestige of their particular departments than about the safety of our nation. Obviously, if the issue had been spelled out in this way and if someone had said, "Look, if you don't stop quarreling, the Russians will have two Sputniks and missiles," the services would not have quarreled, and we would have been protected. But human situations are almost never presented clearly. We rationalize. There is something wrong in American thought and it is not merely our shortage of scientists. If we had twenty times as many physicists, and twenty times as brilliant, we still would be defeated if the moral issue were not faced, and if we spent time quarreling among ourselves when we need unity. That is what makes me realize how central the moral issue is in our lives.

A few moments ago a grateful United Synagogue conferred awards on many congregations and more particularly commended the Levittown congregation for its courageous act on behalf of human brotherhood. Let us consider our situation in the world. We are Americans and Canadians, a small minority in this world and we need friends very badly—we never needed them as badly as now. The world looks at our wonderful standard of living. It is estimated that only 900,000,000 people of the 2½ billion in this world could possibly live on this standard with the resources available today. As it is, most of the people of the world are hungry and would be glad to have the food we waste. We are the "haves" and they the "have nots." Yet everyone knows that if a rich man, taking all his jewels and the money in his pocket, should walk through almost any park in New York after dark, he might find himself in danger of his life, because many people in New York are extremely poor. In order to get what he has, some might also take his life. Throughout history a whole series of people had wonderful standards of living. The Roman people had it, the Greek people, the Persians, the Babylonians, and history is studded with the ruins of every one of them. How does it happen that every success leads to failure, that every empire becomes great and falls to waste?

In the second century of this era the Roman empire was a wondrous thing to behold. In the fifth century it was a heap of ruins because something had happened to the moral fiber of the Roman people. Their wealth and power could not protect them when the moral fiber had gone. It is time for all of us now to find a few more scientists and launch a Sputnik of our own, but how can we handle the disease which is warning us of oncoming destruction—the fate which has befallen each empire before us—the loss of moral character? Time was when rabbis, priests, and ministers talked to us about moral character. Now generals talk about it. Perhaps people will listen to them. I say the spirit of Vilna was preferable to the spirit of New York because the spirit of Vilna was the one which created New York, but from the spirit of New York one can only create a desert or Dark Ages such as followed the fall of Rome.

Now, therefore, what is our problem as Americans, as Jews, and as citizens of the world, and why is the United Synagogue moving on to the world scene in 1957? Conservative Judaism is an effort to recapture the spirit of Vilna and to make it conform to the spirit of our time. It is an effort to do nothing less than save the free world. The Russians have shown and the Chinese are showing that a great deal can be accomplished by regimentation of man, by making people work together. I am told that the man who invented the intercontinental missile for the Russians was held under house arrest for six years. He was given a wonderful salary but could not leave his house. That is not how we

43

do things in America. In America, although most Americans do not know it, there is something of the spirit of Vilna, something of the spirit of the prophets. We don't like outer force to compel us to do what we ought to. We have been relying on inner compulsion, the spiritual power of man, to deal with his problems. Of course, it is much better that it should be so, for with outer compulsion there is no morality. A person who fasts on Yom Kippur because he has nothing to eat and for no other reason is not really heeding the commandment. Following this notion, the Prophets tried to make of us a people dedicated to Judaism out of love for God and man—not out of regimentation—a people struggling to do the right thing because this is the ultimate goal of humanity. How can the United Synagogue help to achieve this goal?

It was difficult to maintain our tradition in poverty and persecution. The survival of Jews generation after generation, in constant terror, and remaining sane, and even becoming great men is one of the miracles of history. Now we have the challenge of wealth. When I was a little boy there was a story in my first reader under the title, "Too Rich to Afford It." All of us are now too rich to afford moral laxity.

Conservative Judaism is therefore trying to deal with a basic human problem: How to retain what the Prophets and rabbis of the Torah taught us, the inner discipline. That has been our purpose from the days of Moses until yesterday and today, to discipline our lives to the worship of God.

Now, dear friends, if we could reintroduce this sensitivity into our own Jewish life; if the time would ever come when a person would come into a room like this and find it kosher—not only kosher in the sense that there is no one who eats forbidden food here, but also in the sense that at this convention no one told an untruth, there was no gossiping in these four days, no jealousy, and no hatred. What a world this would be and how different would be the place of Jews in this world.

What we need here is not more institutional organization, but more devotion and dedication to God. I am not a bit interested in the size, or wealth, or prestige of the Seminary. But I am interested in the honor of God and in whether the Seminary is an instrument to serve God and can take its place with other institutions to serve God. Each time the idea comes to expand this institution I ask, "Is it good for God, or is there some better way of doing His work?" If we could live up to the tradition of Schechter, would we not become a moral force capable of wonderful achievement?

I can document this. What has been the greater force for mankind, the synagogue or the Temple? The answer must be the synagogue, because the synagogue always said it was second to the Temple. From the very first days we always prayed for the restoration of the Temple. The synagogue, a standing institution, prays for its own destruction. We turn to the East: May God come to dwell in this Temple. The realization is with us that while there is no longer a building, the institution which substitutes for it gave birth to the church and the mosque and through them the faiths of the world.

Today we celebrate the establishment of a world union of synagogues. I hope the spirit of Schechter which reflects prophecy and saintliness will somehow find its way into the hearts of our children; that the trend toward demoralization, which is real and threatening, can be stemmed; that somehow we can bring about in these later years that Messianic age which should really come upon us; that God himself may reign over us; that all of us may feel subject to His will; and that together with all the things our children have, they will want to serve Him all the time; that we come really to love Him, and fear Him, and feel His presence among us, and that when we are called by temptation and find it hard to keep the Sabbath because it separates us from our friends, or it feels strange to wear tefillin and recite prayers in an ancient language, we shall persist, nonetheless. It is hard, it is difficult to observe the rituals, and other matters are even more difficult. It is more difficult to tell the truth, to be honest, than to keep kosher and to keep the Sabbath. It is hard, but Hillel said, "According to the labor is the reward." Hillel meant the reward in the future world, but no great thing has ever been achieved easily. Great things are only achieved with great difficulty, and when I come to a passage in the Torah which seems easy, then I know it is not easy, that it is profound, and I study until it becomes hard, and I know what I am talking about. The moral life is difficult, the life of righteousness and prophecy is not easy. The good life of the Vilna Jews is even harder for us because we have temptation all around us, yet there is a great world waiting to be created, and God is bound to create. It is His will that my children and grandchildren may be the instruments to bring about His kingdom.

The Purest Democracy

*Sermon Delivered at the Dedication
of the Military Cemetery on Iwo Jima*

This is perhaps the grimmest and surely the holiest task we have faced since D-Day. Here before us lie the bodies of comrades and friends. Men who until yesterday or last week laughed with us, joked with us, trained with us. Men who were on the same ships with us and went over the sides with us as we prepared to hit the beaches of this island. Men who fought with us and feared with us. Somewhere in this plot of ground there may lie the man who could have discovered the cure for cancer. Under one of these Christian crosses or beneath a Jewish Star of David there may rest now a man who was destined to be a great prophet ... to find the way, perhaps, for all to live in plenty, with

Rabbi Roland B. Gittelsohn was ordained at Hebrew Union College in 1936. He served as rabbi at Temple Israel in Boston from 1953–1977 and was Rabbi Emeritus in 1997. He was Chaplain of the United States Naval Reserve from 1943–1946 and delivered the dedicatory sermon at the 5th Marine Division Cemetery at Iwo Jima. He was President of the Association of Reform Zionists of America from 1977–1984 and President of the Central Conference of American Rabbis from 1969–1971. The author of many books, Rabbi Gittelsohn served on President Truman's Committee on Civil Rights in 1947 and several committees of the Governor of Massachusetts.

poverty and hardship for none. Now they lie here silently in this sacred soil, and we gather to consecrate this earth in their memory.

It is not easy to do so. Some of us have buried our closest friends here. We saw these men killed before our very eyes. Any one of us might have died in their places. Indeed, some of us are alive and breathing at this very moment only because men who lie here beneath us had the courage and strength to give their lives for us. To speak in memory of such men is a solemn privilege. Of them too, can it be said what was said at Gettysburg, "The world will little note nor long remember what we say here. It can never forget what they did here."

No, our poor power of speech can add nothing to what these men and the other dead of our division who are not here have already done. All that we even hope to do is follow their example. To show the same selfless courage in peace that they did in war. To swear that, by the grace of God and the stubborn strength and power of human will, their sons and ours shall never suffer these pains again. These men have done their jobs well. They have paid the ghastly price of freedom. If that freedom be once again lost, as it was after the last war, the unforgivable blame will be ours, not theirs. So it is we, the living, who are here to be dedicated and consecrated.

We dedicate ourselves, first, to live together in peace the way they fought and are buried in this war. Here lie men who loved America because their ancestors generations ago helped in her founding, and other men who loved her with equal passion because they themselves or their own fathers escaped from oppression to her blessed shores. Here lie officers and men, Negroes and whites, rich men and poor . . . together. Here are Protestants, Catholics, and Jews . . . together. Here no man prefers another because of his faith or despises him because of his color. Here there are no quotas of how many from each group are admitted or allowed. Among these men there is no discrimination. No prejudices. No hatred. Theirs is the highest and purest democracy.

Any man among us, the living, who fails to understand that will thereby betray those who lie here dead. Whoever of us lifts his hand in hate against a brother, or thinks himself superior to those who happen to be in the minority, makes of this ceremony and of the bloody sacrifices it commemorates, an empty, hollow mockery. To this, then, as our solemn, sacred duty, do we the living now dedicate ourselves to the right of Protestants, Catholics, and Jews, of white men and Negroes alike, to enjoy the democracy for which all of them have here paid the price.

To one thing more do we consecrate ourselves in memory of those who sleep beneath these crosses and stars. We shall not foolishly suppose, as did the last generation of America's fighting men, that victory on the battlefield will automatically guarantee the triumph of democracy at home. This war, with all its frightful heartache and suffering, is but the beginning of our generation's struggle for democracy. When the last battle has been won, there will be those at home, as there were last time, who will want us to turn our backs in selfish isolation on the rest of organized humanity, and thus to sabotage the very peace for which we fight. We promise you who lie here: we will not do that! We will join hands with Britain, China, Russia—in peace, even as we have in war, to build the kind of world for which you died.

When the last shot has been fired, there will still be those whose eyes are turned backward, not forward, who will be satisfied with those wide extremes of poverty and wealth in which the seeds of another war can breed. We promise you, our departed comrades: this, too, we will not permit. This war has been fought by the common man. Its fruits of peace must be enjoyed by the common man! We promise, by all that is sacred and holy, that your sons—the sons of miners and millers, the sons of farmers and workers—will inherit from your death the right to a living that is decent and secure.

When the final cross has been placed in the last cemetery, once again there will be those to whom profit is more important than peace, who will insist with the voice of sweet reasonableness and appeasement that it is better to trade with the enemies of mankind than, by crushing them, to lose their profit. To you who sleep here silently, we give our promise: we will not listen! We will not forget that some of you were burnt with oil that came from American wells, that many of you were killed by shells fashioned from American steel. We promise that when once again men seek profit at your expense, we shall remember how you looked when we placed you reverently, lovingly, in the ground.

Thus do we memorialize those who, having ceased living with us, now live within us. Thus do we consecrate ourselves, the living, to carry on the struggle they began. Too much blood has gone into this soil for us to let it lie barren. Too much pain and heartache have fertilized the earth on which we stand. We here solemnly swear: this shall not be in vain! Out of this, and from the suffering and sorrow of those who mourn, this will come—we promise—the birth of a new freedom for the sons of men everywhere. Amen.

SOLOMON GOLDMAN

Pro Vita Sua

The careers of all peoples known to history, even as the lives of most human beings, have been marked by selfishness. The strong destroyed the weak; the many engulfed the few. Some executed their tasks with an obduracy that makes us wonder whether human and beastly are not really synonymous; others with a self-righteousness that makes us marvel at the devil's familiarity with Scripture. All peoples assumed their indispensability to the welfare of humanity as axiomatic. Each loudly proclaimed to the world that it was the guardian of a sacred trust, the apostle of a divine mission. Peoples took themselves for granted. To have suggested that even the least amongst them was an encumbrance to the march of progress would have been denounced as treason. Thus, often a nation spent centuries in a slow process of disintegration and decay. Yet no one dared suggest that its moth and rust

Rabbi Solomon Goldman was born in Volhynia. He received his A.B. at NYU and was ordained at the Jewish Theological Seminary. A Conservative rabbi, eloquent orator, and author, he served as the national President of the Zionist Organization of America. He also received several honorary degrees.

created an obstical to humanity's free-breathing. Even when death knocked at the door, suicide was not hinted at by others and certainly not contemplated by itself. As long as there was still a breath of life in its weary body it was unable to analyze itself or anticipate its end with philosophical detachment and equanimity.

To this the Jew has been an exception. Full of the vigor of life with the strength of Hercules in his loins, he has often paused to question the value and purport of his existence. "Is the assimilation of the Jew desirable?" he has asked himself. In other words, shall the Jew live or give up the ghost? This question has been considered pro and con by innumerable publicists. Can one point to such a mark of detachment on the part of any other racial, historical, or cultural group? Try to reword the subject, substituting the name of another group for the Jewish. "Is the assimilation of the French desirable?" "Is the assimilation of the Belgians desirable?" The mere juxtaposition of the words seems to produce an unnatural ring.

Why is it that the Jew is capable of such supreme objectivity? Why can he submit his very existence to scrutiny and debate? Because for centuries he has constituted a minority group in many lands amongst a vast variety of peoples. A minority, in order to exist, cannot for too long a time entertain an uncalculating, overweening loyalty to itself or to any idea or institution, be it ever so lofty and sacred. The majority imposes upon it the need of self-analysis, of self-searching, alas often, the need of self-denial and self-immolation. "Crowd action is the outcome of agreement based on concurrences of emotion rather than thought." The minority to live must think, must be on the alert. It dare not bury its head in the sand if it hopes to enjoy the least modicum of comfort and freedom. It must examine and evaluate traditions and cultures not of its own making. It cannot remain narrow and provincial. It must transcend the limits of its own group and cast its vision far and wide. Its outlook becomes universal, its perspective international.

Our social democracies, or better, majorities of the twentieth century challenge differences. Main Street detests innovations in style, but positively rings the alarm when faced by a new experience or idea. The crowd mind thrives on security and conformity. It has neither the acumen nor the patience to experiment with the unfamiliar. The Jew, too, has often tried to minimize his own divergence and anomalousness. He too picked up the refrain, "Hail, hail, the gang's all here" and all alike, but his endless wandering and ceaseless struggle have purged him of a chauvinism characteristic of most peoples.

"If there is anything distinctive about the temper of Jewish thought today," writes a convinced assimilationist, "it is that it has largely transcended the limits of any localism, however vast or powerful. It refuses to make a fetish of any localism or lineage but insists on utilizing the cultural goods of all localisms and of every lineage for the deeper personal synthesis."

Or, to use the words of another brilliant anthropologist:

> The intelligent Jew today is often an internationalist. Wherever he may reside, he is able to preserve a certain aloofness with reference to purely local issues and thus be saved the bunkum of national conceits. He is also relatively free from narrow traditionalism. More often than not, he is at home in more than one country and not infrequently in more than one continent. Not being fanatically addicted to any nation, he is able to appreciate the worth of all. The sad historical experience of his people has taught him the evils of race discrimination. His national extraterritoriality makes of him not only an internationalist but an individualist, an intellectual freelance, who is capable of judging economic, social, and political issues by their merits, unencumbered by the historic dogmas, prejudices, and biases of those whose egos are shot through with national self-consciousness.

It is of such a "temper" that the world has great need. Humanity has suffered enough through crowds and majorities. Shall Israel abdicate and become submerged in the many procrusteanizing groups and leveling majorities? Shall he give up his international individuality for membership in some particularistic group? Shall he give up his minority individuality merely to add to the numerical strength of the arrogant Nordic or phlegmatic Slav? He cannot become assimilated into an Esperanto-speaking universalist unless perhaps he ascend to Mars. He cannot become a pure universalist. He must be submerged into some nationalistic, particularistic group. Why barter his own nationalism or even tribalism or, if you will, his religious denominationalism for another?

It is no mere accident that the Jew has proved such a vital factor in the development of Western civilization. To survive as a minority he has had to use his wits. His precarious existence imposed upon him moral discipline and mental alertness. His homelessness made him a sojourner in many lands, an interpreter and intermediary among many peoples. He thus became well-nigh indispensable to civilization. "If we were so unfortunate as to have the Jews driven from Europe," declares Romain Rolland, "we should be left so poor in intelligence and the power for action, that we should be in danger of utter bankruptcy." "The Jew," continues Rolland, "is the yeast of the European dough." This great Frenchman expresses amazement at the restless activity of the Jew and his indefatigable impetuosity. One still remembers what a dreary place so good a Christian as Bettauer found the city without Jews to be.

I would not presume to offend anyone's intelligence or tire his patience in an attempt to describe the services the Jew has rendered Western civilization throughout the Middle Ages and in more modern times. In every department of human endeavor, be it commercial, political, scientific, or cultural, Jewish names are legion. This fact has aroused the ire and stimulated the fear of some stupid Nordics. It has developed in Germany a scientific—mark you!—a scientific anti-Semitism. The Bergsons, Freuds, and Einsteins are known to all. Hardly a decade rolls by but some Jewish genius receives universal acclaim. The year 1928 brought forward in the United States two great violinists, one in New York and the other in San Francisco. Both of them are Jews. Of the *New York Times* list of the names of immortals or near-immortals who passed away in 1927, six percent of the total were Jewish names. Remember that the Jew constitutes but a fraction of one percent of the world's population.

Throughout the Middle Ages the Jew was the indispensable intermediary between Orient and Occident. In spite of the laborious efforts of untiring scholars, a proper evaluation of the Jew's contribution is still impossible, so multiple and diversified has it been. In more recent times Heine considered himself primarily an interpreter of France to Germany; Brandes interpreted half a dozen European peoples one to another.

Because of his unique international position, the Jew has often served as the translator of literary works. The great Jewish bibliographer, Steinschneider, consumed eight hundred pages in an effort to enumerate the translations for which the Jews were responsible during the Middle Ages. A modern bibliographer would find his job no less tedious. We, today, are reading Lewisohn's translations from the German, Goldberg's from the Russian, and Meyerson's from the Norwegian.

The great book dealers in France, Germany, and England are Jews; publishers of liberal books are largely Jews. Oswald Garrison Villard has stated to me that his *Nation* is under great obligation to the Jews. Among the founders of the *New Republic* and its first editors there were Jews.

All this is in large measure due to the fact that the Jews, so vastly dispersed, learn and bring together the best cultural goods of all peoples.

The Jewish savant, author, or artist has a better chance than his non-Jewish colleague of becoming internationally known. His own people will transmit his name from land to land. Mendel's theory slumbered undisturbed in the Church archives from 1865 to 1900. Darwin, in the meantime, died without an opportunity of checking his own discoveries on the basis of the new knowledge. This never could have happened had Mendel been a Jew. His service to science would have become readily known wherever there were Jews—that is, at least, to the entire civilized world.

Why should a people so vital, endowed with such "power for action," rendering such valuable service to mankind, be called upon to discontinue its existence? Pathology knows of numerous disease-bearing bacilli, but because the same bacilli are in other respects beneficial to the race, their species is not exterminated. Even if it could be proved that the Jew is also a source of harm, which of course no one but the most rabid anti-Semites have dared to claim—his continued existence is productive of counterbalancing blessings.

I submit that one of these great blessings may well be that of ultimately helping to bring peace to the world. I do not believe in the mission theory and do not agree with those who so boldly and vociferously proclaim that Israel's mission is peace. No people, no more than any individual, starts life with any raison d'être. Its philosophy and ideology is an *arrière-pensée*. Joshua, unless we are much mistaken, did not advance into Palestine with a peace program. Samson, Gideon, Jeptha, Abner, Joab, and David can hardly be designated "princes of peace." Like all peoples, we inherited from our primitive ancestors a fighting predisposition. In the jungle might was right; human society, we thought, would also have to be maintained on such a principle.

Experience, destiny, have willed it otherwise. We early settled in a land that was not flowing with milk and honey but was rather a military encampment, saturated with the blood of many peoples. After much of our own blood had been spilled there, mighty powers forced us into exile; fate caused us to dwell in many lands. The sting of hatred, the disgrace of social ostracism, the pain of persecution convinced us early that might was not right and that human society ought not to be a jungle. Other peoples, too, bled and suffered losses in war, but they soon enjoyed a truce, a time for recuperation and peace. Not so with Israel—suffering and torture were his perennial lot.

Such experience made him reinterpret his entire history in terms of disarmament and goodwill. On the Seder night the Jew, at the mention of the plagues that were inflicted upon Egypt, pours off a few drops from his cup of wine. Originally this was undoubtedly an oblation to the gods as a prophylactic against disaster. But later Jewish teachers gave quite a different meaning to this practice. A cup of wine is a symbol of joy. Seder night, the Jew is rejoicing because he was freed from Egypt. But, say the rabbis, your joy came at the expense of the sorrows of another people; the Egyptian perished. Pour off from the fullness of your cup to commemorate and bewail the fate of your enemy and oppressor. David, according to another tradition, was precluded from building the temple because he was a man of war and had shed much blood.

Peace, peace became the yearning of his heart. Peace, peace, let there be peace. *Shalom aleichem* became his salutation. In every land he worked for universal peace; he has been conspicuous among the pacifists and peacemakers. "The press bureaus or societies of international pacifism," Zangwill remarks, "will be found mainly directed by men and women of the race whose salutation was not 'How do you do?' but 'Peace to you.' " And two Jews, Professor Asser and Alfred Fried, are among the few men who have been awarded the Nobel Peace Prize. It will indeed take an international mind to bring about international peace and who, more than the Jew, is endowed with such a mind? "Multiple cultural allegiance is in itself a force tending to remove the likelihood of war." In the bringing of peace, the most imperative need of humanity, the Jew may well be most helpful.

Western peoples have made rapid strides in material civilization. Beside it, the achievements of the early races, the Greeks and Romans not excluded, fade into insignificance. They, indeed, are subduing nature and making it subservient to man; but has not their history been one of bloodshed, oppression, and brutality? Who can number the wars which Europe has fought within the last one thousand years? How brazenly these peoples set themselves up as the preceptors and mentors of the hosts of humanity—historically not of their stock. European peoples are often the victims of gusty impulses that drive them to vulgar paganism, military aggressiveness, and political intolerance.

A religion of their own they did not evolve and have seldom, if ever, produced a saint. Their spiritual and ethical concepts they borrowed but they soon lost their balance. In the realm of theory, the vague, incipient beliefs of the "heathens" hardened with the march of events into a dogmatic theology that has often constituted the most bitter foe of science and reason. In the world of reality the worshipers of Thor and Wotan abandoned themselves to a hypothetical altruism which degenerated into an antinomianism that is a travesty on human experience and intelligence.

The Jew has valiantly resisted both the theology and the practice of Christianity. Like the Greek, he is endowed with a fine sense of value. He can, therefore, maintain an ethical and spiritual equilibrium but rare among Christian peoples. "Remember the Sabbath Day to keep it holy." How does one keep it holy? "With fresh garments, good drink, and wholesome food," say the rabbis. No Christian theologian could have been guilty of such heresy; no saint of such abandon. Western peoples have been known to swing from one extreme to another; from the most extreme theoretical nonresistance to the most brutal warfare; from bacchanalian revelries to extreme forms of self-torture, and from paganism to asceticism; even marriage is considered a concession to the weakness of the flesh.

It is for these very reasons that they have been unable to show any sympathy with Oriental peoples—China, India, Turkey—it makes no difference. They divide, rule, and exploit. To such peoples the Jew has been frequently a remarkable corrective. Judaism knows of no antagonism between body and soul. The division of life into the secular and religious is foreign to its spirit. The Jew has, therefore, more than once proved to be the conscience of Christendom. Nietzsche, who despised a conscience, most naturally despised Jesus and his race.

But even more than a corrective, the Jew may yet again serve as the interpreter between the Orient and the Occident. "The Jew," remarked Elisée Reclus, the great geographer and socialist, "is destined to play the role of an international link between the different countries of the earth." Contrary to the declaration of a great Christian and

Westerner, East and West, for the safety and peace of humanity, must and will meet. Who can deny to the Jew the privilege of acting as interpreter?

But not only as a corrective and an interpreter does the Jew enrich and serve humanity, but as a vital force for optimism. The Jew has survived; that alone is one of our great spiritual assets. It is the triumph of individuality over the mass; of loyalty to one's personality as "against the power of environmental circumstances." What temptation there is to follow the line of least resistance! How embarrassing it is to be singled out—to appear different! How painful to be whispered about—a Jew, a Jew! How humiliating to be graciously tolerated! How one does want, under such circumstances, to jump out of one's skin! "To think of the course of Jewish History is to stir those thoughts that lie too deep for tears," remarks Zangwill. Said an old, colored mammy one day to a Southern grand dame, "I would gladly suffer the tortures of being flayed alive in order to be vested with a white integument."

But the Jew did remain in his skin. Hounded, persecuted, he was driven from shore to shore, from land to land; nowhere finding peace; everywhere was he treated with discrimination, suspicion and, aye, worst of all, even with fear. Centuries, millennia rolled by; empires rose and fell; civilizations flourished and crumbled to the dust. Egyptian charioteer, Greek hoplite, Roman legion, cross and crescent, all dug their steel into the Jew's flesh, but undaunted, unswerving, immovable, he remained loyal to his ideals—aye, if you please—to his illusions. By all standards of history he should have long ago perished or at least should have become a straggling, despondent vagabond; his morale should have corroded centuries ago, but he refused to submit to an inexorable fate. He fought gloom, despair, pessimism. He doggedly retained his faith in an idea, in truth, in the supremacy of the inner life. He was confident of ultimate victory. He survived.

When the world was hurled into the most destructive of wars, Christian thinkers everywhere despaired of man and his destiny. The most original of England's religious thinkers, the Dean of St. Paul's, painfully cried out against the futility of it all. In a brilliant essay on "Progress" he predicted that the monster Science would sooner or later crush the incorrigible infant—man. The "Gloomy Dean" saw no escape. There is to be no progress. In a preface to a book entitled *The Coming Renaissance*, the same observer is delivering a solemn eulogy over a civilization that was, with hardly a promise of resurrection. Man seems to be caught in the meshes of his own genius. He builds to destroy; he creates to demolish. All the results of his arduous labors prove to be ephemeral. Ruin and transitoriness seem to be his nemesis.

In the midst of the helter-skelter of life—the debris of civilization—stands the Jew imbued with an imperishable faith, hopeful of rebirth. Here is one people in the thick of life's battle and yet undefeated, triumphant! Why shall not humanity, too, conquer its fate and emerge victor?

We would then urge the preservation of the Jew because of the spiritual comfort, the optimism that his very survival must and does inspire in thousands.

But the preservation of the Jew also means the cultural enrichment of humanity. It is a truism that cultural values are enhanced through variety and contrast. "The concept of uniformity and unanimity in culture is repellent." We are not satisfied to hear the music of just one people, see its dances, and read its books. We are blessed with an insatiable appetite for variety. We want the colors of the prism.

A good case for the assimilation of the Jew could have been made out, as a matter of fact was made out, soon after Alexander the Great conquered the Oriental world and jaded Hellas still thought itself capable of imbuing the world with a longing for *arete*, "excellence." The Hellenization roller worked untiringly and effectively. The Ptolemies and the Seleucides did not use the gentle, though not less annoying, tactics of Socrates. Numerous peoples were lost; their cultures were wiped out; the world was Hellenized. Judea alone resisted the arguments, both of gentle persuasion and of force.

Few will today deny that the assimilation of the Jew in the second century before the Christian era was highly undesirable. We have no way of estimating what the Jews might have accomplished as Hellenists. Suppose they had continued the unadulterated Greek tradition and given us a larger share of Attic literature, would that have been sufficient recompense for what the Jews have given to the world? According to Gilbert Murray, all Greek literature that was preserved for posterity constitutes only one-twentieth of the total Athenian product. Suppose the absorption of the Jews into the Athenians had meant saving three-twentieths of the literary output, would we have been rewarded for the loss of the Bible?

We do not at all have in mind the comparative merits of Greek and Hebraic literature. Suppose it were granted that the Book of Job

59

and the Song of Songs as works of art are inferior to Homer and Aeschylus, we are thinking only of the different note the Bible introduced into the Western world and of what that note has meant to art. We are thinking of Michelangelo, Raphael, Milton, Tasso, and a host of composers, essayists, novelists, poets, who seem to be inconceivable without the Bible. English literature, it is generally assumed, excels in the essay. Literary critics are agreed that the essay as a form of composition is directly traceable to the greatest of apocryphal books, Ecclesiasticus. We are thinking of what the note of righteousness has meant in literature. We recall Matthew Arnold's dictum, that conduct is three-fourths of life. That, the Rector of Rugby adds, is Israel's contribution to civilization. Only yesterday the Master of Baliol College, Oxford, stated that the hegemony of the Western spirit is largely Greek and Hebrew.

The Jew has not forgotten Jerusalem and, therefore, has not lost the cunning of his right hand. There is today an amazing renascence of the Hebraic spirit. The muses of Judea have once more unfolded their wings; to Chaim Nachman Bialik they have brought the gift of poetry; they have made him the equal of any living poet. The eloquence of Isaiah, the majesty of Job, the humility of the Psalms lend a poignancy and quaintness to his verse but rare in modern literature. (But for one vote the Noble Prize would have been awarded to one writing in the language of the Bible.) I am sufficiently acquainted with the poet and his art, and I am enough of a behaviorist to maintain that only a combination of circumstances, which we will have to describe as Jewish, could have produced a Bialik. Had Bialik's great-grandfather become assimilated, there would have been no Bialik. There might have been a Robert Frost, a Robinson, a Sandburg, but most certainly not a Bialik. Dreiser is a great novelist, but I must have Hamsun and Rolland and Tolstoi and Tagore and Reymont. Another Dreiser will not do. Even so do I want to see the cultural enrichment that will accrue from the Hebraic strain. I have no reason to believe that its genius is exhausted.

For all these reasons I believe that the assimilation of the Jew is undesirable. Because he constitutes a minority he is compelled to think more and harder than his neighbor; he must be a liberal; his outlook must be international, his perspective universal. Assimilation would mean the absorption of such valuable assets in large crowds and majorities in no way superior. The Jew, too, is in many ways an indispensable factor in European civilization; he is an antidote for Western paganism; he is a force for universal peace. His continued existence is also a tremendous spiritual asset and means the cultural enrichment of our civilization.

But above all, it has a profound esthetic appeal to the Jew himself and to the world. It is glorious to live, to roll up years, decades, centuries, millennia. It is thrilling to look back on vistas of time; there I was— then I was. Age, mere age, evokes interest, admiration, and respect. A diamond wedding anniversary gets a headline in the newspaper. The celebration of the hundredth birthday of almost anyone arouses comment. Medicine is deeply concerned with the prolongation of life; it is making every effort to procure longevity for the individual. An American need not go beyond his own country for natural beauty, but he travels to Rome, Jerusalem, Cairo to worship the old. Napoleon standing in the shadow of the pyramids, begins to poetize and pays reverential homage to the age of Egypt's civilization. How pained we all are to see an old landmark, an age-hoary shrine disappear. Gibraltar is huge, massive, picturesque; some even declare it ugly, but there it stands. Suggest to anyone that it be reduced to the level of the sea and build with its stone magnificent cathedrals. No! We love to venerate the merely old.

Here is the Jew—roll back the book of history; you are almost at its very beginning. Abraham was there to exchange compliments with Hammurabi. Turn a leaf; here is Rameses, well, he had his difficulties with the God of the Hebrew. Rameses, as we now know, was the scion of a great people, but he is, after all, only a mummy. But even as a mummy, because it is so very old and has so admirably defied time, Rameses has attained a commendable reputation; but Moses, mind you, is no mummy and his burning bush is not yet consumed.

Continue to turn the pages—new names, new cultures, new countries, new habits, customs. The Jew, the Jew, he is yet there. You are at the end of ancient times. The whole world is at the feet of mighty Rome. The Jew, amongst many others, is battling for his life; Rome scores a victory.

Some three years ago a collector of coins brought to my study a number of coins of Jewish interest. One of them brought tears to my eyes. It was a coin that was minted between 69 A.D. and 70 A.D. at the request of Titus. There was stamped on it a crouching Jew, symbolizing Judea, and it bore the inscription, *"Judea Capta, Judea Devicta."*

I held the coin in my hand and mused with a pain at my heart. Suddenly I recalled that the firebrand which set the Temple on fire and reduced it to ashes, 1,859 years ago, was hurled by one of Titus' soldiers from Mount Scopus. At the very same moment it occurred to me that the University of Jerusalem was being built on the very mountain and that the world's greatest intellect, "The Tip Topper" of our age, as Bertrand Russell put it to me, Albert Einstein emerged from his laboratory to campaign for funds in order to assure its existence and growth. I turned to the other face of the coin; there was Titus with his helmet and all his imperial Roman dignity. "Perhaps you are best remembered," I reflected, "because of your accursed deed, because you linked your name with an undying people."

"In social as in biological problems, time is the sole real creator and the sole great destroyer. It is time that has made mountains with grains of sand and raised the obscure cell of geological eras to human dignity." Time has made the Jew. Time has thought him thus far desirable. Time alone will have to prove him undesirable.

ISRAEL GOLDSTEIN

Kol Nidre Summons

Kol Nidre, the eve of the Day of Atonement, the holiest night of the Jewish year, is a tribute to the stubborn quality of Jewish faith. Its tones are mournful yet strong, sad yet determined. It is a reminder of the refusal of a stiff-necked people to bow to the seemingly inevitable necessities.

There is a fundamental difference between Greek tragedy and Hebrew tragedy. When the house of Agamemnon is doomed, Electra gives up the struggle and enters the doomed domicile resigned to her fate. Not so with Israel. Encompassed by calamity and surrounded by adversaries, he exclaims with the Psalmist, "I shall not die but live, to declare the work of the Lord." Afflicted and bereaved, he exclaims with Job, "Behold though He slay me, yet will I trust in Him."

Rabbi Israel Goldstein received his A.B. from the University of Pennsylvania, his M.A. from Columbia University and Graetz College, and was ordained at the Jewish Theological Seminary. He served the Congregation Bna'i Jeshurun in New York City and was president of the Jewish National Fund. He also served on the New York Board of Jewish Ministers and was National Chairman of Keren Hayesod.

63

What Polish Jewry suffers one year, German Jewry another year, and what nearly all of European Jewry suffers today are the latest links in a chain of tragedy which stretches from the barbarity of the Roman legions in the first century, to the ferocity of the Christian Crusades in the eleventh century, to the sadistic bigotry of the Inquisition in the fifteenth and sixteenth centuries. To all of these the answer of the Jew has been *Shema Yisrael,* "Hear Israel, the Lord is our God."

Of all peoples which have trodden the stage of world history, the Jewish people is the one people alive today which has been from the beginning a people committed to a moral and ethical purpose. The Jew is the living witness of ageless truths.

If Israel is the living witness, Kol Nidre is the living voice of the living witness. Could we but tune in with all our hearts, with all our souls, and with all our strength, we might hear in the voice of Kol Nidre the majesty of Abraham's response *Hineni,* "Here am I," in response to the divine call demanding his most precious possession as the token of his faith; the daring of Moses laying the command of God upon the most powerful ruler of his time, "Release my people that they may serve Me!"; the bitter sweetness of David singing out of his distress, "When I am in trouble, I cry out 'O Lord'"; the universalistic vision of Micah, "And they shall beat their swords into plowshares"; the passionate warning of Isaiah, "There is no peace for the wicked"; the pathetic lament of Jeremiah, "Woe that a cloud has fallen upon Judea's golden splendor"; the nostalgic yearning of the Psalmist by the waters of Babylon, "If I forget thee, O Jerusalem, may my right arm forget its skill." These are some of the tones and overtones of the vibrations of Kol Nidre. Every year before Kol Nidre, rabbis receive a letter from an organization called "The Free Thinkers of America." The communication purports to open our eyes to see how stupid is religion, and how unenlightened is the observance of the Day of Atonement. Here are a few sentences from the chronic free thinkers' epistle:

> An annual appeal to the Jews of America on the occasion of the observance of Yom Kippur.
>
> The time has come when the enlightened Jews of the world should make a step to emancipate their co-believers from the bondage of their religion.
>
> The Jews do not have to confess their sins; it is Jehovah who should ask forgiveness for the false banner he has given them and for the false prophets he has induced them to follow.

> Yom Kippur is the most humiliating day in all the superstitious annals of religion, so use this day for religious independence, and let it be an emancipation proclamation to the world.
>
> Abandon your temples and renounce your antiquated creed.

If they are sincere, they are to be pitied more than scorned. The doctrinaire "free thinkers" who challenge us are neither free nor thinkers. They are not free because they are confined in the jacket of orthodox atheism of fifty years ago. They are not thinkers because they apparently never heard of such names as Jeans and Eddington. When their epistle was first composed and circulated, probably decades ago, it may have made some impression upon the pseudo-intelligentsia of that day, who, under the first shock of Darwin, Huxley, and Spencer thought immaturely that they were being confronted by a choice between religion and science. It did not take the honest scientists long to learn that in the presence of the ultimate mystery of the universe, science stands in reverence. Correspondingly it did not take intelligent religionists long to make clear that the fundamental premises of religion have nothing to do with cosmologies, whether the world was made in six days or in six eons, nor with folklore and folk ways, but that they have to do with a few basic ideas which Science can neither prove nor disprove.

What are these basic ideas underlying religion in its broadest sense?

1. The universe is not an accident but the result of a creative intelligence.
2. Man is distinguished from the animal domain by virtue of an endowment of spiritual qualities.
3. There is a moral drive in human history which, though slow in fulfillment, ensures the ultimate realization of justice, brotherhood, and peace.

These three affirmations constitute the irreducible minimum of religion, the kernel which will be as safe from the invasion of science in the year 2940 as it is in the year 1940.

The Jew is irrevocably committed to these affirmations. The more they are challenged, the more firmly he espouses them. Individual Jews may be atheists. Our charter as a people, however, is a religious mandate. Read the Bible if you would understand how the Jew conceived of himself and of his place and purpose in the world.

In the beginning, God created the world. It was a good world. Every stage of creation was sealed by the divine approval. "And God saw that it was good." Into this world, He placed man, gave him woman as a companion, a paradise for them to live in, and a few simple commands to obey. Man and woman committed the sin of disobedience. They ate the forbidden fruit. For that, they were punished. Paradise was forfeited. Succeeding generations fluctuated between sin and virtue, good and evil, obedience and disobedience to God's commands. Abel obeyed, Cain disobeyed. Noah obeyed, his contemporaries disobeyed. Then arose Abraham in whom God saw great promise. He decided that out of Abraham's seed he would build the stock of a righteous people, a nation which should be dedicated to God's commands. He bade Abraham abandon his idolatrous environment, and go forth to a new land and to a new destiny, to become the founder of a new people that should be a blessing to mankind. Abraham obeyed the call. He went forth. He needed, however, an heir to carry on his heritage. Isaac became his heir. Regarding his offspring, Abraham received the divine charge that he should command them to keep the way of the Lord, "to do justice and righteousness." An object lesson of what happens when justice and righteousness are not observed was furnished by the destruction of Sodom and Gomorrah.

The early chapters of Genesis are the preamble of Jewish history. They contain the pattern of all that has happened since. The Bible stories therefore are not merely a congeries of quaint fables and commendable maxims, but a connected autobiography of the Jewish people from Genesis to Chronicles, unified by the main theme that this people founded by Abraham was founded not merely in order to be another people on the face of the earth, but to be a unique people, dedicated to God's Law, a people whose title to Canaan rested upon its fulfillment of the Law, but was forfeited when the Law was violated, and whose credentials for survival today are still the same, namely, "to do justice and righteousness in the earth."

There is no other people in the history of nations which has even considered it necessary to justify its existence upon moral grounds. A people is here because it is here. The Jew has read into his destiny a moral purpose. Has he fulfilled that purpose? To a great extent he has, at a tragic cost to himself. He has fathered Christianity only to be recurrently crucified by Christians. He has foster-fathered Muhammadanism only to be sporadically reviled by Moslems.

66

Today, living in a world of force, the Jew is excoriated by the high priests of force because his Bible has imposed a conscience of righteousness and justice upon the world. The "prophets" of might want neither the New Testament nor the Old Testament. Both Testaments are condemned as a menace to the *Kraftanschauung* of the Aryan *Uebermensch*.

So the Jew is attacked in the name of a philosophy. To proclaim high-sounding reasons for hounding the Jew may seem more civilized than bluntly and without explanations to deprive him of jobs, businesses, and careers, and brutally pogromize him. This so-called higher anti-Semitism was rampant in Germany in the nineteenth century. Now it is coupled with the lower anti-Semitism of brute force.

There are also two ways in which the Jew can react to anti-Semitism. There is the reaction on the higher level and the reaction on the lower level. Reacting on the lower level, he can cry out against the physical persecution he suffers, and his cry is as right as the instinctive cry of an animal against its attacker. On the higher level, however, the Jew can rededicate himself to his heritage with all the greater zeal, knowing that he stands for eternal values which will prevail long after the *Uebermensch* era will have been forgotten.

When we understand that, then we lift our burden from a low plane to a high plane. It is one thing to be hated because we are economically envied. It is quite another thing to be hated because we are intellectually and spiritually feared. It makes a great difference in the state of our souls whether we are excoriated for our faults, or we are hounded for our virtues.

There are men, sensitively souled, high-minded men, who when their cause is just would rather be the persecuted than the persecutors. We recall on Kol Nidre such a man in Germany, a German professor, Emil Granauer of Hanauer University, who with his wife and children embraced Judaism as a protest against Nazi persecutions. We recall the great French writer, Romaine Rolland, who said in an open letter to the Jews of Poland, "I regret I am not a Jew, because I am ashamed of the record of my Christian brothers." Let us be sure that if the world's wrath we must bear, we bear it for reasons of which we can be proud. Let us become conscious ourselves and make our children conscious of the best motives of our history and of the highest purposes of our destiny.

Our cause is integrated in the cause which is at the core of the devastating conflict now raging abroad. Never in the history of warfare has the moral issue been more sharply defined than it is today. In the last war a moral basis was discovered three years after war had been in progress. Only in 1917 did President Wilson coin the slogan, "the war to make the world safe for democracy." In the present conflict the moral issue was defined six years before the war began. In 1933, upon assuming power, Hitler and Nazism served notice on the world that they repudiate democracy, excoriate liberalism, scoff at the principles of human equality and brotherhood, revile the religious traditions of Judaism and of Christianity, exalt nationalistic chauvinism, glorify race hatreds, defy international decencies, and extol war as the highest and noblest way of life. At the same time, they proclaimed a special tenderness toward animals. The movement for the prevention of cruelty to animals is very strong in Germany. The Hebrew prophet, Hosea, had a phrase for it—"the murderers of men kiss cattle."

For seven cruel years the Nazi philosophy has been dinned into the ears of the world. Therefore it needs no ministry of propaganda to teach the American people and civilized men everywhere what this war is about. It is a war to defend and maintain the gains of civilization which are threatened with a "blackout."

Anyone who maintains that this is a war between two equally undesirable imperialisms is either a fool or a villain. One need not exonerate the British Empire for its sins of omission and commission against its subject peoples in granting the premise that England today vis-à-vis Germany is on the side of human decency and progress. Let the doubters ask themselves where they would prefer to live today, in England or in Germany. No picture is all white or all black. Life, however, demands a definitive choice between two sets of circumstances on the basis of their general complexions. We are not asked to participate in an academic debate. Civilization, as we know it, imperfect, but better on the whole than what we have known before, is at stake.

In this challenge to civilization, it was no accident that the Jews became the first victim. No greater compliment has been paid the Jew than to have singled him out as the special target of Nazi sadism. Alas, it was a tragic compliment which devastated hundreds of thousands of our people. But it put upon the Jew once more the noble yoke of the suffering "Servant of the Lord."

Some Jews are heard venturing the prediction that Hitler's downfall is inevitable because it is an inexorable law of history that whoever persecutes the Jew comes to grief. To put it that way, as if the

Jew were invested with some magic immunity is to oversimplify and therefore to understate the truth. To believe that would be unworthy and unwarranted chauvinism of which the Jew, least of all, should be guilty.

If history in the long range seems to be on our side, it is only because and to the extent that the Jew has been a living witness of eternal truths, the truths of Sinai which other peoples have adopted in their own characteristic versions.

Israel's place in the panorama of history is quite incidental. The all-embracing theme is that there is a moral bookkeeping system in the ledger of history, that there is a moral nemesis in the affairs of men. "If ye walk in my statutes ye will survive. . . . If ye transgress them ye will perish." The Jew himself is no exception. He is bound by the same moral imperatives. "Are ye not unto Me even as the children of the Ethiopians?" is the cautioning word of Amos. "Because of our sins we have been driven forth from our land," is the memorial refrain of our Prayer Service. His defeats, as his victories, are lessons to himself and to the world. He is the witness that there is a Moral Arbiter in history.

It is no accident therefore that in the challenge which the forces of evil have hurled at religion and civilization, the Jew should have been singled out again as the special victim. His role is incidental but it is not accidental.

Never before in the history of our trials and tribulations has the issue been drawn so clearly. We are proud in the knowledge that Hitler is allergic to Judaism, which means also to Christianity. Never before has the ethical basis of our existence been so convincing. It makes the Akedah, the sacrifice, worthwhile. Jews in many lands stand not only on the physical war front. They are in the frontline trenches of the spiritual war front. The story of Isaac's sacrifice at Moriah becomes a lesson in current events.

A Hitler spokesman has said, "The sword will come into its own again and the pen will be relegated to the place where it belongs." An ancient Jewish Rabbi has said, "A book and a sword have come down to the world" (Leviticus Rabbah, Chap. XXXV, sec. 5). The Jew has chosen the book, the word, the ideal. Let those who will espouse the sword. The future will decide as between the proponents of the book and the proponents of the sword. It is the modern phase of the irreconcilable conflict between Jacob and Esau. And the Jew knows how to wait. Hitler talks about a thousand years. He is merely talking. The Jew, when he speaks of a thousand years, has the warrant of four thousand years of history to which to point. He knows how to wait—a thousand years if need be.

Kol Nidre summons us to remember that there are verities which transcend the changes of time, that there are ageless truths and tasks, that of all the peoples which have trodden the stage of world history, the Jew alone has been from the beginning, a people committed to a moral and ethical purpose, that we of this age must continue to hold the banner high and refuse to bow to the seeming necessities of our age even as our forebears refused in their day.

Leave a Little to God

It is May 24, 1844. A bearded scientist with a group of colleagues is seated at a table tapping out some sounds on a little instrument before him. Moments later, forty miles away in Baltimore, the message is received: "What hath God wrought!" The world stands jubilant and thankful before a modern miracle. The telegraph has been invented, and a new era of human communication has dawned.

It is September 13, 1959. The news is flashed around the world and banner headlines in the newspapers announce: "Russians Land Rocket on the Moon, Time Calculated Within Eighty-four Seconds." Before this extraordinary achievement of man's intellect the free world stands frightened and dismayed. A new era of possible human annihilation has dawned, and some are even tempted to murmur, "What hath

Rabbi Robert Gordis received his A.B. from CCNY and his Ph.D. from Dropie. He was ordained at the Jewish Theological Seminary. This Conservative rabbi, biblical scholar, and author was on the faculty of the Jewish Theological Seminary, President of the Rabbinical Assembly of America, and served on the Synagogue Council of America. Rabbi Gordis was also the editor of "Judaism."

Satan wrought!" And each succeeding achievement in outer space leaves us more terror-stricken or more blasé, resigned to an apparently inevitable course that will lead to cosmic disaster. In fact, we have already transferred the minor hazards of earthbound creatures to the heavens. The inevitable has already happened. A collision has occurred in outer space between two unmanned spacecraft!

The brave new world for which men prayed and hoped for centuries has been ushered in, but it has left us prematurely old and frightened by its prospects. If we seek a refuge from the international scene by turning to the domestic front, we find no peace. Corruption, crime, delinquency, and fraud seem universal. Massive problems create crises, and the massive crises threaten us with catastrophe. No wonder hope and confidence are fled and everywhere there crouch anxiety and foreboding, if not terror and despair. On the threshold of the New Year how can we muster both the energy and the will to face the future?

A century and a half ago, the French tyrant Napoleon was master of Europe. In Spain an embattled English army under the Duke of Wellington was trying to resist his advance. One day a young lieutenant came into the British general's tent with a map clutched in his trembling hands: "Look, General, the enemy is almost upon us!" "Young man," the General replied, "get larger maps. The enemy won't seem so close."

If we wish to understand the shape of things to come, we cannot be satisfied with the headlines of today. We need the perspective of history, the full record of man's past struggles, defeats, and achievements. We are accustomed to speak of the path of human history as though men advanced on a straight highway. Actually, man's progress is best compared to a pendulum, for it is characteristic of human nature that we do not go forward in a straight line, but fluctuate from one extreme to the other. To borrow the language of the physicists, men go from one action to an opposite and almost equal reaction.

When our primitive ancestors first emerged upon this planet, they were animals—with one difference. They were intelligent enough to be frightened, to feel helpless before a vast and unknown world filled with countless dangers lurking everywhere. Hence man, and man alone, peopled the hills and the valleys, the seas and the skies, the rivers and the trees with invisible beings, with spirits, gods and demons, fairies and witches, who were powerful and could determine man's fate.

As time went on and man began to organize his ideas, the gods were now assigned special spheres of sovereignty, given different functions and arranged in families, with elaborate rituals created to win their favor. But in ancient religion, as in primitive times, man saw himself as helpless and dependent on the whims and caprices of the spirits, their favor or their displeasure. Man was the plaything of the gods. The ancient Babylonians, for example, who were kinsmen of the Hebrews, had a tradition about the Flood similar to ours in the Bible. But while the Torah tells us that it was man's colossal wrongdoing that impelled God to visit that catastrophe upon the human race, the Babylonians ascribed it to the fact that men on earth were making so much noise that the gods could not sleep! One can well sympathize with their outraged feelings! The Greek myths in which we take delight today were not legends to the Greeks. The tales of the gods on Olympus, using human beings as the instruments and the victims of their greed, their jealousy, their lusts, and their quarrels constituted religious truth in the Greek world.

When the great religions of the Western world arose out of the bosom of Judaism, man's position underwent a change, but not as radically as is sometimes thought. To be sure, he was no longer a plaything of capricious and unpredictable gods. Man was now the creature of a God of Justice and Mercy. But man's position of total dependence did not change. To accept this total surrender became the mark of piety. The mightiest religion of the West, Christianity, taught, "Believe in Me and ye shall be saved." The most militant religion of the East, Mohammedanism, declared that man's destinies were totally predetermined by Allah, and that the only course for man to adopt was Islam, total submission to Him. For most teachers of religion, man, being a creature of God, was nothing, and God was everything.

But whether or not, as the song writers tell us, "love is a many splendored thing," it is true that man is a many-faceted being. In their churches and cathedrals, men continued to echo the idea that man is nothing, but in their laboratories and plants, their factories and fields, men were acting on the contrary theory that man is everything. The ancient Greeks, who were the architects of our civilization, had a phrase for it, "Man is the measure of all things." The advancing tide of science kept strengthening man's confidence in his own powers. Cynics and disbelievers now whispered that instead of God's creating man, it was man who had created God. As technology progressed and blessings without number poured forth from the cornucopia of invention, man could hardly be blamed for regarding himself as the lord of the universe, the creator and monarch of all he surveyed.

Few stopped to ask, "Whence came man?" who obviously did not create himself; or "Whence came the green earth?" which existed before man; "Or the planetary system?" which existed before the earth; "Or the universe?" which antedated our planetary system. Who could blame the German biologist Ernst Haeckel for announcing triumphantly that he had solved "The Riddle of the Universe."

A little over a hundred years ago, in 1859, Charles Darwin published his *Origin of Species*. Many men were persuaded by the evolutionary theory and other scientific achievements that science had dethroned God as Creator and enthroned man in His stead. From the generous treasure-house of science came not only ships and cars, planes, radio and television, and millions of gadgets and instruments of all kinds. The scientists broke down the barrier between matter and energy. They pierced the mystery of the hitherto unbreakable atom. They peered into the very constitution of the world and fashioned new elements at will. Was it not true that man was the prime creator in the universe? The only hymn that still made sense was: "Hail to thee, great Science, from whom all blessings flow."

The pendulum had swung widely from one extreme to another. First God was everything and man was nothing. Now man was everything and God was nothing.

But the oscillation of the pendulum was not ended. As man's intellect through technology was bringing him one rich gift after another, as homage to a king, man's intellect through science was undermining his position on the throne. Psychology declared that man was a bundle of primitive instincts and his reason merely a false front, an empty facade hiding irrational impulses. Anthropology suggested that there were no moral standards, only varying customs among different peoples, and that these could be discarded at will. The rise of industry in the nineteenth century had led to the mechanization of man and made of man a tool, a hand, a cog in a factory. The twentieth century brought the human race to the brink of a far more horrible fate—the manipulation of man. From being a tool of production, man became a tool of domination. He could be sold anything—a toothpaste, a candidate for public office, or a new fascist or communist order of society, not on the

74

basis of any intrinsic merit or rational evidence, but under the spell of the new technique. There are levels of manipulation. It began, more or less harmlessly, with advertising, went on to "public relations," and reached its highest point or its lowest in organized brainwashing, in propaganda, and the mass hysteria on which dictators have climbed to power.

Suddenly man discovered that he could do everything, but that he himself was nothing. His powers were limitless, but wherever he turned he was helpless. When, toward the end of the nineteenth century, Alfred Nobel invented dynamite, he joyously reported that fact as proof positive that with so horrible a weapon available to the nations, war could never take place again. Now, two World Wars and fifty smaller wars later, we know that we can wipe out the human race completely through nuclear bombs. We can plan the exact place and moment of total annihilation, yet no one is sure that men will not take the fatal step.

If we avert our gaze from the world stage and look about us, we find everywhere else that man is helpless. There always have been criminals in society and malefactors in public office. Now the tragedy does not lie merely in the quantitative increase of wrongdoing. Today we take it for granted that there will be widespread breaches of trust in government, in the corporations, in labor unions, in public institutions, in the press, and on television. The breakdown of the American family is highlighted by the fact that one out of four marriages in the United States now ends in divorce courts. Illegitimacy, abortions, and adultery are increasing alarmingly, bringing in their wake a staggering burden of human misery and degradation.

Our moral crisis goes far deeper than the spiraling rise of juvenile delinquency, vandalism, and crime. This is by no means limited to underprivileged minority groups, but has infiltrated into the so-called better homes and finest communities. The crisis is qualitative. In the past, society as a whole and the offenders in particular recognized the moral standards against which they had sinned. To use the common legal term, they knew right from wrong. Today the criminal derides the judge before whom he stands. He did it for "kicks," or for gain, for "dope," or out of sheer viciousness, and society, deep down in its heart, does not know right from wrong either. That is the essence of the tragedy. In the words of the Psalmist, *Ki hashatot yeharesun, tzaddik mah pa'al.* "For the very foundations are destroyed; what can the righteous man do?" If Oliver Goldsmith were alive today he might be tempted to lament: "Ill fares the land to hastening ills a prey, Where science accumulates and men decay."

Does not that mean that the human race is the end of the road? Have we not exhausted all the possibilities? First man was nothing and God was everything. Then God was nothing and man was everything. Now God is nothing and man is nothing. Behind the alternating bluster and blandness of our enemies, the ineptness and ignorance of our own leadership, behind the wealth of science and the spiritual poverty of man, are we not hearing a voice of doom, "Nothing art thou and unto nothing shalt thou return?" This is the agonizing question confronting mankind.

There is, however, a sound more powerful than the blast of atomic explosions and the noise of jet planes roaring over our heads, a still small voice, first heard on Sinai. Judaism, which first revealed the one Living God to a world steeped in paganism, still has a message in this hour of imminent catastrophe for mankind groping in darkest despair. Against the fear which has gripped human hearts that we stand at the end of the human adventure stands the authentic message of Rosh Hashanah.

Judaism has its own view of man's role in the universe. For the Torah, man is not a plaything of divine caprice nor even a helpless and corrupt creature at the mercy of an omnipotent Power. On the other hand, man is surely not the prime creator of his world, the total master of his fate. In the most profound teaching of the Jewish tradition, man is neither a helpless plaything, nor a worthless creature, nor a self-creator—he is, in the words of the Talmud: *shuttapho shel hakadosh barakh hu bema'aseh bereshit*, "the co-partner of God, the Holy One, in the work of creation." This great cosmic partnership rests upon the profound biblical concept of man set forth in the opening chapter of Genesis, which declares that Man was created *betselem 'elohim*, "in the image of God." What does this vivid Hebrew phrase mean? Obviously, it does not mean a physical resemblance between God and man, because God has no form and man's body has much the same attributes as the animals around him. It means that man possesses part of the nature of God—the gift of reason and thought, the love of beauty manifest everywhere in the world, the unconquerable yearning for righteousness which never dies in the human soul, and above all the capacity to create, to mold and fashion the world, which is the hallmark of God Himself. Man is the only creature who can conceive of a past and of a future. In William Hazlitt's words: "Man is the only creature that can laugh and weep, because he is aware of the gulf between what is and what can be."

What are we doing here in God's world? The hymn of the Daily Prayer Book has the answer *Barakh 'elohenu shebera'anu likhevodo,* "Blessed is our God who has created us unto His glory."

The Midrash boldly spells out the meaning of this cosmic symbiosis, this partnership of God and man. Basing itself on a great passage in Isaiah (43:12)—*attem 'edai, ne'um hashem, va'ani 'el,* "ye are My Witnesses and I am God." The Midrash (*Shoher Tob,* ed. Buber 255a) interprets, *Keshe'attem 'edim 'ani 'el, ukeshe'ein 'attem 'edim 'eini 'el,* "When ye are My witnesses, I am God, and when ye are not My witnesses, I am no longer God." As surely as man cannot build the world without God, God cannot build without man. In Robert Browning's poem, Antonio Stradivarius, the famous violin maker, says, "God cannot build a violin without Antonio."

What does it mean to recognize that God and man are partners? What practical consequences flow from this insight into man's relationship to God? I find the answer in an utterance which the great Solomon Schechter, the first president of The Jewish Theological Seminary of America, was accustomed to repeat, "Leave a little to God." Note what he did *not* say. Not, "Leave it all to God," for then man becomes nothing. Nor, "Leave nothing to God," for then man is doomed to failure. "Leave a little to God"—that is the counsel we need. We must do our share and know that God will do His. *Action and faith both must be our watchwords. To work and to wait must be our program—passion and patience, both are needed for life.*

With this insight we can confront the major crises of our age and conquer. With the threat of worldwide annihilation posed by the Cold War hanging over us, two clear-cut alternatives exist. We may choose to surrender to Communism or wage an all-out war against it and run the risk of blotting out the human race. There are siren voices urging one or another of these courses upon us. But there is a third possibility, slower, more painful, far less simple, making greater demands upon us—the effort to coexist on this planet even with those whom we cannot wholly trust. To this end, we must use the United Nations and direct diplomatic negotiations, trade relations, and cultural exchanges, all as instruments for preserving the peace. But this course of action requires high intelligence and firm resolution, and above all, patience without end.

Whence shall this patience come? It can come only from faith, from the assurance that if we do our part, God will do His and the painful process of "peaceful co-existence" will lead to a happier state of affairs. This faith is no mere whistling in the dark. For God has taught us through His prophet, *Lo'tohu bera'ah lashevet yetzarah* (Isa. 45:18), "He created the world, not for chaos but for human habitation." It is a fact that our social and economic system has undergone vast changes in the last hundred years. So, too, far-reaching changes are taking place in Soviet Russia, and we can be certain that the tempo of change will increase. What will emerge will be in accordance with God's purposes for the world, not Mr. Johnson's or Mr. Brezhnev's or yours or mine, but something different and something better than what either our adversaries or we possess at present. *Lo' tohu bera'ah lashevet yetzarah*, "God created the world not for chaos, but for human habitation." We must work and wait and leave a little to God.

Let us turn to our homes and our families. How often do we see the children we have loved and nurtured wander off into new and perilous paths, apparently becoming strangers to us and all that we hold sacred? Across how many of our homes might we inscribe the title of Shaw's play, *Heartbreak House*. All too often we are tempted to feel that all our efforts in rearing our children, in setting before them standards of reverence and responsibility, and in inculcating loyalty to truth and goodness have been wasted. We know we did not do a perfect job, for perfection is with God alone, but we did the best we could, and behold the consequences! Here again Schechter's words have a message for us, "Leave a little to God." Action and faith, passion and patience are needed in this cosmic partnership. In the words of Koheleth, *Babaker zera' 'et zarekha uva'erev 'al tannah yadekha*, "In the morning sow your seed and in the evening do not let your hands be idle. For you cannot tell which of them will prosper or whether both of them will be good." From faith in God comes patience. If we wait, we shall discover that the seed we have planted has not fallen on fallow ground. Our plowing and planting of the field have not been wasted, because God's sunshine and rain have also been working from above. What will grow in our children will be new, and it may be different from what we are accustomed to, but we can hold fast to the faith that the best of what we have known and loved will not be utterly lost. The good and the true are immortal.

"Leave a little to God." Do your share and He will do His, for He created the world not for chaos and destruction, but for human habitation and joy.

Hayom harat 'olam. "On this day of Rosh Hashanah the world came into being." The majestic Musaf Service in its threefold structure proclaims the life-giving truth of man's relationship to God as co-partner in creation. The *Malkhuyot* proclaim the sovereignty of God—God rules the world as our Father and our King. Nor do we have to go it alone. For the *Zikhronot* recall that God is mindful of man's struggles and agonies, his weaknesses and frustrations, his capacity for goodness and greatness. Out of the sovereignty of God and the significance of man comes the third section of the Service, the *Shofarot*, paying tribute to the shofar, which was sounded on Sinai at the giving of the Law and will be heard again proclaiming the Messianic age.

The shofar is symbolic of the cosmic partnership of God and man. On Mount Sinai it was said: *Mosheh yedabber veha'elohim ya'anenu bekol*, "Moses spoke and God answered him with a loud voice." Let us speak and act for the right and then leave a little to God, knowing that He will not fail us. Together we can go forward to build a world worthy of God's greatness and man's hopes.

IRVING GREENBERG

A Broken Heart/Faith/Love is Stronger: The Lesson of Yom Kippur

Unlike all the other Jewish holidays, Yom Kippur (and Rosh Hashanah) have no outstanding association with major events in Jewish history. But rabbinic tradition insisted that a central biblical episode did occur on Yom Kippur. On this day, Moses finally brought the second set of tablets of the Ten Commandments to the Jewish people. This rabbinic view sheds great light on the psychology of the Day of Atonement.

Judaism is a religion of perfection. Its goal is nothing less than a world become paradise—the kingdom of God in which every human being is treated with infinite value and dignity. The goal is noble but it can be destructive. Perfectionism may be dangerous to your health. Leo Rotan, a psychiatric social worker, made a study of the maxims believed in by men who had heart attacks and matched them to con-

Rabbi Irving Greenberg was the President and co-founder of CLAL—The National Center for Learning and Leadership. He obtained his Ph.D. at Harvard University. This author and lecturer is an ordained Orthodox rabbi and a Professor at Yeshiva University. He founded and chaired the Department of Jewish Studies at the City College in New York.

trol subjects who did not. The heart patients believed "be ye therefore perfect" and demanded perfection of themselves; the healthy ones believed "little strokes fell great oaks" and were more accepting of failure.

Judaism asks human beings to be holy, to become like God in ethics and character. This standard generates superhuman effort but it can result in failure and self-degradation for not living up to the ideal. To offset this tendency, the tradition offers the relief of Yom Kippur, a Day of Atonement and forgiveness—both human and divine.

Those who have internalized the drive for perfection find it difficult to admit their imperfections, so how can they obtain forgiveness? Maimonides asserts that the indispensable, but most difficult, first step in repentance is to admit the flaw/sin. The confirmed sinner is afraid to turn back. He lives in dread that once he lets go and admits the failure, his whole life way will fall apart.

Many also fear that once there has been a serious breakdown, even atonement cannot restore the original wholeness. I had a friend who had a brief affair which he broke off. The guilt preyed on his mind. One day, seeking relief, he confessed to me and asked what to do. I asked whether he considered telling his wife or did he doubt that she would forgive him? He thought she would be angry but truly believed she would forgive. However, he feared that once she knew, their relationship would never be as whole and as trusting again. Here, I explained to him the rabbinic concept of Yom Kippur.

In our fantasy of perfection, once a flaw or break is discovered, things will never be perfect again. In the Arthurian epic of the Holy Grail, only Galahad could find the talisman because he was pure and faultless. Lancelot could not bring in the cup of salvation because he had sinned with Guinevere and has stained his sword with blood. In the rabbis' view, this is a superhuman—therefore, inhuman—conception of redemption. Yom Kippur teaches us that humans inevitably fail or sin: "There is no righteous person in the earth who does only good and never sins" (Ecclesiastes 7, 20). But when people turn, they come out stronger. Loved based on the assumption of perfection in both sides is vulnerable to the almost inevitable crack in the mirror. Each partner probably falsifies the other's image to avoid the reality. Once flaws are acknowledged and accepted, love becomes genuinely unconditional. It may be broken by inescapable failures, but it overcomes and becomes truly whole. Hence the rabbinic statement that a person who sinned and then turned stands in a place where no simple righteous person can stand.

The original tablets of the Ten Commandments were fashioned by the divine, untouched by human flaws. When the people of Israel sinned and created a Golden Calf, God despaired and wanted to get rid of them. Moses was so distressed that he smashed the tablets. It was almost as if the tablets were too pure to be left in human hands. Then came forty days of working through the heartbreak. Reconciliation and catharsis were followed by forty days of Moses' labor fashioning new tablets. This set—product of hard-won repentance—built on realism, forgiveness, and acceptance of others' limitations could dwell among the Israelites and guide them for centuries to come. Such tablets express the spirit of Yom Kippur when out of our brokenness we become stronger than when we claimed to be whole. This is why Rabbi Nachman of Bratslav declared, "no heart is so whole as a broken heart."

When the first Temple was destroyed, the prophets initially feared that God had rejected his sinful people. They came to see that the divine love embraced the human fully. Then they understood that such love can never be vanquished. Today, many are shocked by the suggestion that the Holocaust smashed the covenant. They fear that faith will be weakened by such a statement. They fail to understand that this broken covenant is even more powerful having been renewed by the Jewish people and its covenant partner. To paraphrase Rabbi Nachman, no covenant is so whole as a broken covenant.

Faith based on the expectation of guaranteed succor is conditional, vulnerable to the shattering blows of history. Faith and covenant built again after the Holocaust is proof against the fires of hell. Love which overcomes torment beyond measure is truly "as strong as death . . . the flame of the Lord."

HASKEL LOOKSTEIN

"God—Not Man— Must Be King"

A Rosh Hashanah Sermon (1994)

The central *theme* of Rosh Hashanah is that God is king.

The central *fact* of modern religion, ethics, and morality, is that the human being is king.

Now, the first part of this descriptive couplet is quite clear. Rosh Hashanah marks our *re*coronation of God as King.

1. We start the service in the morning with *Ha-Melekh.*
2. We say "Rule over the entire world in your glory" four times during the day.
3. We say as part of *Oleinu* "May they all accept the yoke of thy Kingship."

Rabbi Haskel Lookstein was ordained at Yeshiva University in 1958. He received his M.A. in Rabbinics and his Ph.D. in modern Jewish History from Yeshiva University. Rabbi Lookstein is Past President of Synagogue Council of America, Past Chairman of the Greater New York Coalition for Soviet Jews, Past President of the New York Board of Rabbis as well as of Yeshiva University's Rabbinic Alumni. He is married and the father of four children and grandfather of twelve grandchildren.

4. The shofar is sounded. One of the reasons for the shofar is that horns were sounded at the coronation of kings.
5. Even *Tashlikh* has a symbolism related to royalty in that kings were crowned alongside a body of water.

The second part—that in modern religion, ethics, and morality where the human being is king—requires explication. It is to that task to which I would like to devote this sermon. The subject is divisible into three parts:

1. To demonstrate that it is so.
2. To explain the ramifications of this phenomenon.
3. To suggest what we might do to counter it.

II

In modern religion, ethics, and morality, the human being is the measure of all things.

Item: In a book entitled *Habits of the Heart: Individuality and Commitment in American Life* (p. 4—quoted by Wertheimer, *Moment Magazine*, August 1994) a woman by the name of Sheila Larson describes her faith: "I believe in God. I'm not a religious fanatic. I can't remember the last time I went to church. My faith has carried me a long way. It's *Sheilaism*. Just my own little voice."

Item: Rabbi Susan Schnur, a Reconstructionist rabbi in the Jewish renewal movement, leads a congregation in New Jersey consisting of mostly intermarried couples and a few singles. She runs her services only once a month, realistically "adjusting to her members' already full lives." She has an eclectic approach to tradition—such as a "Passover seder with bits of Buddhism, Native American religion, and blue collar union songs" (*L.I. Jewish World*, Aug. 27–Sept. 2, 1993, p. 3).

Item: There is a new term coined by Dr. Jack Wertheimer, a Professor of modern Jewish history at the Jewish Theological Seminary of America, to describe the way contemporary Jews approach Judaism. He calls it: "Judaism a la carte," whereby

people pick and choose from a religious smorgasbord of opportunities. Lighting Chanukah candles but marrying a
Catholic. Living Reform but funding Lubavitch. Or a high
school graduate in Florida who was supposed to leave for a
year of Torah study in Israel on August 22nd, but departs the
day after Rosh Hashanah because the Miami Dolphins played
their first game this past Sunday, and he didn't want to miss it.

Now, we have observed before that half-a-loaf in Judaism is better than nothing. This youngster is going to Israel—so he's two weeks
late because of the Dolphins. So what's so terrible?

The answer is: It's not so terrible; in fact, it is very American. But
it is Judaism a la carte. It is founded on individual preferences to pick
and choose. It rests on the ultimate power of the human being and it
does not consider the responsibility to a higher being—to God.

III

And there is a heavy price to pay for a la carte Judaism or, for that
matter, a la carte morality in general.

> **Item:** A young man's father, a very fine, respectable, religious man
> who attends the morning *minyan* daily, is divorcing his wife
> of 25 years because he, too, is picking and choosing and he
> is bored after 25 years. He doesn't get a kick anymore out of
> his relationship. Poof! Gone! That's what happens when one
> lives a smorgasbord existence.

There is a price to pay. If parents pick and choose, so will their
children, and one of their choices may be intermarriage. Why not? In
an age when the individual is king, one has free choice. The fact that I
was accidentally born Jewish may not necessarily be the decisive factor. Love—or choice—may be the determinant. Let us remember: It is
not only choosing within the religion; religion itself becomes a choice,
one alternative among others.

Daniel Bell, a profound student of American culture, a former secularist who has rediscovered the transcendent, describes today's religious
life as a *religion of impulse*. Morality, he says, has given way to psy-

chology. One hears less about "good or bad" and more about whether we feel "comfortable" with this or that. One of my students in a sex ethics class at Ramaz, when I asked about a particular form of sexual behavior, answered: "If it feels good, it is right." Those same words were quoted in a *New York Times* article this summer about Woodstock. Those same words explain the strange twist of values from the old days when, if one committed adultery one at least felt guilty, while today we are taught to feel guilty only if we fail to follow our impulses.

The culture around us, into which many Jews are assimilating, is dominated by the worship of individual preferences. Rabbi Samuel Dresner writes that a family TV script under consideration was returned to its author with the following suggestions: one male should be a homosexual, the love scene should lead to rape, the 45-year-old female should fall in love with the teenager, a shot-gun blast should replace a punch, and a scene should be introduced which would lead to incest. Otherwise, the program will not hold the viewer's interest.

This is all considered normal. In fact, in our topsy-turvy world of individualism run amok, what used to be considered abnormal now must be classified as normal, while what used to be normal is now considered abnormal or, at best, simply one of many alternate forms of behavior. This moved even Russell Baker to be serious in an article on the op. ed. page of the *New York Times* (May 10, 1994):

"Virtually every magazine on the newsstand, every book in the drug store, half the stories in the tabloid press, vast quantities of television, entertainment and movies galore depict sexual philandering as a common and casual pastime. The result can only be that any monogamous folks wandering this cultural Sodom and Gomorrah feel positively freakish, if not distinctly embarrassed by their unorthodox sexual proclivities."

Yesterday, at *S'lichot,* we read a prayer composed by Rav Saadya Gaon in Babylonia 1,050 years ago. With frightening prescience he describes our chaotic world:

"We have rebelled against thy command, and departed from thy judgments . . . we have constantly committed many follies, loved evil more than good, and falsehood rather than truth; we have pre-

88

ferred impurity to purity, the loathsome to the clean; we have
exchanged the everlasting for the transitory . . . We have sunk in a
miry bog, where there is no foothold; we have come into deep
waters, where the floods overflow us; *yet not with thee, O Lord our
God, have we dealt ill, but with our own souls; and not thee have we
vexed, but ourselves*; for when man sins, what effect has it on thee?
If his trespasses are numerous, what does he do to thee? But woe
to the sons of man who sin against thee, and woe to their soul!
For they have rewarded evil to themselves."

That is the way Rav Saadya described it in liturgical accents. Daniel
Bell says something similar in the terminology of the sociologist.

"Modernism," he writes, "is exhausted because the religion of impulse *has been* realized."

> "Drugs, originally perceived as the refuge of marginal figures, have
> in our time been transformed into a 'drug culture.' The social dis-
> eases of family collapse, massive illiteracy, and now AIDS are the
> harvest we reap for the new 'freedom.' Sexual liberation has not
> been the high road to mental health but, rather, to the Russian
> roulette of unwanted pregnancy and/or unwanted disease. A heavy
> price has been paid for a la carte morality in America."

This sad state, which brings us occasional thrills but very little long-
term happiness, is a major ramification of the coronation of the individual and the dethroning of God. Chief Rabbi Jonathan Sacks, of the
British Empire, sums up our predicament as follows: We live in "an
environment in which normal judgment is condemned as being judg-
mental, in which the one concept to have universal currency is that of
rights, . . . in which there is no sexual ethic beyond . . . personal
choice . . . . In such an environment there can be no moral authority
beyond the self . . . there can be no moral institutions such as that of
the family, in which obligations . . . override personal preference."
There can be no moral role-models who epitomize our collective values and virtues, because we are too divided to reach a consensus on
whether to prefer Mother Therese to Madonna.

We cannot even enact a gun control law in our society because of
the enthronement of the individual and the sanctification of his or her
rights to hunt and to defend oneself.

IV

To see the problem and to recognize it as a social and religious catastrophe is to understand what we as Jews must do.

First: On Rosh Hashanah we must re-establish priorities. God is King, not we. "We all must accept the yoke—of His Kingship." That means, as the Ethics of the Fathers says: "Nullify your will before His will." It means concentrating on *mitzvot*, obligations, responsibilities first—and rights and privileges and needs second.

The second step is to study Torah and thereby to *internalize* this yoke of God's Kingship so that we are not automatons but rather responsive, moral, ethical and pious people. In the words of Jeremiah (33:33), "I will place my Torah *within them* and transcribe it *on their hearts.*"

And the third step is to understand that living a life of responsibility to a Higher Law, while it may not always make us "feel good," will ultimately lead to our benefit.

Living a life of moral and religious limits does bring very real benefits. It helps our marriages; it positively affects our children's education and development; it goes a long way toward ensuring Jewish continuity and it brings us a sense of fulfillment. Living a life of commitment to God brings its own reward.

The sainted Rabbi Mendel of Kotzk once asked, "Why the Temple will be built on Mt. Moriah where only an angel appeared and not on Mt. Sinai where God came down Himself and gave the Torah to Israel." And he answered: "The Temple will be built on Mt. Moriah because that was the scene of the greatest commitment of man to God as King and law giver."

On this Rosh Hashanah let us begin to move ourselves and the world a little closer to the fulfillment of that dream by our own total commitment to God and to His Law.

Amen!

SIMON GREENBERG

The Birthright

An honest analysis of our attitude toward the basic problems which confront us is always timely. It is doubly so in days as tumultuous and tragedy-laden as these. Fires kindled and fed by fiends as demonic as any of which hell itself might boast are testing our souls. Arguments as persuasive as any by which Lilith lured Eve are bombarding our minds. If then our souls are not to be incurably seared nor our minds irredeemably corrupted, we must pause even in the very midst of the conflagration to re-examine the principles by which we live, for they serve not only as compass to point the way, but also as the most precious and effective weapons to combat the flame. One of these principles concerns the birthright.

Rabbi Simon Greenberg received his A.B. from the College of the City of New York in 1922, was ordained at the Jewish Theological Seminary in 1925, and received his Ph.D. from Dropsie College in 1932. He was rabbi of Har Zion Temple in Philadelphia from 1925–1946. He taught Education and Homiletics at the Jewish Theological Seminary where he served as Vice-Chancellor from 1957–1986. Rabbi Greenberg was the founder and developer of the University of Judaism in Los Angeles from 1947–1972, President of the University of Judaism from 1958–1963, and President of the Rabbinical Assembly in 1937 and 1938.

Jacob bought the birthright for some bread and pottage of lentils. He felt that he had made a good purchase, but many of his posterity have formed a different estimate of the transaction. It is their considered opinion that Esau got the better end of the bargain. They would, if they could, gladly return that birthright to Esau. They would even permit him to keep the pottage of lentils if only he returned the bread. For while this birthright, with all its spiritual implications, made us an eternal people, it at the same time set us up as the mark at which every arrow poisoned by lust for plunder and thirst for blood has been directed throughout the ages.

We are all only too well acquainted with those modern descendants of Jacob who regret their father's rash acquisition of a life-giving ideal. We all meet Jews who mourn the fact that Moses redeemed our ancestors from Egypt, instead of permitting them to be annihilated there.

We have all had experiences similar to that recently related by a young rabbi. He had been invited to kindle the Hanukkah lights in the home of a lady whose Jewish consciousness awoke after the passage of the Nuremberg laws. She had never before heard of the festival, and she wanted to know its history and manner of observance. After kindling the lights the rabbi related the story of the heroic struggles of the Maccabees and the miraculous victory they won for Israel. He hoped his hostess would find in that account a new pride in her people and an inspiration to carry on in the spirit of the Maccabees. But at the end of his story he was quite stunned to hear the lady sigh, "How sad that the Maccabees won. Had they lost, we would not be suffering today."

This deplorable and ethically revolting reaction is far too common among us to dismiss merely with indignant condemnation. For there are far too many who, though they take pride in the achievements of the past and find spiritual strength in them, nevertheless have their grave doubts about the future. They seriously question why they should bring children into the world if Israel's lot is one of unrelieved suffering, or why they should urge those children who are already born to remain Jews if there is any way by which they can sever their relations with this perennially persecuted historic group. Calling these people ugly names is not enough. Labeling them as cowards and renegades does not answer their questions. Because these queries disturb so many warm and loyal Jewish hearts, and because they are roused by cruel persecutions and unparalleled sufferings, they should be analyzed carefully and sympathetically.

Let us then start by asking a few pertinent questions about this frequently encountered Jewish desire to disappear as a distinguishable entity from the stage of human history. Can it be fulfilled within a reasonably short time by a well-ordered, consciously directed, and ethically acceptable process? Is it a morally justifiable, edifying ideal for a whole people or any considerable segment of it? Has the disappearance of any historic group or any important portion of it ever been exhibited as evidence of the commendable idealism, courage, wisdom, or spiritual vitality of that group? Is this comparatively widespread Jewish craving for spiritual and physical self-annihilation anything more than a child's futile weeping for the moon? Or what is much more pitiable and tragic—is it not rather the expression of that physical exhaustion inevitably accompanied by an intellectual weariness which tempts and often persuades even strong men to sell their souls in return for a chimerical safety for their skins? These are some of the questions every Jew should ask himself before condemning Jacob and attempting to reject the birthright.

Let us consider the case of the parents who may say, "True indeed that mass assimilation is impracticable and will not solve the whole of the Jewish problem. But we are not interested in the whole problem. We are interested only in our own child. We want to give him a chance for a happier life. We want him, therefore, to grow up as little conscious of his Jewishness as possible so that he may have an opportunity to disappear into the mass of the majority." The motive of such action, then, is always transparently clear. It does not start with a condemnation of the Jewish heritage, though for purposes of self-justification it often ends that way. The motive is the child's welfare.

To the spiritually and intellectually superficial, the intentions of such parents may be noble. To one having a deeper appreciation of human values, nothing can be more reprehensible than this exposure of a child to a life of inner hypocrisy, of playing a role demanding insincerity, and eternal watchfulness lest his true nature be discovered. And all for what purpose? That the child be physically secure! But we know that if there is a violent wave of anti-Jewish feeling in the land he will be spared as little as any other Jew. Let us assume, however, that for a few generations there is no active anti-Semitism and that this child intermarries and succeeds in obliterating completely the memory not only of his people but of his own parents. What is achieved then? Are he and his children secure? Who knows? The Jews are not the only minority in the world. There are always other minorities, political, religious, economic, or social. Once majorities begin to persecute minorities they do not stop with any one of the minorities. Totalitarian societies do not tolerate any kind of variations. Nor are minorities constant. One can never know when a present-day majority may become tomorrow's persecuted minority. Such are the whims of fortune that the grandson for whose membership in the majority of our own day we were ready to cripple our souls and our child's souls, may in reality find himself a member of a new ostracized minority. But let us assume that he remains always with the ruling group. What a comforting and inspiring thought it must be for parents to contemplate the possibility that their son or grandson having become a triumphantly accepted member of the majority may, to prove his allegiance to the new group, become a virulent anti-Semite. Nor is this a farfetched and imaginary bogey summoned for this occasion. The sons of the Russian Jewish apostate, the learned Professor Abraham Zimmerman, actually participated in a pogram against Jews. History records altogether too many instances of anti-Semites whose ancestry was Jewish and whose anti-Semitism was therefore all the more bitter and uncompromising, for there is no hate like self-hate. The case of Bela Imredy, Premier of Hungary, instigator of the anti-Semitic legislation in Hungary, though himself a descendant of Jews, is too recent to require elaborate comment. The discovery of his Jewish ancestry caused his own downfall, but did not diminish the evil of his legislation. The thought of such a possibility, be it ever so remote, should be sufficient to deter any self-respecting parent from exposing his child or grandchild to such ethical decay.

In contemplating this possibility, Jewish parents might do well to take to heart the fears disturbing the minds of the best among the non-Jewish mothers of our days. Jewish mothers dread the thought of raising children who may be persecuted by anti-Semitic barbarians. Non-Jewish mothers today dread the thought that they may raise sons who will be anti-Semite barbarians capable of torturing their innocent fellowman and peaceful neighbor, as if they were indulging in some sport. Erika Mann, daughter of the great Thomas Mann, in her book *School for Barbarians*, describing Nazi education, records the fear of one such "Aryan" mother who spoke not only for herself, but for all decent "Aryan" mothers of Germany. She has this to say, "I want my child to become a human being, a good and decent man who knows the difference between lies and truth, aware of liberty and dignity and true reason. I want the boy to become a decent human being and man and not a Nazi." Dorothy Thompson in many of her brilliant columns calling for a united front against anti-Semitism echoed the same sentiments. Writing to a Jewish friend who expressed fear regarding her son's future in a world controlled by Nazi ideology, she expressed even greater concern for her own son in such a world, for he might be among those who would accept that ideology as his own. There is little doubt that the world will have to move either in the direction of greater tolerance or in the opposite direction of an ever-increasing intolerance. In the first instance, being a Jew will involve a decreasing amount of discomfort. In the second instance, we ought to prefer to take our chances to be among the persecuted rather than among those who delight in persecuting others or remain callously indifferent in the presence of such persecution.

Therein lies the crux of the whole matter and our rabbis saw it clearly. "What is it," they ask, "which prompted Jacob to endanger his very life to get the birthright—was it the desire to escape a burden, or to achieve physical security or economic advantage?" On the contrary, we know that it caused him to flee from his home and to give up all peace and safety. It endangered not only his life but later the lives of his wives and children. The rabbis answer: "Jacob wanted the birthright because he saw that until the Temple in Jerusalem would be erected, the first born had the responsibility of bringing the sacrifices, of being the priest in the service of God. It was he who was to carry on the purposes for which Abraham was chosen—'to command his children and his grandchildren after him to do justice and righteousness.'" And Jacob said, "Can I expect that an irresponsible, ethically insensitive creature like Esau should fulfill his duties properly?" There was holy work to be done and he offered himself!

That has remained throughout the ages one of the many implications of that birthright. This Temple of God, of righteousness and justice of which Isaiah prophesied that "all nations would go up to it to worship," is still to be erected. There is still much holy work to be done. There is still need of men who like Jacob will offer themselves to assume that task when all around them they see so many Esaus with no other care in their hearts or heads than how to use their swords and fill their stomachs. In the doing of that holy work each one has his part to play. The poet put it succinctly and well when he said:

> You cannot choose your battlefields,
> The gods do that for you—
> But you can place your standard
> Where your standard never flew.

Our place on that battlefield has been chosen for us by God and by the voluntary actions of our ancestors. We are to be the world's most permanent, most widespread, most articulate, most self-conscious minority, remaining true to our birthright and carrying high our standard with its divinely inscribed injunctions:

> To love the stranger
> To love thy neighbor as thyself
> To do justly, love mercy, and walk humbly with God.

By this standard we and all men are to be tested. Without tolerance, brotherly love, and justice, all other attainments of civilizations are mere Frankenstein's monsters leading to their creator's destruction. Any Jew believing that the whole Jewish people can be forced or persuaded to give up this standard or the strategic, though enormously dangerous, position which it occupies on the battlefield of the human spirit, has simply misread the whole of Jewish history and lacks the most elementary understanding of Jewish character. If he desires to run away by himself or with his family to the other side of the battlefield, let him try to do it. But let him know that his desire is rooted neither in wisdom, nor in mercy, nor in self-respect. Let him know that it is prompted by little more than the simpleton's impression that the windows in the other fellow's castle are made of gold, or the weakling's belief that the position occupied by his opponent is safer than his own, or the coward's readiness to take the gambler's chance of saving his skin by selling his soul. In the world in which we are living, no nation has a palace with gold windows, no position is absolutely safe, and no skin was long secure if that security was paid for by the soul.

Esau, the rabbis further teach, agreed to sell his birthright because he believed only in the immediate present and had no faith whatsoever in the distant future. Therein, too, Jacob differed radically from his brother. Jacob and his descendants after him never wavered from their faith in the coming of the day when "they shall not hurt nor harm in God's holy mountain for the earth shall be full of knowledge of the Lord as the waters cover the sea." It is because many of Jacob's descendants have become like Esau and lost faith in the future of mankind, that they now would deny their birthright. Believing that mankind will never outgrow its persecution of the Jew, they seek to transfer their child from the ranks of the persecuted to the ranks of the persecutor. And what great sacrifices they are ready to make in order to achieve so ignoble an end!

We are no longer alone among those who have faith in that future. All true believers in the reality of the living God, all true lovers of His teachings and of His children have that faith.

If others have the confidence, the spiritual courage, and the physical stamina to live and struggle and suffer until the day of the universal brotherhood of man arrives, certainly our fathers have proved that they had that confidence, courage, and stamina. Surely we, their children, who are physically stronger and more numerous than they ever were, surely we are not going to give up the struggle now. Surely we will not deny our birthright and abandon our positions. Surely we will not be found engaging in the morally reprehensible acrobatic stunt of always seeking to join the ranks of him whose star is temporarily ascendant. Let us hold firmly to our positions in the ranks of our father Abraham, whose star is that of one God and one mankind, the star of justice and brotherhood, and the right of each man to "hold firmly to the right, as God gives him to see the right." Let us not lose heart because the luster of that star may temporarily be clouded. It is destined ultimately to rise supreme and to rule in unchallenged splendor in the benign skies which canopy this globe. It is our noble aspiration and firm faith that Israel should and will be there to rejoice in its light.

DAVID HARTMAN

Aliya: The Transformation and Renewal of an Ideal

The call to aliya today often creates feelings of estrangement and hostility among Diaspora Jewry. At a recent gathering of leaders of world Jewry, the President of Israel called for aliya as the obvious solution to the Diaspora's concern with Jewish continuity. After all, assimilation would cease and their continuity would be assured if Jews would only leave the fleshpots of the Diaspora and join the historic renaissance of the Jewish people in its homeland.

Rabbi David Hartman was born in Brooklyn, New York and attended Yeshiva Chaim Berlin and the Subavitch Yeshivah. He received his M.A. in Philosophy from Fordham, and his Ph.D. in Philosophy at McGill University. He was ordained at Yeshiva University's RIETS by Rabbi Joseph B. Soloveitchik. In Montreal, he served as rabbi of Tiferet Beit David Jerusalem Congregation. He made *aliyan* with his family to Israel in 1971 and joined the Department of Jewish Philosophy at the Hebrew University. In 1976, he founded the Shalom Hartman Institute in Jerusalem. Twice he received the National Jewish Book Award. Rabbi Hartman is a leading Orthodox thinker, blending *halacha* with modernity.

The President's speech was misunderstood as patronizing and humiliating, ignoring Diaspora Jewry's efforts at building its own viable social and cultural frameworks. They were turning to Israel for partnership, not salvation.

Is this encounter symptomatic of a deep cultural schism within the Jewish people? Must Israeli leaders be silent about aliya—the central motif of the modern Zionist revolution—in order to maintain meaningful dialogue with the Diaspora?

In the following essay I shall argue that the concept of aliya must undergo a radical transformation if it is not to become extinct and irrelevant. But, before continuing, I shall discuss a feature of Jewish law which informs my position.

THE LANGUAGES OF MIRRORING AND ASPIRATION

Jewish law can be understood in terms of the distinction between mirroring and aspiration, that is, between norms which reflect the moral sensibilities of the community and those which point to new moral and spiritual values.

One function of law is to provide political stability, order, and continuity by incorporating and mediating existing standards and values. *Dibra Torah bileshon b'nei adam*, "The Torah speaks in the language of human beings." A law that ignores what the majority of people can appreciate and appropriate in everyday life is in danger of losing its normative credibility. Law thus mirrors where people "are at."

Another function of law is to awaken the community to strive to higher goals and ideals. From this perspective, law educates rather than mirrors. Its goal is to challenge and to inspire the community to aspire to new spiritual heights. Maimonides' interpretation of the different forms of worship, that is, sacrifices, petitional prayer, and contemplation, is an excellent model for understanding the educative, leading function of Jewish law (*See The Guide of the Perplexed*, III:32,51).

In the final analysis, law must balance the conservative need for stability against the progressive pull to educate and change. A law which mirrors the moral and spiritual status quo without awakening alternative possibilities becomes lifeless and banal, a law which speaks the language of aspiration without recognizing what people are really like ceases being a workable framework because of its distance from accepted notions of what people can achieve.

This distinction can shed light on the problematic meaning of the concept of aliya in contemporary Jewish life.

THE CONTEMPORARY PROBLEM
OF ALIYA LANGUAGE

In the past, aliya was a response to political crises which threatened the existence of Jews. Massive aliya to Israel was directly related to persecution and anti-Semitism. Jews "escaped" to Israel. Aliya was more often a "running away from" than a "striving for something higher."

The North American experience, however, differs radically from this paradigm. In America, Jews are very, very comfortable. Even when experiencing a sense of marginality, Jews basically feel safe and at home. There is no physical danger driving them to seek aliya as an answer to their survival needs.

This is the crux of the dilemma. We can no longer talk an aliya language that is nurtured by fear and physical crisis. The overriding threat to the future of North American Jewry is assimilation, not anti-Semitism or marginality.

No matter how serious a threat assimilation is, it is not experienced as a life-threatening crisis. Although caring Jews do consider assimilation a real crisis, those who assimilate view their behavior as free and uncoerced. They are not reacting to an external threat. Some might even recommend assimilation as a liberating alternative to the burdensome guilt of feeling responsible for Jewish history and culture.

Ironically, assimilation can be understood as a Jewish longing for normalcy—the very same notion which traditionally inspired many Zionists. If our aliya pitch is to live a "normal" life, we expose ourselves to the response that intermarriage and assimilation are perfectly good ways of achieving normalcy.

The limited range of human lifestyles of the Eastern European ghetto is not the social reality which Jews experience in Toronto or Los Angeles. For many Jews living in pluralistic democracies which offer an unlimited range of opportunities for personal self-fulfillment, the Zionist dream of normalcy has already been realized. For them the promise of aliya has been fulfilled!

We must understand this new historical reality and instead of hunting for signs of anti-Semitism in order to reignite the cause of aliya, we must face the fact that North American Jewry is not a community in crisis.

A CONCEPTUAL TRANSFORMATION
OF ALIYA LANGUAGE

However difficult it is for the Zionist movement to admit it, the community of crisis, which fueled interest in aliya in the past by making it alive and relevant for Jews, no longer exists. The traditional survival- and normalcy-oriented appeals of aliya no longer resonate in the hearts of Jews today. If Israelis are to avoid the frustration of issuing endless aliya proclamations which fall on deaf ears, they must understand that you cannot speak about aliya to people who do not appreciate the significance of living an intense Jewish life.

The quality of daily Jewish life in the Diaspora is the necessary groundwork for turning aliya into a relevant live option. If you enjoy life as a Jew in Dallas, then one day you may want to realize your Jewish self in Israel. But if Jewish living in Dallas has no vital moral and spiritual significance, then living as a Jew in Jerusalem is a dead option.

The "safe haven" and "normalcy" appeals which gave vitality to the language of aliya in the past must be replaced by an aliya language which conveys the spiritual and moral excitement that Israeli life makes possible. Before worrying about the future of Diaspora Jewry, Israeli leaders concerned about aliya should first address themselves to the problematic moral and spiritual quality of Jewish life in Tel Aviv and Jerusalem.

Receptivity to the language of aliya is a function of the sense of Jewishness that permeates a person's daily life. For my father, being Jewish and living as a committed Torah Jew were natural and self-evident. His instinctive answer to my asking him about the meaning of Jewish observance was "This is how my father lived and how his father lived!" For him, my questions were irrelevant because of the inherent power of the past that it informed his present identity and practice. He could only sing a Jewish *nigun.*

While this was true of my father's world, for me and my generation these were no longer pointless questions. The importance of the tradition and of being Jewish had ceased being self-evident. Knowledge and personal conviction were necessary now if the tradition was to be a live option in my life. In some very important sense, I chose—and I must continuously choose—to live a committed Jewish life.

Although I know that my family, my teachers, and my early Yeshiva education shaped my identity profoundly—leaving the Jewish family is not a real option for me—I nevertheless realize that, in contrast to my father's Jewish experience, my commitment to continue my father's and grandfather's way of life has to be reappropriated through knowledge and personal conviction. Living in dynamic pluralistic societies challenges me continually to confront and reclaim the spiritual vision of my ancestors.

Leaving Montreal where I had built a synagogue and worked tirelessly to further Jewish institutions and university studies wasn't simple. Leaving productive rabbinic and university careers and uprooting a family from a normal and comfortable way of life were not easy decisions.

I often say to people who ask me what inspired me to make aliya, "I was among the few members of my congregation who listened to my sermons! What could I do? I was so inspired by the rhetoric of aspiration that I forgot what Israel was really like."

After making aliya, however, I soon realized that Israel was not exactly what my sermons were about. It took me several years to bridge the gap between the Israel of my *drashot* and dreams and the manic-depressive quality of daily life in Israel.

Without the powerful and inspiring image of a Jewish national spiritual renaissance—of what I innocently believed Israel to be like—I would not have had the strength to uproot my family or to persevere in facing the strains and tensions of Israeli life.

I have come to understand from my own experiences that the language of aspiration is both a catalyst for change and an important counterweight to the feelings of futility and despair that can undermine serious attempts at effecting change.

The "rhetoric" of hope and the belief in future possibilities is not a regressive escape into childish fantasy. It is essential for sustaining the vitality of a broader perception of what human life could be. In this sense, I am happy and grateful that I listened to my sermons!

Articulating a new vision of aliya and of what Israel could be, or rather of what "Israel really is about," is not a form of escape or a denial of the vulgar parts of Israel political life but is necessary for reinvigorating the Zionist ideal of aliya.

Focussing exclusively on the Holocaust and the possibility of future anti-Semitism will not move Jews to leave the comforts of Los Angeles for Israel. We must let go of the crutches of anti-Semitism and alienation in order to create and sustain conviction—in order to move aliya from "mirroring" to "aspiration."

INDIVIDUALISM, HISTORY, AND NATIONAL CONSCIOUSNESS

How do you make the language of aliya resonate in people's souls without sounding anachronistic or pointless? How do you move the focus of "aliya language" from crisis to personal conviction?

Jews in Israel and throughout the world must understand the significance of our dream to return to Israel and Jerusalem. The themes of Jerusalem and *kibbutz galuyot*, the "ingathering of the exiles," are central themes of our liturgy.

Why did the tradition make our return to the land, to Jerusalem, an essential feature of Jewish identity? Why did land and nation become constitutive elements of Jewish spiritual self-understanding? What makes Jewish nationalism distinct from other forms of nationalism? Serious Jewish leaders must offer intelligent answers to all these questions.

To be a Jew is to be claimed by three thousand years of history. The individual is the carrier of a legacy, of a covenantal promise of the Jewish people to become a holy nation (*goy kadosh*). The Jewish family, therefore, was always imbued with a national purpose to mediate the founding memories of the Jewish people for the next generation.

> And make them known to your children and to your children's children; The day you stood before the Lord your God at Horeb, when the Lord said to Me, "Gather the people to Me that I may let them hear My words, in order that they may learn to revere Me as long as they live on earth and may so teach their children." (Deut. 4:9–10)

The central concern of the Jewish family was to cultivate a sense of being claimed and an appreciation of the ultimate significance of daily life.

In contrast to this notion of the family, the modern Jewish family understands itself in psychological terms. Individual happiness and social adjustment are the central parental concerns. The family is essentially future-oriented. History and memory are peripheral if not totally irrelevant to the overriding preoccupation with the child's psychic and economic well-being.

Aliya is predicated on the premise that the "I," the individual, can shape and be shaped by the "we," the nation. The drama of community informs the drama of self-fulfillment. For aliya to become a serious option, the notion of the individual self must become more relational and community-oriented. Individual self-realization must be informed by notions of shared history and memory. Unless we overcome the ethos of self-sufficiency, aliya language will have little chance of being heard.

The power of community and family must be among the most important Israeli efforts to the Diaspora. The new Zionist dream for Israel must be infused with the belief that the liberal concern with individual rights and dignity can flourish together with a deep commitment to history and community.

ISRAEL: THE PUBLIC FACE
OF THE JEWISH PEOPLE

Aliya must regain the inherent force of *aliya*—a word that implies "going up," aspiring to, striving for something higher. It must become a concept that challenges, that points to new possibilities and alternatives, that disturbs complacency and self-satisfied acceptance of the status quo.

The message of aliya should convey the idea of privilege—the privilege of bringing up children with a sense of history and community. This must become the central thrust of aliya as a language of aspiration.

As a Jew who lives in and loves Jerusalem, who feels privileged to have brought his family here, I can testify to the excitement and authenticity of living in a nation still involved with shaping its future identity.

In contrast to my religious life in the diaspora, my celebration of the Sabbath and Jewish festivals does not place my identity in opposition to my environment. On Yom Kippur the streets of Jerusalem mirror the inner sanctity of the day. Here my public self talks to my private self, my outer world shapes and is shaped by my inner world.

Even though I feel anger and frustration when I read the morning papers and realize that many of our efforts at changing things through education are being undermined by short-sighted Knesset members bent on legislating Judaism, yet I feel alive. I am angry, I am pained, but I am energized by the excitement of fighting to shape a nation that doesn't yet know who it wants to be or how to appropriate the Judaic tradition in the modern world.

Israel is the public face of the Jewish people and aliya is a call to shape that public face. *Time* magazine follows us wherever we go. Whatever happens in Jerusalem is immediately broadcast on CNN worldwide. With the establishment of Israel Jews can no longer hide. For better or for worse, Jews have gone public.

Anyone who cares about the legacy of Jewish history must realize one thing: the future of Jews in America and everywhere else will be defined by the type of Jewishness we build in Israel. If we fail, Diaspora Jewry will be ashamed to show its public face. If fundamentalism and delegitimization of others grow here, we won't be able to talk about the ethical legacy of the Jewish people. We won't be able to repair the public shame of Yigal Amir's fanaticism.

The issue of aliya then is: Who are we going to be? Jews who value pluralism and tolerance, who understand the meaning of freedom of conscience, or Jews who returned to their own country only to act as if they never heard about democracy or fought to preserve the rights of minorities?

Israel is not only a call to normalcy, to be like the nations. Israel is a call to fulfill the vision of Moses, "And you shall be to Me . . . a holy nation" (Exod. 19:6) in a new way. Aliya is a call to the individual to arise, to assume a dramatic role in history, to participate in nation-building.

If we can overcome the embarrassment of the biblical and prophetic understanding of the role of Israel in history, and if the Jewish spiritual legacy can become personal conviction, then aliya will regain the compelling power of an ideal worth striving for.

It is not speeches and proclamations that will move Diaspora Jews but rather a Jewish society which inspires the individual to want to participate in the three-thousand-year-old legacy of the Jewish nation. Aliya must first address Israelis and educate them to appreciate the crucial role they can play in determining the future of Jewish life throughout the world. Israelis are not only asked to address the persecuted and frightened Jew, but also, and above all, Jews who have lost their sense of memory and history and whose Jewishness has ceased being necessary and self-evident.

Israeli society must convey the excitement and importance of living as modern Jews who combine a sense of history and tradition with a profound belief in new human possibilities. The final chapter of our people's spiritual drama has not yet been written.

Israel as a vital Jewish society will awaken Jews to become active participants in shaping the future of the Jewish people's moral and spiritual legacy.

ARTHUR HERTZBERG

The Trouble With God-Talk

God seems to be replacing anti-Semitism as the "hot" subject of contemporary Jewish discussion.

Books keep appearing in which He is portrayed with astonishing certainty by theologians who tell us they know His limits or who assert, with even greater certainty, that they can tell us how to find the union of the soul with Him. On the Jewish lecture platform, God-talk used to be very rare, appearing usually in the form of an occasional debate between Orthodox and liberal rabbis. It is no longer so.

Every "politically correct" Jewish lecture series must bow towards "Jewish continuity" by having a lecture or two about God.

I have no doubt that right-thinking people would expect a traditionalist like me, who has been standing on the roof for forty years

Rabbi Arthur Hertzberg received his A.B. in 1940 from Johns Hopkins University, was ordained at the Jewish Theological Seminary in 1943, and received his Ph.D. at Columbia University in 1966. He has served various Conservative Congregations and served as Chaplain in the U.S. Air Force from 1951-1953. This prolific author has also served as President of the American Jewish Congress from 1972-1978 and as editor of the "Journal on Jewish Social Studies."

shouting the demand for more Jewish learning and more religious seriousness to be trembling with joy that God has seemingly been asked back into the Jewish community. But I am not.

The supposed theological revival is not about God at all. It is, mostly, about the obsession with self, against which I was preaching in the 1960s and 1970s.

So let me explain.

In my parents' home (my father was the rav and rebbe in Baltimore of the Chasidic shteibel that he founded), everyone obeyed the injunctions of the religious tradition, and we often talked about what courses of action these rules prescribed or indicated, but we never talked about theology.

My father did once quote Maimonides to me to make the point that any description of God is essentially a limitation that we are imposing on Him.

For example, to say that He is good suggests that evil, as we feel it, cannot come from Him. To Maimonides, and not only to him, such a notion which defines God as a "limited" being is perilously close to blasphemy.

Very early in my youth, I was taught the midrash that the Torah begins with the second letter of the Hebrew alphabet because the *bet* is closed on all three sides and open only in the front, thus imparting the lesson that man should not speculate on what is above, below, or behind. Man is charged to look only forward, to the path that he must take to live a decent, godly life.

Of course, I was brought up to know that one must not only love God but must tremble in awe before His judgments and that each of our souls is both part of him and stands naked before Him, but all these states of spirit were essentially private, personal, and intimate. The essence of Judaism was its demands on our behavior. Indeed, as Solomon Schechter wrote a hundred years ago in one of the essays in *Studies In Judaism*, the Jew communes with God every day by performing the deed that the religious tradition demands. Such behavior is, in Schechter's definition, the "normal mysticism" of Judaism.

Most of the contemporary God-talk is in a different key. The pop theologians of today have picked up on a theme that was first stated in the 1940s, by Rabbi Joshua Loth Liebman in his wildly successful *Peace of Mind*.

Liebman wrote that book when psychoanalysis was in fashion, to suggest that judicious doses of religion would effect a quicker (and, not incidentally, a cheaper) cure for the torments of neuroses. His successors of the last decade have been addressing themselves to the seemingly undeserved pain from which most people suffer at some point in their lives, to the desire for ecstasy safe from the hangovers that can come from mood-altering drugs or to the need for healing when wholeness seems remote and even unattainable.

At the center of most of the God-seeking is "the hungry i," the name that was on the front of a famous club in San Francisco in the late 1960s when the "advanced" thinkers were obsessed with the self. A quarter of a century later, the hungry self is still troubled by its own pain. It is now trying God, the old-new and supposedly most potent mood-transforming drug. Perhaps He will make me happy.

I have no doubt that some of those who have read so far are already reaching for their computers to fire off letters of protest.

How could I possibly not understand that the present God-seeking is carrying forward the basic impulses of Chasidism and many centuries of the kabbalah.

Let me answer these letters in advance: Nonsense! The Chasidim, even at their most ecstatic, were always anchored to the practices that tradition prescribed and to studying the sacred Jewish texts. My Chasidic ancestors regularly ascended the ladders of the kabbalah towards the En-Sof but not in order to make themselves feel better.

Always, they were concerned about others; they were trying to persuade God to forgive the sins of the Jews and to hasten the redemption. Their own happiness was expendable or irrelevant.

The classic Jewish doctrine of realizing the self is that it can be realized only in self-forgetfulness. "Do not be like slaves who serve the master for the sake of receiving rewards." By giving up even the advantage of reward in the world to come (we are told in this passage of the "Ethics of the Fathers"), a human being reaches his fullest stature, because he has gone beyond any need to calculate pleasure or pain. Pain and grief are the given of human life, for all of us live all the time on the edge of an active volcano which will erupt irregularly with deadly consequences.

The prime task of those who remain after each eruption is not to work through their personal grief through psychoanalysis, drugs, or God. It is to rebuild society on moral foundations.

The most alarming aspect of much of the present God-talk is that it is transforming Judaism into a passive religion. Take adequate amounts of God, so we are being told, and you will achieve serenity and optimism and you will become a well-adjusted person.

But authentic Judaism is about none of this. The righteous have no rest in this world and probably not even in the world to come, so the Talmud tells us, because their lives are dedicated to the work of perfecting the world. Not a single one of the prophets or the masters of the Talmud was a "well-adjusted" person, comfortably at home with the society in which he lived or with himself.

On the contrary, prophets and rabbis were plagued by the need to make themselves more godly, that is, more righteous in His service.

There is some God-talk today that does point toward the work of perfecting the world so that it might become God's kingdom.

There is some God-talk today that is leading toward study of sacred texts and realizing the teaching of these texts in the life of the individual and his society.

But too much of today's God-talk is self-involved and self-indulgent.

To those who are, again, in quest of "peace of mind," one should quote again the profound insight of the 19th-century moralist, Israel of Salant: "If you want to save your soul, save somebody else's body."

To this one needs to add the insights of a younger contemporary, Solomon Schechter: "If you want to feel that you are united with God, stop talking and go do a mitzvah: any mitzvah."

RICHARD G. HIRSH

The Power of Silence

A story:

Once the evil king Ahab and the wicked queen Jezebel sought to kill Elijah, for he spoke against them. Elijah traveled for forty days and forty nights as far as the mountain of God at Horeb (which is also called Sinai). There he went into a cave, and there he spent the night.

Then the word of the Lord came to him saying, "Why are you here, Elijah?" He replied, "I am moved by zeal for the Lord, the God of hosts, for the Israelite people have forsaken your Covenant, torn down Your altars, and put Your prophets to the sword. I alone am

Rabbi Richard G. Hirsch was ordained at Hebrew Union College-JIR in 1951. He is a civil rights activist and founding director of the Religious Action Center of the American Union of Hebrew Congregations. While serving several Reform congregations, he initiated many pioneering activities particularly in the area of interfaith relations, as well as establishing and appearing as the Jewish representative on the first interreligious prime time television program in the United States. He has testified often before Senate and Congressional committees on such issues as church vs. state, civil liberties, poverty, and foreign policy. Rabbi Hirsch is both an author and orator.

left, and they are out to take my life." "Come out," God called, "and stand on the mountain before the Lord."

And lo, the Lord passed by. There was a great and mighty wind, splitting mountains and shattering rocks by the power of the Lord; but the Lord was not in the wind. After the wind, an earthquake; but the Lord was not in the earthquake. After the earthquake, fire; but the Lord was not in the fire. And after the fire, "Kol D'mma Daka," variously translated as:

> a small murmuring sound;
> the sound of fine stillness;
> a thin voice of silence;
> the soft barely audible sound of almost breathing;
> a still small voice.

When Elijah heard it, he wrapped his mantle around his face and went out and stood at the entrance to the cave. Then a voice addressed him, "Why are you here, Elijah?" He replied, "I am moved by zeal for the Lord, the God of hosts, for the Israelite people have forsaken your Covenant, torn down Your altars, and put Your prophets to the sword. I alone am left, and they are out to take my life." The Lord said to him, "Go back by the way you came. . . ."

Jewish tradition is a tradition of words, language, and speech. To speak of silence within a Jewish context is almost an oxymoron, certainly a paradox. We are uncomfortable with silence, perhaps afraid, certainly ambivalent. Even that section of the liturgy known as the "silent Amida" is not really silent. For the Amida, tradition requires that our words be audible to our own ears; like God, we too are required to speak in a still, small voice.

There is something mystical, magical, and moving in the power of silence: the holy and positive power of sanctified silence, and the hurtful and damaging power of angry silence. There are many things that can be heard in the sound of fine stillness.

The power of angry silence is the silence we impose on ourselves in relationship to others; it is the silence that closes off relationships and often remains unrepaired. It is the silence we experience and interpret as rejection, as abandonment, or as punishment.

The power of angry silence is often associated in the Bible with the withdrawal of God. As envisioned by the prophets, God's angry silence is a consequence of the faithlessness of the Jewish people, who have failed to fulfill the commandments of the Covenant, and from whom God now withholds that most essential element: the power of the word.

Thus the prophet Amos says to his generation, "A time is coming, says God, when I will send a famine upon the land; not a hunger for bread or a thirst for water, but for hearing the words of the Lord" (Amos 8:11).

When, in ancient Israel, the first Temple was destroyed and the remnant of Judea was exiled to Babylonia, our ancestors voiced their anguish in the metaphor of silence, "When I cry and plead, He shuts out my prayer" (Lamentations 3:8). As much as restoration to their land, they sought assurance of the continued relationship with God that they feared had been broken forever.

Like our ancestors in their ancient national Covenant with God, each of us comes to rely upon the words of those we love in order to reassure us that our relationships, however strained, are not severed.

Here is how the Psalmist put it in the psalm we read morning and evening for the entire month before Rosh Hashana, "Hear, O Lord, when I cry aloud; have mercy on me, answer me . . . do not hide your presence from me; do not thrust me aside in anger; do not forsake me, do not abandon me . . ." (Psalm 27:7-9). Without the assurance of relationship, how can we embark on the process of atonement and repentance?

We too are familiar with the power of angry silence. We withdraw and withhold, out of a need to punish or a need to hurt; and we thereby create a distance which continues to grow in proportion to our ability to stay angry.

Sometimes, like God, we are angry because we are disappointed: in our partners, in our parents, in our progeny. Some expectation went unfulfilled, some promise was broken, something that was supposed to be said was not spoken, or something that was not supposed to be spoken was said.

And sometimes we are angry at ourselves, and someone else has given us a convenient place to displace that anger, about which we prefer to be silent even to ourselves.

Sometimes the power of angry silence makes us feel good, at least for a while. Elijah was, after all, filled with righteous anger, "I am moved by zeal for the Lord, the God of hosts, for the Israelite people have forsaken your Covenant, torn down Your altars, and put Your prophets to the sword. I alone am left, and they are out to take my life." And so he withdraws. In return, all he gets to be is alone.

Too often we use silence as a form of withholding or of control, denying to those we love the reassurance that it is what they have done, rather than who they are, that has made us angry. Especially when dealing with our children, we often forget their vulnerability, and their need to know that our love for them is reliable. And sometimes we even let our anger eclipse our love. There ought to be a confession for "the sin of withholding love in the guise of angry silence."

We pay a price for the silence of anger; and often so do those we love. Jephtha was one of the chieftains of ancient Israel. In a rash moment, he swore an oath to God that if he was victorious in battle he would sacrifice the first thing to come out of his home upon his return. Tragically, the first thing to come out of his home was his daughter.

In the midrash, the rabbis ask: Why did Jephtha not go to the High Priest and ask for a Bet Din, a religious tribunal, to revoke the vow? Because, they answer, when the High Priest heard about Jephtha's vow, he said, "I, after all, am the High priest; why should I go to him? Let him come to me!"

When Jephtha heard this, he said, "I, after all, am a chieftain in Israel; why should I go to him? Let him come to me!" And so the arrogance became anger and escalated until Jephtha and the High Priest retreated into silence . . . and for Yiftach's daughter there was no reprieve. Too often it is children who get caught in the lonely space between two parents who have retreated into silence.

Letting go of the power of angry silence often begins when we realize that it is no longer hurting anyone but ourselves. Rabbi Lawrence Kushner, teaching about grudges—near-cousins of anger—says this: "Each grudge takes on a life of its own. Like a parasite, living in our past, demanding ever-increasing amounts of unconscious attention, it feeds on our vitality. And as the grudge anchors us to something long-gone, it denies a part of us from being here in the present." Healing the angry silence begins when, like Isaiah imagines God speaking, we can say, "I have kept silent far too long" (Isaiah 42:14).

Not all silences are hurtful, and not all are angry. There is also the holy and positive power of sanctified silence. This is the silence in which Elijah heard the Kol D'mama Daka, the still small voice of fine stillness.

116

Writing in his recent book *In Speech and In Silence*, Rabbi David Wolpe teaches, Elijah was witness to a titanic show of natural force in order to prepare him to listen for the silence. He was anticipating a word and needed to learn to hear its absence. God's self-disclosure to Elijah is not with a word, but with the voice of silence. Elijah is renowned for his zeal; he understands the God of awesome declarations, of dazzling wonders. And now, when God needs to speak to him, Elijah expects thunder. He learns silence.

What does it mean to learn silence? What can it mean to look within, to hear in the sound of our own breathing the voice that we seek?

First, it can mean being prepared for the unexpected, being prepared to change and be changed in ways we did not anticipate. Each of us comes to Yom Kippur with some expectations; we think or hope or wish that some transformation will occur, that something dramatic will happen and we will somehow be different.

But like Elijah, what we seek is not in the wind, not in the earthquake, and not in the fire; it is not even up on the mountain. It is, as the Torah puts it, "very close to you, in your mouth and in your heart . . ." (Deuteronomy 30:14). What we seek is the awakening of our inner voice, the awareness of the conduit of conscience through which God calls to us.

To learn silence is also to learn to respect silence, to allow a place for it in our otherwise over-programmed and over-scheduled lives. Do you know what they call it when you turn on the radio and there is silence? "Dead air." Our answering machines are voice-activated; pause for a moment and you are cut off. We seem to have an insatiable need to fill our lives with sound or at least with noise.

To learn silence is to begin to regain control over time. Jewish tradition mandates daily recitation of three standard prayer services. While this may no longer be within the reach of most Jews, making time once, twice, even three times a day for a few moments of silence might well help us to regain perspective and to refocus our energies.

To learn silence means learning to pause before speaking and to pause before doing. "What do you do before you pray?" the hasid asked the rebbe. The rebbe answered, "I pray that I might be able to pray."

Silence can thus be a prologue to ritual. A moment of silence before kindling the candles allows everyone to gather themselves together and to make the transition from weekday to Shabbat. A moment of silence before donating to *tzedaka* can make us conscious that we are doing a holy act, not merely depositing coins in a can.

Learning silence can help us to hear, and not just to listen. Too often, we wait for someone else to finish talking so we can tell them what we think about what they just said; before they have even finished their thought, we have formulated our response. A moment of silence before replying would help us focus on what we heard and perhaps remind us that not everything that is said requires a reply.

Finally, silence can help us to respond when response is called for. According to one rabbinic legend, when God descended on Mount Sinai to reveal the Torah, all that God actually spoke was the sound of the first letter of the first word of the Ten Commandments. The word is *anochi*, "I am . . .," and the first letter is an *aleph*, which in Hebrew is a silent letter. The rest of the Torah is our response to that silence.

Perhaps most important, silence can help us to hear ourselves; and after all, that is surely part of the reason for Yom Kippur.

When Elijah first comes to the mountain, the text reads, "Then the word of the Lord came to him. God said to him, Why are you here, Elijah?"

But after the wind, the earthquake, and the fire; after the still, small voice; the text reads, "Then a voice addressed him, Why are you here, Elijah?"

Something has changed. What was "the word of the Lord" is now described in the text as "a voice." What seemed to come from only one place now comes from nowhere . . . or perhaps from everywhere or perhaps from within Elijah himself.

But something else has not changed; the question is still the same, "Why are you here, Elijah?"

This is the question that really matters. This is the question that God asks. This is what is whispered in the silence.

And this is the question for each of us on Yom Kippur when we gather in the synagogue, "Why are you here?"

The answer is not in the wind, nor in the earthquake, nor in the fire; the answer is in a small murmuring sound, the sound of fine stillness, a thin voice of silence, the soft barely audible sound of almost breathing, a still small voice.

LAWRENCE A. HOFFMAN

The Message and Meaning of Pesach

Ask anyone when the Jewish New Year falls, and you will be told it is in the autumn. Indeed, what we call Rosh Hashanah does fall then, but for most of Jewish history, the New Year that mattered was the beginning of the month of Nisan, which is to say this very Shabbat. The autumn month of Tishrei is actually the seventh month of the year.

There were other New Years, too, once upon a time, corresponding to the agricultural calendar of ancient Israel (like our different fiscal new years in the world of business and accounting). We still have Tu B'Shvat, for example, the new year for trees. But the two most important new years are the calendar's new year (corresponding to the creation of the world) that became our Rosh Hashanah and the spiri-

Rabbi Lawrence A. Hoffman was ordained at Hebrew Union College–Jewish Institute of Religion in 1969 and received his Ph.D. in 1973. He has served as Professor of Liturgy since 1973 and has served as director of its School of Sacred Music. He is also the past president of the North American Academy of Liturgy. Rabbi Hoffman has written or edited 15 books and is a regular columnist for *The Jewish Week*, the largest Jewish newspaper in North America.

tual new year (corresponding to our creation as a nation) that arrives this Shabbat. They have much in common.

Both new years are occasions for rabbinic sermons. Since the nineteenth century, most modern synagogues have featured at least a d'var Torah, and maybe a full-fledged sermon, every Shabbat. But it was once usual to limit sermons to the two new years. On Shabbat Shuvah between Rosh Hashanah and Yom Kippur, the rabbi spoke of *teshuvah,* the need to repent for our personal failings before the time for atonement passes us by. On Shabbat HaGadol, preceding Passover, people were usually instructed on matters relating to Passover, such as how to cleanse a home of *chametz* ("leavened food") before Passover arrived.

On the face of it, the two topics are as different as can be—repentance in the fall and disposal of leaven in the spring—until we consult the rabbis on what they included in the category of leaven. *Chametz,* they said, is not just the food we avoid during Passover week. It is also a metaphor for sin. Cleaning our homes of *chametz* implies cleaning them also of the accumulated improprieties that get closeted away in our family life over the course of a year. In the autumn Rosh Hashanah, then, we cleanse our inner selves; in the spring new year that presages Passover, we begin the equally arduous task of cleaning out the physical and spiritual dross of our homes.

Because it takes a while to own up to personal failures, our calendar anticipates Rosh Hashanah with the preparatory period of Elul, a whole month when a daily shofar blast calls us to repentance. So, too, the springtime recognition of our family's moral and spiritual crises does not come easily. People might think that all they have to do is clean their cupboards of actual bread, cake, flour, and such. But that part is easy. The hard part is cleaning the nooks and crannies of our family relationships. For that difficult task, we need a preparatory period like Elul, and we get it—starting this Shabbat.

For this Shabbat is called Shabbat HaChodesh, and it features the Torah's reminder, "This shall be a first month for you." This is the month to start all over. It is the time to restore our family life to spiritual soundness. It is our annual chance to do some moral housecleaning together.

By moral housecleaning, I do not only mean the monumental sins like incest and child abuse, though of course these are included too. I mean also the little things on which families start to founder: the bad habits that eat away insidiously at our family's spiritual health, the moral "bread crumbs" (so to speak) to which we became so accustomed that we hardly notice them after a while.

They do their damage by collusion as when a husband and wife stop sharing their feelings, then forget how to be mutually supportive, and eventually begin lying "just a little bit" to each other now and then. Or when parents stop asking what their children are doing because they don't want to know, while children stop telling them because they don't want to say. I mean the bouts of anger or mutual recrimination that poison relationships over time, and the petty grievances that make brothers and sisters stop talking to each other eventually. I mean the subtle barbs we use because we know best how to hurt the people we love most. I mean the spiritual toxicity that collects over the long hard winters of our discontent.

Are you headed for a divorce but don't really want one? Are communications breaking down with the people you want most to be in loving contact with? Do conversations hurt more than they help? The next two weeks are set aside to examine these things. If you find your life polluted by them, toss them out along with last year's stale bread crumbs. Try actually writing them down on a composite family list and literally burn them as your spiritual *chametz* this Passover.

Then later, that very evening, sit down for your seder with the sure knowledge why this night is different from all other nights. It won't just be the food. It will be the absence of destructive behavior patterns that you burned as the real *chametz* of the soul. You will look into the eyes of the people you love, recognizing that you have just left bondage far behind.

Let this month be a new beginning for you.

LEO JUNG

The Grace of Tolerance

The Sidrah of Lek Leka commences the story of the first Hebrew, Abraham. The earlier chapters of Bereshith dealt with the origin of the world, the development of life, the creation of man, and the vicissitudes of the human race up to the time of Abraham. Father Abraham has been a luminous personality of abiding influence in the whole course of Jewish history. He brought God to a heathen world and he taught religion in the most effective manner—not by preachment alone nor by merely conveying theological concepts, but by the calibre of his life. He will forever be associated with the basic virtues: *Tzeddeq* or "righteousness"; *Chesed*, "grace or kindness"; and *Rachmanuth* or "mercy."

Rabbi Leo Jung was born in Moravia in 1897, and came to the United States in 1920. He attended Hildersheimer Rabbiner Seminary in Berlin and obtained his A.B. and Ph.D. at the University of London and his A.B. and AM at Cambridge University. He was an Orthodox rabbi as well as a Professor of Ethics. He was on the faculty of Yeshiva College and the Stern College for Women. He was also an officer of the Union of Orthodox Jewish Congregations. He was the Spiritual Leader of the Jewish Center in New York City, and active in the Joint Distribution Commission, Jewish Agency.

The rabbis paid close attention to every aspect of his life. They knew that he had left Ur Kasdim, a city of a flourishing civilization, for the primitive life of Canaan. He was called *Ibri*, and the normal interpretation of that word is "one who crossed" the river Euphrates on the way from Mesopotamia to ancient Canaan.[1] But, reading between the lines of Holy Writ and endeavoring to exhaust every meaning of the word, one of our sages said that Abraham was called an *Ibri* not in reference to *Abar*, meaning to cross, but to a most precious capacity, to remain alone in a good cause: *Kol ha'olam kulo m-'eber 'echad v-hu-m'eber 'echad.*[2]

We moderns remember the dictum of Henrik Ibsen: Only he is strong who can stand alone, only he who can say, "I have arrived at my judgment carefully. I have based my action on that judgment. I am not to be swayed by public applause, not to be diverted from my goal by public disapproval."

There are legitimate objections to tolerance itself. Too often it implies a superior attitude towards people "below us," though, fundamentally, there are no people below us. *B-tzelem 'eloqim bara otham*[3], "God created every human being in His image, the image of man which He had created Himself."[4] No race theory was ever accepted in Judaism. A man is not superior or inferior because of the pigmentation of his skin, or because of his belonging to any geographical, linguistic, or social group. Everyone has a divine spirit in him, his immortal soul. "*N-shamah shenathata bi, t-horah hi*"[5], "The soul which Thou hast given me and every fellow man is pure." Essential equality is the basis of the Jewish way of life.

We in America appreciate this principle because we have learned through trial and error that the essence of democracy is the right to be different, both in the field of religion as in that of any other cultural approach. We "expect differences and respect them," grounded on the right of the individual who is law-conforming and promotive of general welfare, to be different where his conscience, his background, or his foreground incline him towards a particular philosophy of life, form

---

1. Sir Leonard Wooley, "Ur of the Chaldees"
2. Genesis Rabbah A. L.
3. "An Enemy of the People," end
4. Genesis I, 26
5. The version of Symmachos: *betzelem—'eloqim bara 'otam*

of worship, social group; by whatever ways, small or large, by which he may be distinguished from his neighbor. This elemental equality implies the right to be protected against all discrimination, to be spared all indignity, and to be granted those benefits of democratic living which all citizens expect to enjoy.

Nevertheless, tolerance has its uses. It applies to two types of people, even in our modern world. One is a citizen of an underdeveloped country, of a group that could not supply him with basic education, training in social amenities, in hygiene, and in awareness of some of the generally accepted forms of social life. Americans occasionally were censured by their own government and by even the most tolerant of Europeans, for a certain kind of snobbishness. Any American, temporarily in a country less developed than our own, who speaks contemptuously about the imperfect arrangement in his hotel, about poor provisions for comfort, about national or individual low-level in any host country, is a source of much evil to the United States. He does not know that one must try to understand, and then one would tolerate other people's handicaps, which make them less pleasant to behold or convenient to associate with. In the *Ethics of the Fathers*, we are admonished not to judge our neighbor *'ad shetagia lim-qomo*,[6] until we have labored ourselves down, painstakingly, comprehendingly, to his lower place, to the conditions which have determined his attitude.

Tolerance is mandatory, too, towards wicked persons or groups. On the basis of his belief in human equality, Abraham was pleading with the Lord for the city of Sodom,[7] which, according to the tradition of our sages, was one of callous indifference to human woe, of ruthless oppression, of violent hatred towards those whose helplessness one might benefit.[8] Yet Abraham pleaded, "*There may be some people—perhaps fifty, perhaps twenty, perhaps ten*—who deserve to be helped and whose example, as a potent minority, might ultimately change the character of the inhabitants of the city." When Lot received the Divine messengers, the ruthless conduct of the Sodomites showed that not one person in that city deserved consideration. But Abraham had established an immemorial reputation when he did plead for them!

---

6. Siddur, Shacharit
7. II, 5
8. Genesis 18:2r–32

We, in America, are faced with similar situations. What shall we do with the godless mob that attacks Negroes, with the agitators who are responsible for the bombing of synagogues and churches and public schools? We must fight evil. We must use every lawful endeavor to discourage mobsters. Yet we ought to try to understand what makes these fellow-citizens of ours act in such an un-American, inhuman way. The real culprits are the professional agitators, the men who make a business out of preaching hatred. It is they who frighten what is called "the white trash." It is they and conscienceless politicians who encourage riots in order that they might attain their ulterior purpose, either jobs or political preferment or financial gain.

Tolerance, then, for those who are bereft of opportunity for moral or spiritual or social self-advancement; tolerance for those who act not out of full appreciation of any situation, but out of reaction to fear,[9] themselves half-innocent victims of ruthless plotters who incite them—such tolerance is included in the teaching of Abraham, nay, it may be the crown of his teaching.

The prophet holds out this divine promise[10]: "*I will make thee a new threshing sledge, having sharp teeth. Thou shalt thresh the mountains and beat them small and shalt make the hills as chaff. Thou shalt fan them and the wind shall carry them away and the whirlwind shall scatter them!*" Isaiah refers to ideas as weapons. The Abrahamic idea of justice shall penetrate the cruelest mob, the thickest skull of tyrants. "The mountains and the hills represent the powerful worldly forces that seek to block the spiritual and ethical ideals in Israel's message and work. These shall be reduced to powder and scattered by the whirlwind." History and their suffering will teach them that abuse abuses the abuser, that oppression oppresses the oppressor, that eventually it brings its own punishment. In the battle for a more abundant life for all His children, we must remain determined for right and uncompromising foes of wrong. In matters of differences—religious, cultural, social—we must agree to disagree and do so agreeably. This philosophy of tolerance some have derived from our sacred tradition, others from a pragmatic view of history. But where did Father Abraham achieve this timeless aware-

9. Genesis Rabbah, A. L.
10. J. B. Cabell's "Reactionaries"
11. Is. 41:15–16

ness? How, almost four thousand years ago, did he arrive at this formula, the soul at once of religion and democracy?

In one of the classics of modern Hebrew literature, a story is told which would explain the source of his wise-heartedness. The house of Abraham, according to tradition, was situated on top of a hill. There were doors in all directions, so that the weary traveler, seeking its famed hospitality, might find his way up without undue delay. One morning he saw an old man struggling painfully up the hill. In accordance with his way, Father Abraham rushed out of the house to meet the stranger. He helped him reach the top. He bathed his feet, he offered him food and drink. The old man was profoundly grateful and when he was sufficiently relaxed, Abraham said to him, "And now that you are happy, let us say grace to God." The stranger looked at him without comprehension and said, "What is God? Who is God?" "Well," said Abraham, "He is the creator of the world. He is the father of human beings. He is the provider of everything we enjoy." Said the old man, "I don't know anything about that God. I worship the fire." Abraham lost his patience and he said, "You wicked man! I can't have in my house someone who doesn't acknowledge God. You had better leave." The old man went out, unconvinced, unhappy, more lonely than ever.

That night, God appeared to Abraham in a dream, and He said, "I have suffered the foolish old man for seventy years, Abraham. Couldn't you have been patient with him for one night?"

That dream changed the course of Abraham's life. Through that dream he found God truly, he came closer to Him. That dream has been the promise and the challenge and the whole purpose of Jewish history. That dream is of profound significance for every one of us, today and tomorrow.

ROBERT I. KAHN

Leftover Turkey

The day after a holiday is almost always a sad and lonely day. The climax of a celebration is frequently followed by the anticlimax of a morning after. Almost inevitably the high points in our lives leave a low place in our hearts on succeeding days.

It is rather like a stadium after the game is over and the crowd is gone. It is a depressing sight. All that is left are empty sacks and bedraggled banners. Our homes look a little like that after a birthday party is over, all the guests have gone, the floor is littered with ribbon and torn wrapping paper, and the children have turned a little peevish.

Rabbi Robert I. Kahn received his B.A. at the University of Cincinnati and was ordained at the Hebrew Union College—Jewish Institute of Religion in 1935. He received his doctorate in Hebrew Literature in 1950. Rabbi Kahn is a prominent preacher, lecturer, and author who has been President of the Central Conference of American Rabbis, President of the Houston Rabbinical Association, a Chaplain during World War II, the National Chaplain of the American Legion in 1959, and Chairman of the CCAR Liturgy Committee. He is also Rabbi Emeritus of Congregation Emanual, in Houston, Texas.

The same thing can be observed in our synagogues on Shabbat Shuvah, the Friday night after Rosh Hashanah. What is an average Shabbat-size congregation looks so small by comparison. They look about at each other and wonder where everyone has gone. And so it is in our homes, after some occasion which has brought all the family together and the house has rung with laughter. It seems so empty when everyone has gone.

It is probably for this reason that Monday is known as Blue Monday. It comes so close after a weekend of relaxation and family togetherness. A husband goes back to work, the children to school, and mother is left with dirty dishes and dirty clothes.

It is no different on Thanksgiving. It is a happy day, a day of feasting, of family unity, of both physical and spiritual joy. But the day after—well, I do not think I would be far wrong if I wagered that this evening for supper most of you had leftover turkey.

Leftover turkey—somehow the phrase itself tells the whole story. It is the day after the holy day, when all that is left of that beautiful golden brown bird, stuffed to overflowing with dressing, surrounded by cranberries and other good things, is a bony carcass and a few scraps of meat. Yes, on the day that follows Thanksgiving, the menu is likely to be cold sliced turkey or turkey salad or even turkey hash.

Somehow I feel as though there is a sermonic message in this matter of leftover turkey, a thought we would do well to think through with care. For our whole life has something of this quality. Our joy is followed by sorrow, our days give way to night, our happiness is succeeded by problems, and for every turkey we enjoy, there is leftover turkey the day after. One day our home is full of childish laughter and the joys of growing up, and then off they go to college, to the army, to marriage, and the house is quiet and empty and our hearts are lonely. One day we are young and healthy and full of the sap of life, and the next, it's the doctor's office or the hospital, and we must live out our lives with aches and pains and sometimes much worse. One day we sit hand in hand with those we love, and the next, they are snatched away and we are left with only our memories to warm the hearthstones of our hearts. This is the pattern of our lives: Thanksgiving and the day after, the golden bird and the leftover turkey.

Now the real test of a good housewife is not what she serves on Thanksgiving, but rather how she handles leftover turkey. It is no trick to please a family with fresh turkey, or broiled steak, or standing rib-roast every night and just throw away the leftovers. All that takes is money. The test of a housewife is to take the leftovers and turn them into some appetizing, attractive, and tasty dish.

And so, too, with all of us, it is no trick to enjoy life's Thanksgiving days. Everyone enjoys opening gifts on a birthday; everyone is happy relaxing on a Sunday; everyone loves turkey freshly sliced; but the test of life, when life strips us as bare as a Thanksgiving bird on the day after, is how we conduct ourselves, how we pick up the leftover pieces and live out our lives.

When we are in good health, it is easy to be gay and peppy and happy. But what when our health fails and we have to limp through life? When things are going our way, when the money is rolling in, it's easy to laugh and be joyful; but when things are going the other way, it's bills coming in and money going out, what then? When life is kind, when the sun shines warmly and everyone around us shares our love, it's not hard to smile and be cheerful; but when the darkness comes at midday, or when the days get short and the weather turns rainy and cold, when all we have is leftovers, what then, what then?

Believe me, friends, sooner or later, most of us must make do with leftovers, and if we have not learned to take the scraps of our lives and out of them make something new and worthwhile, then all the rest of our lives, we'll just gnaw on bones and be consumed with bitter memories. The test of an individual, the test of a people, the test of a nation, is what it does with leftover turkey.

From the personal point of view, this can be illustrated with two life-stories.

I do not know how many of you knew, or know of, Rabbi Michael Aaronson of Cincinnati. I saw some members of his family just this past month and it brought back a flood of memories. Michael Aaronson was a student at the Hebrew Union College in 1917 when World War I broke out. Being a theological student, he was exempt from the draft, but he waived his exemption and enlisted. In the Meuse-Argonne offensive in France, Aaronson earned the Purple Heart at the price of his eyesight. He was blinded on the battlefield and sent back home. Certainly of all the losses our bodies might undergo, I think all of us would agree that blindness would be the most difficult. And not much would have been expected of this young man whose eyes had lost their vision. But he took what he had left and put it to work. He went on to finish his rabbinical work and was ordained a rabbi in 1923.

Can you imagine learning Talmud and theology, and Rashi and history by ear alone? But that was only the beginning. He went on to serve his people as a field representative of the Union of American Hebrew Congregations, went on to found the Jewish Braille Review, went on to serve as Chaplain of the Disabled Veterans, went on to write articles and books, went on to live a life as active and as fruitful as any rabbi might wish. Here was a man who took leftover turkey and served up a life beautiful to behold.

While Rabbi Aaronson was fighting with the American Army, Franz Rosenzweig was with the German army on the Austrian front. His life is another good example of our theme. Rosenzweig, who is still not well known to us in America, was a German Jewish scholar and thinker whose work is just beginning to appear in English translation. One of his books was written in the trenches on postcards, which day by day he mailed home. Any of us who have lived on a battle front, even an "all quiet" one, know how much concentration this must have taken. But at that time he was young and vigorous. After the war, he was overcome by paralyzing disease which little by little disabled him until he died. Yet, during even his last year, when there was so little left that he could not hold a pencil and could not shape a word to be heard, he managed by finger taps and eye-blinking to communicate with his wife and to continue to think and to write about God, about Israel, about Torah. Talk about leftover turkey! This man knew what to do with nothing at all!

Nor need we feel that Michael Aaronson and Franz Rosenzweig are men whose courage and character are beyond our reach; men so great and so strong that we could not hope to emulate them. Perhaps we cannot match their achievements, but their character is no more than any person can show *if* he but will it. I know many people here in Houston who are equally oppressed and equally valiant. When you come to think of it, this is the fate of every widow and widower, isn't it, to pick up the pieces of life left shattered by death and build anew. This is the challenge to every man whom age has robbed of his powers, of everyone who goes to the hospital for an operation, of everyone who has lost a job; to pick up the pieces and begin again with cheerfulness and optimism, with faith and with hope. Yes, the test of a housewife is what she does with leftovers, and the test of all of us is what we do with the leftovers of our lives.

This same thought goes further, friends. It reaches out beyond the individual and touches the lives of peoples and nations.

Who, after all, were the men and women who celebrated the first Thanksgiving but the leftovers of England. Look back in American history. Who came to Georgia? The off-scourings of debtors' prisons. Who came to Massachusetts, to New York, to Maryland? Who made up the waves of migration from Germany or Ireland, from Italy or Yugoslavia, from Poland, from Russia? Were they the people who had been comfortable in Europe? Were they the happy, the well-to-do? Did they own broad acres, live in sumptuous houses, eat turkey every day?

Far from it. They were the poverty-stricken, the unsuccessful, the outcasts, the leftovers! Well did Emma Lazarus put it, "Give me your tired, your poor, your huddled masses yearning to breathe free, the refuse of your teeming shore, send these, the tempest-tossed to me."

The leftovers, and they came to this country with nothing but hunger and hope. They plowed the fields and built cities and helped grow a way of life where every day is Thanksgiving day for freedom. Yes, the test of a nation is what it does with leftovers. Look what America has done!

But not only America. Look to our own history, to our own people. In more ways than one we Jews have been the leftover turkey on the banquet tables of the world. Our flesh has been consumed by hatred, our bones broken on the rack of suffering, and yet again and again we have taken the broken leftovers of our lives and rebuilt it anew.

Other nations succumbed, other nations died. Their stripped carcasses were thrown into the refuse cans of history, but we have managed time and again to survive. We didn't call ourselves leftovers, of course. In Hebrew we put it *sh'erit*, "remnant." But if you have ever sold yard goods, this too is not a compliment. The remnant is the scrap that is left when all the usable yardage has been cut and sold. Remnants are also leftover.

It was Isaiah who first used this thought to comfort a people conquered and scattered. Their nobles were held captive, their king had been blinded, the soldiers who had once protected them had been carried far beyond the horizon. All that was left in Israel were a few shepherds and farmers, a ragtag and bobtail of a people, remnants, leftovers. But Isaiah preached that the faithful remnant would be the foundation of a renewed people, that the leftovers would rebuild and be rebuilt, that a Temple would rise again, and God's truth be preached again, and Israel live again. The stone which the builders rejected would one day become the chief cornerstone.

And it did, and time and time again. The Roman boot may have pressed our necks, the Saracen's sword may have dripped with our blood, the Inquisitor's exquisite tortures flayed our flesh, the Cossack's knout driven us down the bloody roads of exile, but always there was a remnant, always a leftover to carry the word, to live and teach, to pray and to renew.

Look at the land of Israel in our own day. There is a whole country of leftovers developed by a people of leftovers.

The land itself, the forests that once covered its hills had been consumed by Bedouins' goats. The cisterns that once held its Negev rainfall were filled with sand and silt. The valleys that once flowed with milk and honey were swamps where the malaria mosquito had his home.

And the people, yeshivah students so frail they grunted when they lifted a Talmud volume, bookkeepers from Munich who never had a calloused palm, the pitiful remnants of concentration camps, children who have never known their mothers, backward people from the *mellahs* of North Africa who had never seen an electric light nor a hypodermic needle.

These leftover people took a leftover land and there they built. On eroded hillsides they planted trees, in swampy valleys they dug ditches, silted cisterns they cleansed and used, and they built hospitals and a university and a modern democratic government, all of leftovers.

This is why I do not despair even in these dangerous times. No one knows what tomorrow may bring; the world is on the brink of a new age. But I do not fear, for I know that whatever happens our people will not succumb. Somewhere and somehow there will be Jews left over, a faithful remnant, who will take the broken fragments of their lives and build Arks for this Torah, and teach their children, as we have taught ours, to say the *Shema* and follow in God's way.

But, lest I seem too gloomy, let me add this one thought.

Life is not all leftovers. To have leftover turkey for dinner tonight, you had to have turkey yesterday. Life has its ups and downs, its triumphs and defeats, its sweetness along with its bitterness. Let us savor the Thanksgiving days when the sun shines; let us enjoy the laughter when it fills our homes; let us rejoice in the health we have; let us be happy in the freedom and peace in which we live. For it is in the joyful times of life that we store up the memories and the hopes with which to face its sorrows. And if we must make do with leftovers, at least we shall know that there was something to be leftover from. And more . . .

Thanksgiving will come again, next year, and the next year still again. In this spirit and with this sure knowledge, let us give thanks to God both for sunshine and rain, for joy and pain, knowing that one day there shall be a universal Thanksgiving, in which mankind shall come of age, and history be fulfilled. Amen.

SAMUEL EGAL KARFF

The Human Condition

Monday night in my Rice University class it was time to explore the Jewish view of human nature. What does Judaism teach about the human condition? Are we good or evil? What can God expect of us?

What can we expect from each other? Is Judaism's view optimistic or pessimistic? Hopeful or despairing?

That class discussion coincided with the commemoration of the 50th anniversary of the Allied liberation of Auschwitz. The enormity of the Holocaust is so difficult to grasp. That's why a single little book focusing on a single family—a book titled *The Diary of Anne Frank*—caught the attention of millions around the world. It has been translated into many languages.

Anne and her family were hidden in the attic with the help of Christian friends in Amsterdam. The Nazis finally found them and

Rabbi Samuel Egal Karff is senior rabbi of Congregation Beth Israel in Houston, Texas. He was Adjunct Professor at Rice University and President of the Central Conference of American Rabbis. He is the author of several works on Judaism, and a collection of his sermons has been published.

transported them to the death camps. Anne's father survived the war and so did her diary. In one of the most often quoted passages, this 13-year-old Jewish girl hiding from the Nazis wrote, "In spite of everything I still believe that human beings are really good at heart." No doubt she believed this and no doubt her parents had taught her this, but does this view enable one even to begin to understand Auschwitz? Is this an authentic Jewish view of the human condition? It is not.

WE BEGIN WITH ADAM AND EVE

How do we begin to formulate a Jewish view? We start as do our Christian neighbors with the story of Adam and Eve in the early pages of Genesis. Adam and Eve are instructed by God that though they may eat of the fruit of every tree in the garden, they must not eat of the tree of knowledge of good and evil. Adam disobeys. He eats; so does Eve. Adam blames Eve and Eve blames the serpent.

Through that act they gain a unique level of self-consciousness. They know they are naked. They lose their innocence. The knowledge of good and evil means that they become aware of their power and freedom to say "Yes" and "No" even to God.

The bad news is that this self-conscious power, this freedom to defy God, makes humans the most dangerous creatures on earth. Here is a creature who has the power to imagine that he is God and to act accordingly; a creature capable of worshiping self and of shrewdly and even brutally manipulating others to serve his needs; a creature capable of Auschwitz; a creature capable of destroying his own habitat on earth.

The good news is that this creature is also capable of unique acts of self-sacrifice and faithful love, as was the case with those who hid Anne Frank and her mother and father. Because we are free, our "No" is awesome—but so is our "Yes."

We have a unique capacity to make promises and to keep them. I like to watch the swans from our cottage in Michigan. Swans pair up for life. Swans are programmed for fidelity. There is no choice, no conscious promising to be faithful, no vows exchanged. And, to the best of my knowledge, there is no experience of temptation as we understand it.

A female swan is not capable of writing a book as did author Madeline L'Engele in which she describes her marriage of forty-plus

138

years to actor Hugh Franklin. She describes how, as a writer, she does her work in the solitude of her study and so has not been subject to the threats to their marriage that have assaulted her husband who is surrounded by all those beautiful, often younger, women in the theater.

Madeline L'Engele writes, "I didn't like it, having never completely thrown off insecurity. But Hugh had taken the marriage vows as seriously as I had and I had no cause for worry. Together we learned the meaning of faithfulness." It is much easier for a swan. They are programmed. Faithfulness is a more awesome achievement for us humans.

THE MEANING OF *YETZER*

The human creature's freedom to say "No" and "Yes" together with our powerful intelligence makes us potentially the greatest force for good or evil on earth. If we take as our text the early pages of the Torah, humans do plenty of evil. Cain kills Abel. The generation of Babel builds a tower only to make a great name for themselves. The generation of Noah was so corrupt as to require a purging flood. The ancient rabbis don't ignore this darker side of the human story. They speak of *yetzer*, that uniquely human primal energy, and they speak of two urges: the *yetzer tov*, the good inclination, and the *yetter hara*, the evil inclination. Some rabbis add that the evil inclination is thirteen years older than the good inclination. The evil inclination is present virtually at birth, the good inclination at age thirteen. This is the rabbis' way of declaring that young children are not innately good. Who among us has not discovered that children can be very cruel to one another?

Although our tradition places such a high value on learning and intelligence, the ancient rabbis did not believe that brilliant minds or scholarly dispositions are spared the evil impulse. Quite the contrary. One Talmudic sage contends: "The evil urge is greatest among scholars (or intelligent or powerful people)." One rabbi wisely observes: "The greater the person, the greater the *yetzer*," the greater the energy that can be used for evil as well as for good. It seems we have traveled a long way from Anne Frank's declaration that people are basically good at heart.

The bad news is that the impulse to misuse our God-given energies is strong. The good news is that we are capable and often do use our endowment of energy constructively, creatively, nobly. The good news is we are capable of growth. Who has not heard of that mischievous child in the room who is a real challenge to the teacher. He is into all kinds of things. If the teacher is able to turn him around, this kid may become the leader of the class. How about those students who get kicked out of religious school for totally disrespectful behavior and who are now constructive and fine members, even leaders, of this congregation, some perhaps even on the bimah tonight. I mention no names!

We have heard of ingenious thieves, second-story men, who now work passionately to keep young people away from crime, or of passionate atheists who become impassioned proclaimers of a religious view of life.

And yes, more good news. While none may be totally righteous, some persons are better than others. If fortunate, we have seen models of decency and nobility in our family life, models of significant success in overcoming the evil impulse, profiles of good character.

THE IMPORTANCE OF TORAH

Our sages teach that the greatest weapon against the evil impulse has also been given to us by God. That weapon is the Torah, that very scroll which we symbolically passed from generation to generation this night. Torah is many things. In the context of this message tonight, Torah is moral commandment. It speaks of a moral order of life that must not be violated with impunity.

Respect for Torah is what makes us shudder at the thought of doing certain deeds that must not be done. The old Yiddish expression was *M'turnisht*—"You must not!" Torah gives us the awareness that we are created in the divine image and so is the other person.

I'll never forget visiting the death camp at Dachau twenty-five years ago. There were three tiny chapels, one a Jewish chapel, and it was in the shape of a crematorium. Words from the Bible were inscribed on an outside wall. What do you place on the outside of a Jewish chapel in a death camp? Certainly not "My house shall be called a house of prayer for all peoples." The verse chosen by the chapel builders was Chapter 9, verse 21 of the Book of Psalms: "Set fear of You over them, O Lord, let the nations know that they are but men."

A world without Torah, a world without the fear of God leads to Auschwitz and Dachau. A world with Torah is a world in which when we have violated the moral law, we know it. We feel guilt and remorse and shame and are in need of repentance and forgiveness.

THE AMERICAN MORAL CRISIS

There is much concern in our country today about values, about an erosion of the reverence for human life. There is cause for that concern. Item: In a Grief Assistance Program in Philadelphia, families whose loved ones have been murdered are counseled and helped to carry on with their lives.

One family survivor remembers going to court and confronting the person who killed her teenaged son. The parent said, "He is looking at you like 'What's your problem? So what if I killed your son?' " A counselor in the program says that of 1,200 families she met with during the past 3 years in Philadelphia, only 10 of those 1,200 families, 1 percent, had seen remorse in the person who had killed their loved one.

Closely linked to remorse is a sense of shame. Dennis Prager recounts that during a television show in Cleveland, students from six different high schools, of different ethnic, racial, religious, and socioeconomic backgrounds were asked this question, "How many of you would shoplift from a department store if you really wanted something badly and were certain you wouldn't get caught?" Virtually every student raised his or her hand.

Prager comments, "Some people in my high school generation would also have shoplifted from a department store, especially if they knew they wouldn't get caught. But few, if any, would have raised their hands and admitted it on camera."

It is bad enough that virtually all would steal if assured they would not be caught. Worse still, they are not even ashamed to admit that they would steal and to admit it on camera for their parents, their neighbors, their teachers, the world. That says something about them, but it also says something about the moral climate around them.

Joe Klein of *Newsweek* monitored three television shows in one day last week. One of the programs featured the theme: "One Night Stands—Jilted Lovers Begging to Be Taken Back." Another featured women obsessed with their looks and another featured a mother and daughter discussing their desire to be intimate with the same man. The man in question was then invited on camera to choose between mother and daughter.

Our sages taught that the most prominent and powerful manifestations of *yetzer hara*, of the evil impulse, are acts of idolatry (when we treat what is less than God as our god) and the abuse of our sexuality.

The television program just mentioned is a triple manifestation of the impulse to degrade ourselves and others by abusing our sexuality: first, the fact that the mother and daughter have such a story to tell; secondly, that the producers, out of a greedy obsession with ratings, search for and televise such programs; and thirdly, that apparently many Americans watch such programs.

There is a good deal to worry about in our society today.

SIGNS OF HOPE

Thank God, there are also signs of hope. For one thing, many Americans of all political leanings seem genuinely concerned about the need to restore boundaries, personal accountability, decency, and family values to our lives. That's hopeful.

There is something in most of us which ultimately rebels against that which degrades us; something from the deeper recesses of our souls which impels us to battle against this evil impulse.

Sometimes the evil impulse, itself so real, so powerful, so potentially destructive, triggers the *yetzer tov*, the good impulse, which knows that we need Torah. We need to recover respect for an order of life and for standards that are greater than ourselves. When we act accordingly we call this *teshuvah*, repentance.

Our rabbis say that the worst thing that can happen to a person is to lose the ultimate ground of his dignity, the sense that we are created in the image of God. Almost as bad is to abandon the vision that there is a path, a way of life ultimately God-given, a Torah, which it is possible for us to live by and which remains the ultimate measure of the significance of our lives.

WE KNOW ...

To me the most hopeful sign of all is that, for all our lapses and imperfections and for all that I have said about what is happening in certain segments of our society, most of us have not lost the vision. I am most reminded this is the case when there is a death in the congregation, and I am called to speak with the family, actually to hear them speak about the person who has died in order that I may frame my own parting tribute to that person's life.

Oh, the family may recount some foibles and shortcomings and mistakes, but they need to accentuate the good stuff. "He was a proud self-respecting Jew." "She was so loving and caring, she was there for us. She was so giving. She was kind even to strangers." Or "His word was his bond. He was honest in business. It made him happy to see others happy."

Why this need to affirm the significance of life in moral terms? Because we know that the most important story of our lives is that we are created with the freedom to do good and evil and we know that we fulfill the deepest meaning of our lives when we are faithful to the covenant, with the Source of our being, when we live like a *mensch* and embrace Torah.

Nobel Laureate Saul Bellow said it best when he portrays a man who loved his uncle. His uncle's name was Elya. The uncle was a very important factor in his life, like a surrogate father.

> Uncle Elya has died. His nephew stands at the grave. After the funeral service is over, the nephew says these words: "Remember, God, the soul of Elya Gruner. He was aware that we must meet, and he did meet through all the confusion and degraded clowning of this life, he did meet the terms of his contract, the terms which in his inmost heart, each man knows, as I know mine. For that is the truth of it, we all know, God, we know, we know, we know."

ABRAHAM J. KARP

Adding Life to Our Years

We offer up many prayers these High Holy Days. We pray for pardon and for forgiveness, health and bodily vigor, security, good sustenance, salvation for Israel, peace for the world. There is one prayer, a short and simple supplication that we breathe with added fervor, *Ribon ho-olom zohrainu l'hayim aruhim*, "Lord of the Universe, remember us for a long life." We pray and we long for a long life. We turn our thoughts to length of days, anxious to add years to our life.

I well recall a discussion on this matter with the oldest man I ever met, my great grandfather, Ha-Rav Shmuel Yehudah, rabbi for more than sixty years of the community of Adelsk. Great grandfather was the family patriarch and a family legend. His age at the time of our

Rabbi Abraham J. Karp received his A.B. from Yeshiva University in 1942 and was ordained at the Jewish Theological Seminary in 1945. He has served several conservative congregations. He was visiting Professor at the Jewish Theological Seminary, Dartmouth University and the Hebrew University in Jerusalem, a Professor at the University of Rochester, Jewish Theological Seminary, and President of the American Jewish Historical Society. A prolific author in the field of American Jewish History and Literature, Rabbi Karp is the recipient of many awards.

145

meeting was reckoned to be well over a hundred. No one knew his exact age, and no one dared ask him. Before our family left for America, I was taken to him for his blessings. He sat, as I recall, at a small table near the window, a folio of the Talmud before him, studying. With the boldness of youth, I asked him, "Grandfather, how old are you?" He replied with a smile, "I've long since passed my allotted years of three score and ten."

I made bold to ask again, "To what do you attribute your length of days?" "You ask me? The Talmud contains a section devoted to just this matter. When you'll be older, you'll study and learn."

I have recently studied that extremely interesting and informative portion of our lore. Students ask their teachers, "Through what merit have you reached old age?" And the sages give their formulas for longevity. It is one of these formulas that I would discuss with you this morning.

R. Nehunia b. Hakonoh was asked by his disciples, "In virtue of what have you reached such a good old age?"

The sage replied, "Never in my life have I sought honor for myself through the degradation of my fellow man, the curse of my fellow man has never followed me to my bed, and I was free with my money."

Psychosomatic medicine, which has shown that many physiological ills are caused by psychological disturbances, would tell us that the human failings, which the sage carefully avoided in his own living, could actually take years from a man's life. Unprincipled ambition to get ahead; using human beings and human misfortune as stepping stones to success; worry, continuous and growing, over the acquisition and retention of money—a person beset by these shortcomings, one who surrenders his being to their service, such a man actually subtracts years from his life.

So, R. Nehunia's answer is a true answer and a good and valid lesson for life. But not a full lesson! There is another side to the coin! The Talmud records an interesting addition to this discussion, a comment, which must have occurred already to many of you. The sage Rava is quoted as saying: "Long life depends not so much on merit as on fate." How right he is! There is little we can do to make long a life that is destined to be short. There isn't much we can do to add years to our life. But the Talmud teaches: *Yaish shanim shel hayim, v'yaish shanim she-aynon shel hayim.* "There are years which are filled with life. There are years which are empty of life." Now, we can fully understand the words of R. Nehunia. Nay more, we can live them! We may or may not be able to add years to our life, but it is fully in our power to add life to our years.

The formula of the sage is to be viewed not merely as that which takes years from life, but that which takes life from our allotted years. The life of a man who raises himself on the misfortune of others—is that a life? You've heard these boasts, "Did I give him a licking. If his business survives, it'll be a miracle!" Or, "I'll make good, and no one is going to stand in my way." Such people can't "make good." They can only make it bad for their associates and employees, a bad name for themselves and families, a bad life that really is no life. What is the life of a man, who labored a lifetime, only to merit this description, "He's the wealthiest and loneliest man in town." No, the life of a man, who views fellow man as a rung on his ladder of success—to be stepped on in order to reach the next rung—is no life at all, for it is bereft of all friendship, serenity, true accomplishment.

The story is told of a wealthy Jewish manufacturer, who was the most beloved man in town. He was especially admired for his wonderful relationship with his employees. Particularly beautiful was his friendship with the old superintendent of his buildings. He often spoke of him as "the man who saved my life." But no one knew what he was referring to, and the superintended swore that he never did anything to merit that praise nor would the man explain. The rabbi of the town, intrigued with the matter, finally took courage and asked for an explanation. He heard this reply:

> In my early days, when I was first starting out, I was the toughest and the most hated employer in the whole town. I once needed a janitor, so I put an ad in the paper "Hand wanted" and waited the applicants. A man came in response to the ad. I had to put him in his place immediately. I was rough with him and gruff to him. I was trying to beat down his wage by beating down his spirit. I kept referring to him as a "hired hand, a hired hand."
>
> Suddenly he interrupted me, "I don't know whether I'll get this job, and what's more I don't care, but don't call me a 'hand.' I am a man. I have a name. In me, as in you, there beats a heart, there's a mind and a soul. If you want a man—I'm available. If you want a 'hand'—good day!"
>
> "That day, he saved my life!" continued the manufacturer. "He caused me to see men not as tools, but as individuals, human be-

ings, co-workers, associates. Had my life continued as before, I would have been hated and despised, without friends and without honor. He saved my life. He showed me how truly to live."

R. Nehunia tells us that a life of strife is no life at all. To live with a curse against your fellow man always in your heart is not living, for it is a life that causes curses to be heaped upon you, that makes people hate you.

But people will question, "What can I do about it? If he hates me, if he curses me, what can I do?"

It once happened that two newcomers to a community were visited on the same day by the local rabbi. During the course of the conversation, the first new resident asked the rabbi, "What kind of people live in this town?"

The rabbi answered with a question, "What kind of people live in the town you came from?"

"Oh," replied the newcomer, "they were wonderful people. Friendly, neighborly, real genuine people."

"You'll find," said the rabbi, "the same kind of people in this town."

During the rabbi's conversation with the second newcomer, the same question was asked of him, and he gave the same answer. The new resident replied: "The town I came from was a horrible place. The people were unfriendly, disagreeable, the worst sort of gossips, always feuding!"

The rabbi replied, "You'll find that this town has the same kind of people."

In truth, it is our own actions and attitudes that bring out the good or the bad in people. To live a life that brings out the evil in people why that's no life at all. To live so, as to bring out the goodness in fellow man, that's putting life in our years.

Finally, R. Nehunia admonishes us that the life of the grasping miser is no life at all. Years spent in merely gathering, those are years bereft of life. The lust for money is a progressive disease. The more you accumulate, the more you grasp for. You and I have seen men, whose whole life is grasping for more and thirsting for yet more.

Such a person was Takom, a peasant, who worked hard upon his land, and then bought more land and was thus able to live in comfort. But he was stricken with the disease of wanting more. He heard that across the Volga, land was being given away free. He went there and found that it was indeed so. There was but one stipulation. A man was permitted to retain only the land he could cover before sunset. So, at the break of dawn, Takom began to walk. As he surveyed the vast stretch of land that was to be his—he began to yearn for yet more. So he hastened his pace, and began to run. He was getting weary. His heart was beating heavily, his feet were aching. But he wanted just a bit more, just a few acres more. The sun began to set and he began stumbling in utter exhaustion. Still he had to have just another bit more. And as the last rays of the sun were sinking behind the horizon, Takom fell. Exhaustion had taken its toll.

Takom got his land, six feet of it!

How many do we know who spend their lives always trying to grasp for just a little more who end up like Takom? Men who don't pause to use their gains for the benefit of their community, for the welfare of others, or even for themselves! Is that life?

The question that life asks is not "How much have you made?" It is rather, "What are you doing with it?"

We add years to our life and life to our years if we respect man and call him fellowman; if our life brings out the best in people about us, in "scattering" and not in "gathering."

A truly effective prayer has a twofold message. It is a plea to God. It is also an admonition to the one who utters the prayer. On this day of Rosh Hashanah, as we pray for *hayim aruhim.*

We petition God to add years to our life.

We must also admonish ourselves—to add life to our years!

HAROLD S. KUSHNER

The Missing Piece

Yom Kippur 5739
In Memory of Aaron Zev Kushner 1963–1977

My Friends,

Though we are all here in the same place at the same time for Yom Kippur, each of us comes with his own very personal agenda, his own hopes, dreams, fears, hurts, memories. I guess that's always the case when a large number of people congregate, but especially today, when the setting calls forth so many deeply personal responses. The prayerbook tries to pull us together, by asking us to share the same words, but it's not really enough.

The prayerbook tries to get us talking about sin and repentance, about cleansing and atonement. But our hearts resist. We don't respond to sin, to atonement. We want to pray about the brevity of life, the

Rabbi Harold S. Kushner graduated from Columbia University in 1935. He was ordained at the Jewish Theological Seminary in 1960 and was Rabbi Laureate of Temple Israel in Natick, Massachusetts. Rabbi Kushner is the author of five best selling books, including *When Bad Things Happen to Good People*. He was also honored by the Christophers as one of fifty people who have made the world a better place in the last fifty years.

pain of death and loss, the sustaining power of memory. So strong are we in our insistence, in the gravitational pull we exercise on the service, that it finally has to accommodate us. When we open the Torah on Yom Kippur, to study the ancient rituals of purification, the opening words deal not with Yom Kippur but with life and death: "The Lord spoke to Moses after the death of the two sons of Aaron the High Priest," as if the Torah itself had to concede that it can't begin to talk of atonement and cleansing until it has spoken of grief and bereavement first, because that is where our hearts are.

Let me begin by telling you a story, a strange kind of story which can best be described as a children's story for grown-ups. It was written by a man named Shel Silverstein and it's called "The Missing Piece."

Once upon a time, there was a circle that was missing a piece and it was very unhappy. It went all over the world looking for its missing piece. Over hills and across rivers, up mountains and down into valleys, through rain and snow and blistering sun, it went looking for its missing piece. Wherever it went, because it was missing a piece, it had to go very slowly. So as it went along, it stopped to look at the flowers and talk to the butterflies. It stopped to rest in the cool grass. Sometimes it passed a snail, and sometimes the snail passed it. Wherever it went, it kept looking for its missing piece.

But it couldn't find it. Some pieces were too big and some were too small; some were too square and some were too pointy. None of them fit. Then suddenly one day, it found a piece that seemed to fit perfectly. The circle was whole again; nothing was missing. It took the piece into itself and started to roll away. Now, because it was a whole unbroken circle, it could roll much faster. And so it rolled quickly through the world, past the lakes and past the forests, too fast to get a good look at them. It rolled too quickly to notice the flowers, too fast for any of the insects to fly by and talk to it. When the circle realized that it was rolling too fast to do any of the things it had been doing for years, it stopped. It very reluctantly put down its missing piece, and it rolled slowly away, heading out into the world, looking for its missing piece.

Now that's such a beautiful story, I almost don't want to soil it, to violate its poignancy, by taking it apart and trying to understand it. But it's saying some important things. The most important thing it's saying is that, in a strange, mysterious way which we can't really understand, a person is more whole when he's incomplete, when he's missing something. That little bit of incompleteness cures him of his illusion of self-sufficiency, opens him up—as it did to the circle in the story—to feeling more, seeing more, experiencing more. In a paradoxical way, the man who has everything will never have some of the most poignantly beautiful experiences in life. The man who has everything will never know what it feels like to yearn, to hope. He'll never understand the songs and poetry which are born out of longing, out of grieving, out of incompleteness. You can never make him happy by giving him something he would enjoy, because by definition, he already has it. In a strange way, the person who has everything, who is missing absolutely nothing, is a very poor person indeed.

We're more complete if we're incomplete. That's the paradoxical truth of the story. We are made more whole by the things we don't have. I think that's true at many levels. When it comes to giving charity, we become more whole through what we give away. I think we instinctively understand that the person who can afford to be generous, who can afford it psychologically, not only financially, is a more whole person than the man who is afraid to part with what he has, because he's afraid that if he gives something away, he's giving away part of himself. The wealthy man who needs to be asked three times before he gives and thanked three times afterwards, strikes us as, in some ways, an incomplete person; he may have a lot of money but he's lacking something more important. The man who is not afraid to be generous, because he knows he is not giving his self away, comes across as really more whole.

It is perhaps indicative of the culture we live in that many of us are familiar with the parable of the Fish and the Loaves from the New Testament—how a whole crowd of people were miraculously fed with just two fishes and seven loaves of bread—but we don't know that the story originally comes from the Hebrew Bible, where it's told about the prophet Elisha.

V'ish ba miBaal Shalisha vayavey l'ish HaElohim lechem bikkurim v'carmel.

A man came to Elisha with a present of a loaf of bread and an ear of corn. And the prophet told him, "Distribute it to the entire crowd!" The man said, "What! Am I supposed to divide this among a hundred people?" And the prophet told him, "Distribute it to all the people for the Lord has said, it will suffice." And he gave it to them, and they ate, and left some over, as the Lord had promised. (2 Kings 4:42–44)

It's a nice trick to know when you have unexpected company. But the real point of the story is a more profound one. Each of us has the resources, the financial and emotional resources, to help a whole lot of people, but we don't know how much we have until we start giving it away. It's a scary thing, I can tell you from my experience as a rabbi, to have people make emotional demands on you, to have them ask you to give them strength. That's why it's so much easier to find people to work with machines, with numbers, with pieces of paper, and so much harder to find people who can work with people. You're afraid that if you give them strength, you'll be left weak. But in fact, it works just the other way. The act of strengthening others makes you even stronger. The process of giving away leaves you more complete for having done it, like the pitcher of wine in Greek mythology that grew magically more and more full as people tried to empty it. You never know how rich and full you are till you start sharing yourself with others.

The person who has grown comfortable with the fact that he's missing a piece is, in a sense, more whole than the person who thinks he has to be complete, unbroken. When someone you love has died, there is no replacing that person. His death leaves an emptiness which will never be filled. A husband or wife can remarry and be very happy, a son can invest more of himself in his own family, a grieving parent in her remaining children. But whatever you do, you will go through life with a piece of you missing. No matter how full, how crowded your life may go on to become, there will always be that empty space.

But the person who has survived bereavement (and that's all you can ever do with it, survive; you can't prevent it or undo it or ignore it)—the person who has survived and learned that losing part of yourself is an inevitable part of life, has become a more complete person than he could ever have been before. Nothing can scare you because you have been through the worst and come through it.

I think the person I feel closest to in all the pages of the Bible is a man whose name I don't even know. All I know about him is one poem he wrote 2800 years ago, the thirtieth Psalm, *Mizmor Shir Hanukkat HaBayit*. We recite this psalm every morning at the beginning of the service and after we've said it, if there is a minyan present, the mourners say Kaddish.

The thirtieth Psalm is the story of a man who used to believe that nothing bad could ever happen to him. *V'ani amarti b'shalvi teal emot l'olam.* I once thought, while at ease, nothing could shake my security. He was profoundly and sincerely grateful to God for being so good to him. In exchange, the man lived a moral life, prayed regularly, and gave charity. The suddenly, a series of terrible calamities befell him. *Histarta panecha, hayyiti nivhal.* You turned your face from me, and I was terrified. His whole world threatened to fall apart.

But then he made a vital discovery. He learned something about himself he could never have known before—that he was capable of believing in God and in God's world even when tragedy happened to *him* instead of to strangers. Before that, he could never have been sure of the quality of his faith. Did he serve God because He was God, or because He was good to him? Now he knows what he could only have hoped before, that there is nothing tentative, nothing conditional or self-centered about his faith. In a sense, God has given him something he never had before, the strength to go on despite his wounds, despite his sorrow. That's a great thing for God to give him; how could he have found his way without it?

In that same mysterious way of which we have spoken, there is something whole about his faith now, where it was immature and incomplete before. Missing a piece has somehow made him whole. The religion of, "I love You as long as You're good to me," has been replaced by, "I love You because You're God and because without You, I couldn't have made it."

It's not only bereavement that forces us to go through that profound growth. Everyone of us, in one way or another, is missing a piece. Everyone of us has come here an incomplete, unfulfilled person in one way or another. Some of us have been left incomplete by death, some by a divorce. A part of ourselves has moved out of our lives and somewhere out there, somebody is walking around with some of our most intimate memories; others of us by disappointment, the job we wanted and didn't get, the talent that would have made us so happy, that we somehow never managed to develop, the child who didn't turn out as we hoped he would. Every one of us is incomplete in one way or another. We're missing something from our lives, and its absence weighs us down, slows us down (like the circle in the story), compels us to see everything in our lives a little bit differently.

155

Yet I would insist that we're made more whole by the experience of missing something, missing out on something. We learn reality, we come to see the world as it really is. The world isn't a birthday party, where if you've been good, everything happens the way you want it to. It's a very mixed-up unpredictable place, where hours of sunshine alternate with hours of darkness, redeemed by occasional flashes of bravery and love.

We learn gratitude; precisely because we can't have everything, we learn to be grateful for what we do have. Children don't understand that. For them, the world is divided into what they have and what they don't have yet but intend to have. The idea that there are some things they won't ever have, and that some of the things they have may be taken away from them—that's hard for them to understand. And probably that's just as well. They deserve a few years to be children; they'll be wise long enough. But we who roll through life slowly, with our missing pieces—we understand that.

In the Grace after Meals (and you'll have to forgive me on this of all days for speaking earlier of feeding the multitude, and now of the *Birkat Mazon*, the Grace after Meals), there is a line toward the end: May God bless me and those around me as He blessed Abraham, Isaac and Jacob, *biv'racha shlemah*, with a complete blessing, with everything, a blessing from which nothing is lacking." The Midrash, the commentary, notes, "Maybe Abraham, Isaac, and Jacob were blessed by God with a *bracha shlemah*, a blessing from which nothing was missing. But nobody since then has been."

In fact, when you think about it, Abraham, Isaac, and Jacob had their missing pieces as well. They had problems with their parents, their wives, their children. Abraham broke with his father over a matter of religion, left him, and never saw him again. He sent one of his wives out of his house into the desert. He had a son who intermarried and caused him grief.

Isaac was almost killed by his father as a child. When he grew old, he lived with his wife and children but had nothing to say to them. They were living in opposite directions, they had forgotten how to trust each other.

Jacob ran away from home as a teenager. He quarreled with his father, with his brother, with his father-in-law, and he saw his sons quarrel viciously with each other. And they came as close as anyone in the Bible to receiving a *bracha shlemah*, a complete blessing with nothing missing.

The fact of the matter is, there is no such thing as a life that isn't missing a piece. It can't be a full life without disappointment, without pain, without loss. Maybe that's what the prayer really means when it says that Abraham, Isaac, and Jacob received a complete blessing. Maybe it doesn't mean that they got everything they wanted and kept it. Maybe it means that God gave them a *full* life, a life full of love and full of pain (because how can there be love without pain?), a life full of hope and full of disappointments (because if you hope grandly enough, you'll have your share of disappointments). Maybe instead of giving them an easy life, God gave them a full life, a *bracha shlemah*, the blessing of fullness, a life full of joy and full of tears, full of accomplishment and full of failure. We ask that God give us that kind of fullness, that kind of wholeness, too.

To be missing a piece, to have to go through life carrying around an emptiness where something important and precious to you used to be, and to understand despite the pain that you are a deeper and richer person because you're missing that piece—that's what it means to be whole. That Hassidic master, the Kotzker Rebbe, used to say, "There is nothing in all the world as whole as a broken heart," and sooner or later in this life, each of us comes to understand what he meant.

The Torah makes the same point. In the opening lines of the Book of Leviticus, when it speaks of how our forefathers used to worship God with animal offerings, it says *adam ki yakriv*, when a man brings a sacrifice. Several times, for each of the categories of offering, it repeats those words, *adam ki yakriv*, when a man brings a sacrifice. Then, when it comes to the very last kind of offering, the *mincha*, the poor man's offering, it suddenly changes the wording, and now it says *nefesh ki takriv*, When a soul brings a sacrifice.

The commentators respond to the change of language: what kind of sacrifice does a soul bring? This is their answer: Sometimes there is something you want very badly, to the very depths of your soul. You work for it, you pray for it, you say to yourself and to God that if you could only have that, you'd be happy, you wouldn't want anything else. But one day you have to acknowledge that it's not going to come your way like Moses at the end of the Torah, realizing that he's never going to reach the goal he has spent his life working for. If you can do that without losing your soul, without becoming so embittered that life will have no further meaning for you, if you can be like the circle at the end of the story, if you can let go of your missing piece and roll away to face life without it, that's *nefesh ki takriv*, that's the sacrifice of one's soul which we bring and lay on God's altar, and turn away, feeling whole in a way that we could never feel whole before.

NORMAN LAMM

Today

Judaism is meant for today—not only for yesterday, and not only for tomorrow, but for today. That does not sound like a startling thesis, yet it is an idea that is sadly neglected not only by the detractors of Judaism, but even by some of its staunchest advocates.

Of course, Jadaism has always had the greatest reverence for the past and its sacred traditions. We refer to ourselves as the children of Abraham, Isaac, and Jacob, and we never tire of remembering the exodus from Egypt. History is sacred for the Jew. We also have an unshakable faith in the future of our eternal people; that is why we believe in the Messiah, in the world-to-come, and the *malkhut shamayim,* the Kingdom of Heaven. It is foolish to dismiss the past and it is dangerous to ignore the future.

But it often happens that in our preoccupation with preserving the past and in keeping faith with the future, we overlook the present.

Rabbi Norman Lamm is President of Yeshiva University, a Professor of Jewish Philosophy, and founding editor of *Tradition: A Journal of Orthodox Jewish Thought.* He is also the author of several books.

Between a modified ancestor worship and a euphoric optimism, we forget that there is a today in which God addresses man, in which obligations await us, in which life must be lived responsibly. Once we forget that, we are, for all practical purposes, obsolete. If Torah, with its demands and inspiration and duties, is not for today—with its excitement and complexity and anxieties—then we have nothing to offer to the young Jew whom we are trying so hard to win over to Judaism.

The task of all Jews, then, on the eve of the year 5727, is not merely to search out ancient texts or to undertake sociological studies which will predict future trends, but to live Jewishly today, to show the world that Jewishness was meant for now, that we are alive and dynamic and meaningful and relevant for man in the last third of the 20th century. We must determine to give a new interpretation to that beloved verse we recite after each sounding of the Shofar: *Ha-yom harat olam*. That is usually translated, "Today is the creation of the world," that is, today is the anniversary of the divine creation of the universe. Let us, however, resolve that we shall interpret it thus: *Hayom*, if the "today" of each of us is dedicated to full Jewish living, if our "today" is the scene of our practice of Torah and its sublime *mitzvot*, then indeed this *hayom* can become *harat olam*, the creation of a new world. There is no greater creativity that we can bring to the world than to demonstrate that Torah was meant for *hayom*, today.

Let us, then, stop living in the past or in the future alone while the present remains for us unreal and chimerical. R. Israel Salanter once overheard two people speaking. One moaned to the other, *"das Leben is a Chalom,"* (life is but a dream). The great rabbi interrupted their conversation, "Pardon me, but that is true only if you are asleep!" Those who do not believe that Torah Judaism can and should be fully lived in 1966 are asleep. They are dreaming. For them, as Maimonides pointed out, the Shofar is meant as a kind of spiritual alarm clock: *uru yeshenim mi'shenatkhem*, wake up, O ye slumberers, from your sleep. God calls you here and now. Judaism is the religion of contemporary man. That is why to the challenge of Shofar we respond: *Ha-yom harat olam*, today is the time that we must build new worlds.

One of the most bedevilling of all ideas, which afflicts believers and nonbelievers alike, is that the Godless self-indulgers have taken over *ha-yom*, the contemporary scene, and have left us benighted souls who still believe in God and Torah as the antiquarian caretakers of yesteryear or the starry-eyed visionaries of the year after next. This world and this day belong to the emancipated secularist, who may rightfully eat, drink, and be merry because tomorrow he dies and he might as well take over today; while the next world and some distant time can be safely left to the man of religion.

Orthodox Jews must never take that kind of defeatist attitude, relinquishing their rights to *ha-yom,* and retreating into the past or retiring into the future. That is a solution we cannot afford. We dare not abdicate our claim on *hayom*—our role in meeting and sanctifying *all* of modern life: modern science and modern thought, modern business and modern technology, and the modern Jewish community here and in Israel. But unfortunately, we sometimes tend to do just that, both in our communal and our individual lives. We surrender either Torah or today. Sometimes we react by giving up on the world of today; sometimes by embracing today but rejecting Torah.

Communally, Orthodox Jewry sometimes shows an inclination to run away from *ha-yom.* Some Orthodox Jews act as if we ought to be afraid of secular learning and keep our children away from the universities. They are apprehensive about modern science. They feel we ought to pull out not only of the general community, but even of the Jewish community. That is not as illogical as it sounds. When you remember that so many Jews have through assimilation cut themselves off from the past and have through intermarriage forfeited their future, there is a strong appeal for the idea of not identifying yourself with this kind of community.

But there is also a deeper reason why observant Jews in America have so often taken such a negative attitude. Why this fear that we are today weak and defenseless? Why have we largely failed to become spiritually mature and confident about our chances?

To an extent, it is because we are still overwhelmed by our great yesterdays. We look back to the heritage of European Jewry—both East and West—and we feel like dwarfs in comparison. How gallant and glorious those Jews were, how rich their lives, how we look like pygmies beside them! We have neither *gedolim* nor *gadlut;* greatness is not ours. "My father was so learned," says the second-generation American Jew, who denies that he is pious, even if in fact he *is.* Such is human nature: how many sons of distinguished men suffered because of the erroneous idea that they could never equal, let alone surpass, their illustrious fathers!

Yet, the American Jew of today must not deny himself the opportunity to create a today as great as his European father's yesterday. Spiritual eminence is possible today, *ha-yom,* in America, in the Space Age.

The renowned Rabbi Nathan Adler, the Rav of Frankfurt, and known as the "Great Eagle," recognized this problem as one that is well nigh universal. Isaac had no experience of revelation until after Abraham died: *va-yehi aharei mot Avraham va-yevarekh Elohim et Yitzhak.* Jacob was quite ordinary whilst he was at home, under the shadow of Isaac. But when *va-yetzei Yaakov mi-be'er sheva,* when he left and went on his own, *va-yahalom,* he experienced his great prophetic vision. Joshua was only a *naar,* a young disciple, while Moses flourished; only afterwards did he rise to history's call. Indeed, all of Israel suffered, in this sense, from the greatness of Moses. And Moses recognized this; that is why, in recounting the story of the revelation at Sinai, he says to his people: *Anokhi omed bein ha-Shem u-venekhem,* I was standing between God and you. He does not mean that he was the one who mediated between God and Israel, but quite literally, *I stood between you,* I prevented you from achieving your full spiritual stature, from contacting God, because in the presence of master and father, disciple and son usually suffer.

But this situation does not exist forever. That is why, at the end of his life, the great Moses calls all his people together and addresses the assembly with the immortal words: *Atem nitzovim ha-yom kulkhem lifnei ha-Shem Elohekhem;* now that I am about to pass away, all of you can stand on your own, *ha-yom,* this very day, before God. Now *ha-yom,* "today," belongs to you!

Certainly, American Jewry looked pale beside European Jewry in its hours and centuries of greatness. But, alas, that great and fertile source of Jewish life and thought is no more. The spiritual father of American Jewry has been murdered. Yesterday is gone and it will never return. Whether we like it or not, it is now *our* turn to blossom, to mature, to play our role on the stage of Jewish history. *Atem nitzovim ha-yom kulkhem lifnei ha-Shem Elohekhem,* we must stand, erect and proud, before God, and it must be *ha-yom,* today, with *our* initiative, *our* enthusiasm, *our* sense of mission. We must strive for *our* achievements, as we meet our challenges in *our* times. *Ha-yom harat olam,* by realizing Torah in the world of today, we shall create a great new Jewish world of which even the past can be proud.

But while a significant part of the community tends to deny *ha-*

yom, others ecstatically embrace every aspect of contemporary life while neglecting Torah as a vital element therein. Jewishly, we live in all tenses except the present.

Some of us live altogether in the future: I will study Torah and Talmud—when I retire. I will give *tzedakah*—in my will. I will become active in Jewish organizations—when my son begins to take over more duties in the business. Meanwhile, rabbi, forget about me; there's no hope for my generation. Concentrate on the children instead.

What a sweet and charming faith—and what a devilishly clever way to avoid the responsibilities of *ha-yom*, today! Of course, retired people should study Torah, and semiretired people should be active in organizations, and people should leave their money for clarity in their wills, and synagogues should be concerned with youth. But that is no excuse for forfeiting Jewish and human obligation today—now, right now. For there is one thing wrong with this procrastinating into the dim future: who knows if there will be a future, if there will be a tomorrow? *Im lo akhshav—ematai:* if not now, when then? If there is no today, there can be no tomorrow.

There are some people who avoid the present by living in the past. "My father conducted such a beautiful Seder"—but how about yours? "My mother prayed so warmly"—well, why don't you? "Once upon a time there was so much fervor in our observance"—but why "once upon a time," why not now? Should we not strive for a Jewish today at least as good as the Jewish yesterday? On the verse of the *Shema* that we must observe the commandments which the Lord commands us, *hayom*, the rabbis commented: *ha-yom—bekhol yom va-yom yiheyu b'einekha ke'hadashim, k'ilu kibaltem otam ha-yom methar Sinai;* "This day"—let the commandments appear to you every day as if they were brand new, just given to you at Mt. Sinai this very day. To live Jewishly *ha-yom*, today, means to experience marvelous discoveries, true zeal, fervor, passion, love, and enthusiasm. Today, as Franz Rosenzweig once put it, is not only a bridge to tomorrow; it is a springboard to eternity. *Ha-yom harat olam.*

Let us, then, leave the synagogue today with this message of the Shofar: *ha-yom*, today and not only yesterday and tomorrow. This very day we shall be more agreeable, more responsive, more cheerful, more charitable. This very day we shall make a friend feel good, compliment a neighbor, forgive a wife or husband or parent or child. *This Musaf* we shall pray with renewed *kavvanah. This* year we shall make the effort to pray with a *minyan* even during the week, *this* year we shall study Torah and attend classes, *this* year we shall be more observant to Jewish law, *this* year we shall strengthen as never before our devotion to and love of everything Jewish.

Let us be Jewishly creative: *ha-yom harat olam.* And in return, we shall hear the affirmative response of Almighty God to our closing prayers: *ha-yom te'amtzenu, hayom tevarkhenu, ha-yom tegadlenu.* May God give us courage—today; may He bless us—today; and may He endow us with genuine greatness—today.

The True Artist of Life

A popular philosopher of our times, Havelock Ellis, makes a remarkable statement in one of his books, which seems to have caught the spirit of an ancient rabbinic comment. It is so true, it reveals such a deep understanding of the Bible and of the Jewish genius, that it is almost worthy of a place in the literature of our Midrash.

Speaking of the artist, he says that the Jewish people have shown real artistic genius when, in the Biblical description of the creation of the world, they assigned to God not only the six days of active creational work, but also one day, the Sabbath, for passive contemplation. That one-seventh part—an immensely important factor—this philosopher asserts, has not commanded our sufficient consideration.

Rabbi Israel Herbert Levinthal was born in Vilna in 1888 and came to the United States in 1891. He received both his B.A. and M.A. from Columbia University and his J.D. from NYU. He was ordained at the Jewish Theological Seminary and received his Doctorate in Hebrew Literature. He was spiritual leader at the Brooklyn Jewish Center and taught homiletics at the Jewish Theological Seminary. He was a prominent preacher as well as the author of books of sermons. Rabbi Levinthal died in 1982.

He tries to make his thought clearer with the following illustration. When does the painter really create his picture? Is it only when he takes the brush, dips it into the paint, and runs it over the canvas? Is that the only time that he fashions the painting? Or does he also create, or perhaps create even more, when he stops and examines his work, when he contemplates and reflects upon what he has done and what needs yet to be done? Is it not true that when he rests for contemplation, that is also a vital part of the process of creation; that reflection is also an activity—an activity of vision that helps to create the thing of beauty?

Herein is the difference between the true artist and the sham artist, between the one who fashions a perfect creation and the one whose work never achieves the distinction of art. The latter just works; the former works but also pauses to study his work, to review it, to examine it, and to reflect upon it. Ellis quotes an ancient Greek philosopher, Plotinus, to the effect that "contemplation is an active quality, so that all human creative energy may be regarded as the byplay of contemplation."

God is thus revealed, according to Havelock Ellis, as the true artist in that He had a Sabbath on which He not only rested but also contemplated His handiwork, studied His accomplishments, and reflected upon what improvement might be made, and upon what had yet to be done.

I have said that this observation of Ellis caught the spirit of the old rabbinic masters. Indeed, one of the ancients, R. Judah ben Menashia, commenting upon the words of Hannah, *En Tzur K'Elohenu*, "There is no rock like our God," makes a significant change in the Hebrew text so that it reads: *En Tza-yor K'Elohenu*, "There is no *artist* like our God!"—thereby emphasizing the very thought developed by this ultramodern thinker of our day. Because God was the supreme, the master artist, He knew the value of utilizing a Sabbath as a day of contemplation and thought, as part of the process of creating His world. That the Sabbath was not only a day of rest and surcease of work but also a part of the Divine act of creation is hinted in the very text of the Bible story: "And on the seventh day God finished His work which He had made; and He rested on the seventh day from all His work which He had made." The question has often been posed, why does the Bible say that God concluded His work on the seventh day? Was it not the sixth day on which the work had ended? Indeed, the

Septuagint regards the Hebrew text as faulty and amends the text to read "the sixth day." The translators of the Greek text did not grasp the deep truth that the original text here reveals—a truth which Havelock Ellis understood and appreciated—that God, the true artist, really finished the task of creation not on the sixth, but on the seventh day, on the day on which He examined His work, studied it, reviewed it, and reflected upon it, to see whether it measured up to His ideals of perfection. Our Hebrew text of the Bible goes even further. Speaking of the reason for the institution of the Sabbath, it says: "and on the Sabbath day *Shovat*, He rested, *Va-yi-na-fash*." This latter Hebrew word is also translated in our English version as "rested." There is, however, a significant distinction between these two words—*Shovat* and *Va-yi-nafash*. The first means "rested"; the second is derived from the root *Nofash*, and literally means "and He took on a new soul." God not only rested from work done, but refreshed His Spirit with new inspiration; He took on a new soul for new work yet to be done!

The Day of Atonement in Jewish literature is designated as the Sabbath of Sabbaths. In that very term is revealed its true purpose and function. If we are true artists of our lives, then this day must mean to us what the Sabbath meant to the Master Creator, God—what the moment of contemplative pause is for the artist with brush or chisel. On this Sabbath of Sabbaths, we are to pause and examine what we have achieved, what we have done with our own lives, to ask ourselves, in the words of our liturgy: "What are we, what is our life, what is our strength, what is our goodness, what is our righteousness?" All through the year we drive ourselves and rush hither and thither. If we are artists of our lives, we need not only activity, but thought and reflection. We need a Sabbath of Sabbaths to study and to examine that activity, to pause and to ask ourselves: "Whither art thou going?"

Jewish life was rich in former days because Jews were master builders of their lives. They lived in squalor and misery. They were spat upon and regarded as outcasts by their oppressors. And yet, they were able to fashion lives of spiritual beauty and perfection. They were true artists, utilizing not only the Sabbath of Sabbaths—the Day of Atonement—but every Sabbath of the year for that very purpose, the contemplation of the work of their lives. They studied themselves, they studied their children, they studied the life of their people; they noted wherein they failed, the errors that had to be corrected, the improvements that had to be made.

The tragedy of our lives today is that we have banished the spirit of the Sabbath from our midst. We are no longer genuine artists. We work and build and fashion, but never do we pause to contemplate, to think how we are working, what we are working for, what we are achieving. Not only do we fail to utilize the weekly Sabbath for that artistic value, but even the Sabbath of Sabbaths we no longer utilize for that sacred purpose. The result may be seen in the poorly fashioned lives that we behold. We are no longer artists—simply botchers, crude artisans, of life!

Ellis concludes the development of his thought with this beautiful illustration. What does the sculptor do when he contemplates? He sees a line crooked that ought to be straight, a curve where it should not be, too little light here, too much shadow there. He takes a chisel and hammer and shapes the block of marble into a form of beauty. This is our task, too, if we are true artists of our lives. Let us study our work. Where there is vulgarity, cut it away; where there is coarseness, smooth it off. Chisel away what is crooked. Where there is the darkness of ignorance, let the light of learning fall. Let us, like the Divine Artist, not only pause to contemplate on our work done, but let us also have the Sabbath and the Sabbath of Sabbaths to take new spirit and inspiration for the new work that needs to be done in order to achieve a perfect life and a perfect world.

This analysis also touches upon the problem of all American–Jewish life. There is feverish activity in every sphere, there is constant driving and campaigning, there are *Y'me Ha-moaseh*, "the days of action," but alas, no Sabbath of contemplation. What are we driving for? Whither are we going? Perhaps we are on the wrong track; perhaps we are tackling the problem in the wrong way. Never a moment of reflection, for thought, for analysis, for "taking on new soul!" That is the reason why, despite all our activity and all our driving, so little of real value is actually accomplished. Look at the problem of Jewish education that faces us today—how far we are from solving that fundamental, yet vexing, problem in Jewish life. Buildings are erected, drives are conducted, but the essence of the problem—winning the child for Jewish study—seems to remain unsolved.

Look at the problem of Jewish philanthropy here and abroad and the problem of the rebuilding of Palestine. See the apathy of so vast a number of our people in every section of the land.

Above all, look at the problem of our religious life here in

America. Millions of dollars have been raised in the last few decades for the erection of synagogues. Magnificent temples adorn the fashionable avenues in our cities. But have we developed a creative, a dynamic, religious life that shall give true meaning to the Jewish name?

The diagnosis is the same in every field of Jewish endeavor. We have not learned the truth that Plotinus emphasized, that "all human creative energy may be regarded as the byplay of contemplation." Our energy is divorced from contemplation and therefore is not truly creative. Again, we come to the sad conclusion, we are not artists, we are botchers of Jewish life!

Let us, on this Sabbath of Sabbaths, resolve to restore the spirit of the Sabbath to our lives. Let us not be content with only the *Y'me Ha-maaseh*, days of action. Let us bring back the Sabbath, too, for thought and contemplation.

In our individual lives, let us study, let us examine our failures and our faults and then rectify that which needs correction. Let us always seek to improve the lives that we fashion, so that we too may be privileged to say of our lives—as God so proudly said of His handiwork—*Re'u Briyah She-barati Vettzurah Shetzarti*, "Behold the being that I have created, the countenance that I have fashioned!" Let us become true artists also of our Jewish life. Let us add the Sabbath of contemplation to the days of action in all our communal endeavors; let us give more thought as well as more work to all our Jewish problems, and then, like true artists, we shall build a Jewish life of beauty and meaning and richness in which the *Shekinah* will dwell and reveal its blessedness.

JOSEPH H. LOOKSTEIN

Yesterday's Faith for Tomorrow

Will yesterday's faith do for today or tomorrow? Can the religion of
the fathers satisfy the needs of the children? Are the spiritual patterns
of a bygone day suited to our nuclear age?

These questions agitate the mind of modern man more than many
realize. It is not correct to regard ours as a secular society and to speak
about the irreligious orientation of the modern mentality. The modern mentality is very much preoccupied with matters of religion. God
is most certainly on the agenda of man, and it it not difficult to understand why that is so.

Our world has not been a very happy place to live in during the
last half century. In two world wars we suffered one hundred million

Rabbi Joseph H. Lookstein was the Rabbi of Congregation Kehilath Jeshurun
from 1923 until the year of his death, 1979. He was founder and first principal of the
Ramaz school, president and then chancellor of Bar Ilan University and a leading
preacher in the American Rabbinate. He taught homiletics at The Rabbi Isaac Elchanan
Theological Seminary of Yeshiva University for over forty years.

dead and at least three times that number in total casualties. There is hardly a spot on the globe which at this very moment is free of hostility, of the hot or the cold variety.

The world has become a huge arsenal stockpiled with lethal weapons of every kind. We are told that there is in reserve today the equivalent of thirty thousand pounds of TNT for every man, woman, and child in the world. Not a happy place this world of ours!

There are some four billion people in our world. It is estimated that from one-half to two-thirds of them are seriously underfed or malnourished to the point of starvation. Do we realize that more people have been killed by famine than by war? Are we simultaneously aware that America is spending one million dollars a day merely to store the huge food surplus of our country? What a painful paradox—the crisis of hunger and the crisis of abundance! No, not a happy place in this world of ours.

Of such a world Matthew Arnold said that it,

> hath neither joy, nor love,
> nor light,
> nor certitude, nor peace,
> nor help for pain.

In such a world man is looking for something strong, steady, and stable to hold on to. He is seeking what one teacher of religion called some "invisible means of support." Twentieth-century man is desperately searching for God.

Not long ago a book appeared with a strange subtitle—*L.S.D. and the Search of God.* How frantic must be man's need for God if he will even resort to psychedelic drugs in order to find Him.

A new school of theology flaunts its slogan, "God is dead." The God of the past and the religion that was built around Him simply will not do. A Jewish member of that school of thought has declared that for him God died at Auschwitz. One can understand the bitterness and rebellion out of which such conclusions are formed. But as one listens to the theological eulogies over the Divine, he cannot help but detect the desperate desire to discover a living God and a viable faith.

What sort of faith shall it be? Our generation is not unique in asking this question, and many have been the answers over the ages as man pursued his troubled quest for intellectual certainty and emotional stability. Man experimented with many gods and bowed before countless idols. He worshipped Nature, he enthroned Reason and even deified Man. In his spiritual odyssey he touched many theological ports before finally entering the secure harbor of monotheism. It took millennia for man to achieve religious maturity and to realize with the Psalmist that it might be well to "try the Lord and you will find Him good."[1]

Well then, what sort of faith is suited to our generation? Do we need a new faith, or will the spiritual patterns of the past satisfy the needs of our age and of ages yet to come?

Scripture might perhaps suggest an answer. When our forefathers stood in the ancient Temple two thousand years ago, they chanted a song of thanksgiving over their offerings. The last verse of that song states our position with the utmost clarity. "The Lord is good; His mercy is everlasting; and His truth endureth to all generations."[2]

When our ancestors chanted "and His truth endureth to all generations," they were enunciating a sober philosophic fact. There are some truths that are immutable. The founding fathers of America referred to such truths as "self-evident." The Magna Carta of England, the Declaration of Independence of the United States, and the Universal Declaration of Human Rights of the United Nations contain such truths, and they are immutable and eternal.

Religion is such a truth. "I the Lord do not change," said the Prophet Malachi.[3] In the chapter in which this statement appears, the Prophet lists a whole catalogue of sins. He speaks in the name of God and says: "I will be a prompt witness against sorcerers, adulterers and perjurers; against those who defraud widows and orphans, and laborers of their wages; against those who wrong a stranger . . ."[4]

What was the reaction of the Prophet's generation? They wanted a different God, a newer religion, a more agreeable way of life. Listen to them and you can almost hear some of our contemporary voices: "It is useless to serve God; what gain is it to do His bidding; to walk

---

1. Psalms 34:9.
2. Psalms 100:5.
3. Malachi 3:6.
4. Malachi 3:5.

mournfully before the Lord of Hosts? It is the worldly who are happy; evildoers prosper; they that defy God, escape."[5]

It is then that the Prophet sets them back on their heels. "I the Lord do not change." Religion is not a matter of fashion, worn sometimes knee-length and sometimes mini-length. Right is right in every century. Good is good in every generation. And evil is evil whether in the horse-and-buggy days or in the jet age. "The Lord is good; His mercy is everlasting; and His truth endureth to all generations."

The timelessness of religious truth is not entirely due to any inherent property of religion itself. It is primarily due to the fact that those for whom religion is intended remain basically and fundamentally unchanged. Yesterday's faith is valid today because the world of today is fundamentally the world of yesterday. God is a God for all seasons because man is essentially a man for all seasons. There are, indeed, three constants to reckon with—the world, nature, and man.

Let us begin with the world. To be sure, we know more about the world than our ancestors ever knew. We have measured her dimensions and clocked her speed around the sun. We know how old she is, how warm she is, and how cold she can be. We have scaled her highest peaks and descended to her lowest depths. We are familiar with her periodic convulsions and can predict her temperamental spasms. We have surveyed her surface, explored her outer space, and seismographed her heartbeat.

Yet with all this knowledge we must conclude that the world we inhabit has fundamentally changed hardly at all. "A generation comes and a generation goes but the world remains forever," said Ecclesiastes,[6] and his words somehow ring true. We are still puzzled by the mysteries of the world. We still wonder how it came into being and marvel at its stupendous architecture. Our awe and wonder of the world have not changed.

Nor has our world changed qualitatively. We talk about the contraction of the world and proudly feel that it is slowly becoming one world. Is it? The inhabitants of our world are further apart than they have been in centuries. The iron curtains of our day are more impregnable than the Chinese Wall millennia ago. How much has the world changed?

---

5. Malachi 3:14.
6. Ecclesiastes 1:4.

We boast of the conquest of the desert through irrigation and of the triumph over the jungle through civilization. Is our boast justified? Has not the jungle and its violence invaded our cities? How much, really, has the world changed?

An unchanging world does not need a change of religion. After Auschwitz, contends a Jewish exponent of the "God is dead" school of thought, a new faith is needed which will be intellectually more tenable than the old one. He forgets, in the heat of his theological indignation, that the Auschwitzes *were* the products of a new faith. Nazism was the new faith. The Nuremberg laws were the new decalogue. The old God was pronounced dead and was replaced by a deified Führer. The old Biblical doctrines of love, justice, and mercy were ruthlessly uprooted and were replaced by the false and vicious theories of race supremacy. It was the *new* faith that spawned the Auschwitzes and exterminated six million of our brothers and turned an entire continent into a wasteland.

No, a world which is capable of such convulsions, which is subject to periodic spasms of fury and violence, has not changed much from the days of Noah and the flood. The old faith still has quite a job to do.

If the world remains a constant factor in the experience of man, the same may be said of nature. From the beginning of time man has been contending against the natural forces of existence, trying to subdue them, or at least to assuage them, but never quite succeeding.

"Cursed is the earth for you," was the divine penalty imposed upon the first man. "In toil shall you eat of it all the days of your life. . . . By the sweat of your brow shall you eat bread, till you return to the earth from which you were taken; for dust thou art, and unto dust shalt thou return." [7]

This harsh statement determined for all time the relationship of man to nature. There is a perpetual battle between the two, and in that battle man must frequently turn to God for help. Included within every faith-tradition are prayers for rain, for sunshine, for bread, and for protection against the caprices of nature.

Nature's severest weapon is disease, and man's genius is busy devising counter-weapons of every variety. When these fail, and all too

---

7. Genesis 3:17–19.

often they do, man turns to God as the supreme physician for help. There is no medical substutute for the ancient prayer: Heal me, O Lord, and I shall be healed." [8]

Sometimes nature claims the final victory and death comes. Even then man does not accept defeat. His faith has prepared him for the inexorable and inevitable moment. Crushed but not beaten, he stands over a fresh grave and says, as Robert Ingersoll the atheist once said, "O God, can this be the end?"

All this—the strength to resist nature, the privilege of appeal against the cruelty of nature to a God who is above nature, and the capacity to hope that nature's victory over man is never final—all this comes from yesterday's faith. Is there an alternative to such a faith? "For the Lord is good; His mercy is everlasting; and His truth endureth to all generations."

If the world remains fundamentally constant and unchanging, and if nature continues cruel and implacable, what can we say of man, the principal inhabitant of the world and the supreme creature of nature?

Does man change? Of course he does, and anyone who fails to recognize the change is either blind or cynical.

Man has come a long way since primitive times. His remarkable progress from the stone age to the jet age, from the bow and arrow to the hydrogen bomb, is a gallant odyssey indeed. "For dust thou art," was the original estimate of man. "And You have made him but little short of the angels," was the eventual evaluation of his personality. The poet was right:

> And step by step, since time began
> I see the steady gain of man.

But man, in his essential nature and in his basic attributes, remains the same. He is still capable of good and evil. He is still subject to anger, rage, and hostility. He can still fall prey to envy, to greed, and to lust. He is still assailed by passion, and he still succumbs to temptation. He cannot easily shake his frustrations and cannot readily be rid of his fears. He is familiar with the mood of elation but is no stranger to depression and sorrow. In a word, he is a human being and not a machine.

---

8. Jeremiah 17:14.

In all of these aspects of his manhood, he is no different from his ancestors or from his earliest antecedents in the human family.

I recently saw a UNICEF poster showing a primitive-looking mother from a backward country holding starving child in her arms and bathing it with her tears. Phase out the picture. Replace the primitive mother with a modern and elegant mother bowed over the crib of her child dying of cystic fibrosis, the new killer of the young. She has come a long way from the mother on the UNICEF poster. But she is still a mother, and her child in torment is still her child, and death is still death.

That mother needs deep inner spiritual resources to pull her through. "Even though I walk through the valley of the shadow of death, I will fear no evil."[9] What spiritual strength that can provide!

Does, therefore, man, inherently unchanged through the ages, need a new faith? He does need the new medicine to heal him, the new science to serve him, the new psychology to understand him, and the new psychiatry to adjust him. But he dare not be deprived of the old faith. The god of some theologians may be dead but not the God of man.

Modern man, confused and perplexed, intellectually still groping, physically still plagued, emotionally still distressed, can still turn to his old God for relief and salvation. With the tortured and tormented Job, symbol of the eternal struggle of man against the forces of life, modern man can still say, "I know that my Redeemer lives."[10]

George Santayana summarized our thought poetically and philosophically.

> I know no deeper doubt to make me mad,
> I need no brighter love to keep me pure.
> To me the daily faiths of old are daily bread;
> I bless their hope, I bless their will to save.

This is precisely what the Psalmist said and what our ancestors chanted long ago: "The Lord is good; His mercy is everlasting; and His truth endureth to all generations."

---

9. Psalms 23:4.
10. Job 19:25.

SIMEON J. MASLIN

This Is My God

This is my God, whom I glorify,
The God of my father, whom I exalt.
                    —*Exodus* 15:2

My father, who died exactly one month ago, taught me to believe in God. My sermon on this eve of the New Year is about God, about what it means to believe in God.

From this evening through that final blast of the shofar that we shall hear at the conclusion of Yom Kippur ten days from now, we shall be addressing a lot of words to God—words spoken, words sung, words whispered or thought—thousands, tens of thousands of words, all addressed to God. But who is this God? Does He/She exist at all, or is He/She a figment of our historic imagination? An opiate, as Karl Marx suggested, to soothe the pains of toil and tragedy with promises of pie in the sky?

If you and I have come here this evening for some more exalted purpose than conforming to Jewish social norms, if we have come here

Rabbi Simeon J. Maslin was elected the sixth senior rabbi of Keneseth Israel in 1980. Holding degrees from Harvard, the University of Pennsylvania, Hebrew Union College–Jewish Institute of Religion, and Chicago Theological Seminary, he also served as President of the Central Conference of American Rabbis 1995-1997. Rabbi Maslin is the author of three books and numerous articles and pamphlets.

so that we might indeed be moved to attempt to live more noble lives, then we must have some conception of the object of our prayers. And so I ask two simple but ageless questions. Is there really a God? And if so, what can we know of God?

I said a moment ago that my father taught me to believe in God. But even before I achieved adulthood, my concept of God began diverging radically from his. We both loved and revered God, but he in his way and I in mine. (If it were my father speaking now, he would have said that I loved God in my way while he loved God in God's way.)

Jewish tradition teaches that we should conclude the initial thirty days of mourning with a memorial tribute. This sermon, then, is my tribute to *Avi Mori*—to my father, my teacher. I dedicate this sermon to his memory, and I take as my text the verse from the Song of the Sea in Exodus that reads: This is my God, whom I glorify, The God of my father, whom I exalt.

One of the leaders of early nineteenth-century Chassidism was Rabbi Mendl of Kotzk. When the young Mendl began leaning toward Chassidism, his father, whose beliefs were more traditional, rebuked him. Rabbi Mendl then quoted that verse from the Song of the Sea to his father, with a marvelous commentary. Rabbi Mendl said, "This is my God"—first I must find God for myself so that I may glorify Him; only then can I accept "the God of my father" and exalt Him properly.

That exchange between Rabbi Mendl and his father reminds me of an exchange between my father and myself back in 1974. I had been invited to give a lecture on prophetic values in Reform Judaism at the convention of the Central Conference of American Rabbis in Jerusalem that year. Although I looked forward to visiting with my father, I did not tell him about my lecture because there were certain comparisons that I would be making between the Reform response to the social justice message of the prophets and the Orthodox response. Reform Judaism may have many weaknesses, but surely its strength is its devotion to human rights; Orthodoxy certainly has great strengths, but its great weakness is its silence on issues of human rights. I was going to focus on that weakness, and so I did not mention my lecture to my father.

Somehow my father found out that I was lecturing, and he told me that he would be there. He was quite busy that afternoon, but he would take the hour to come to the convention hall to hear my lecture. I could not disinvite him, and I remember considering whether or not to soften certain passages in my lecture out of deference to him. But then I decided: no, he has strong opinions of his own, and I have to be true to my convictions.

From time to time during the lecture I recall looking at my father. He sat there, attentive but expressionless. When I finished, during the customary applause before the questions, he rose and made his way to the exit at the rear of the hall. But before he went out the door, he turned to me and he raised his hand in a gesture of real approval—his thumb and forefinger in a circle as he waved to me. I was truly baffled; I knew that he could not have agreed with most of my message. Yet how to interpret his gesture?

That evening I called my father, and I asked him what he had meant by that signal of approval. Had he really agreed with my critique of Orthodoxy? "No, no," he answered. "I didn't agree at all with what you said, but I liked the way that you said it!" And so, while I dedicate this sermon to the memory of my father, I do so knowing that he would disagree with much of it, but that he would approve of my search for God according to my own lights.

Has it ever occurred to you that nowhere in the Bible are we commanded to believe in God? The Bible takes the existence of God for granted, from the opening verse of Genesis through the entire twenty-four books. Every chapter and verse rests on that opening phrase that declares, with perfect faith: "In the beginning of God's creation of heaven and earth . . ." It is as if the narrator understood, long before philosophers and theologians began to argue their various proofs for the existence or the nonexistence of God, that such arguments are futile.

There is no way that anyone, no matter how brilliant, has ever proven or will ever prove empirically the existence of God. If God exists, then God is, by definition, beyond the comprehension of finite creatures. God is infinite, *supernatural*, the subject of metaphysics. So I readily admit defeat as to answering the first question that I posited, "Is there really a God?" There I take my leap of faith, and I join the company of Abraham, Moses, Job, Maimonides, and Einstein in turning to the second question, the question that should be on the mind of every Jew in these first hours of the New Year, "What can we know of God?"

Some of you may be tempted to answer: God is God. Whatever Jewish tradition says about God, whatever my wonderful parents and grandparents believed about God—that's good enough for me. But no, dear friends, that is not a Jewish answer. The real Jew, the Jew who takes his or her Judaism seriously, must engage the mind and continue the search. That's what these High Holy Days are all about.

On this eve of Rosh Hashanah, I urge you to join Abraham as he asks, "Is it possible for the Judge of all the earth not to do justice?" (Genesis 18:25). I urge you to join Moses as he implores, "Explain to me Your ways, so that I may know You" (Exodus 33:13). I urge you to join Job as he cries, "Why do You hide Your face, [O God], and treat me like an enemy?" (Job 13:24). I urge you to join Maimonides as he struggles with logic, writing, "God exists without the attribute of existence; God lives without the attribute of life; God knows without the attribute of knowledge" (Guide for the Perplexed, ch. 57). I urge you to join Albert Einstein who articulated his search by explaining to Martin Buber, "What we [scientists] strive for is just to draw [God's] lines after Him." To a colleague at Berlin University he said, "I want to know how God created this world . . . I want to know His thoughts."

Let me proceed with our search for the meaning of God by describing two hypothetical instances. In one of them, God acts; in the other, God does not act. Hypothetical 1: A beautiful little baby is crawling toward the edge of a cliff. His family's attention is momentarily focused elsewhere. He has somehow escaped from his playpen and he has reached the edge of the cliff. His mother spots him just as he leans out over the edge, loses his balance, and falls over. He is dashed on the rocks a hundred feet below . . . with God watching. Hypothetical 2: A beautiful little baby is crawling toward the edge of a cliff. His family's attention is momentarily focused elsewhere. He has somehow escaped from his playpen and he has reached the edge of the cliff. His mother spots him just as he leans out over the edge, loses his balance, and falls over. The hand of God catches him before he hits the rocks and returns him gently to the bosom of his mother.

Question: Which of these stories describes a God who has meaning for us?

Dear friends, at the risk of sounding cruel and heartless, oblivious to the pain of a mother, I will opt for the former God, the God who allows that beautiful innocent baby to be broken on the rocks along with the hearts and the hopes of loving parents and grandparents. Why?

Why, in Heaven's name—literally, in Heaven's name—why do I choose the God who allows an innocent child to die?

Why, hearing of the death of that innocent baby, or the crash of an airplane loaded with innocent people, or the starvation of hundreds of thousands of innocents in Somalia, or—to come closer to home—the six million innocents who perished in the Holocaust, or—to come even closer to home—those young men and women and even children in our own community who have died by accident or disease this past year—why do I prefer the God who allows these tragedies, these injustices to happen, over the God who would intervene miraculously and prevent them?

Or let's put the question the way that Job put it:

> Why do the wicked live, prosper and grow wealthy? . . .
> Their homes are secure, without fear;
> They do not feel the rod of God . . .
> They let their infants run loose like sheep,
> And their children skip about . . .
> They say to God, "Leave us alone,
> We do not want to learn Your ways.
> What is the Almighty that we should serve Him?
> What will we gain by praying to Him?"
>
> (21:7–15)

That genius author of Job was sorely tempted. All around him he saw the wicked prospering and the innocent suffering. He saw the deaths of lovely little children. And as chapter follows chapter we realize that the author is telling us that suffering and loss, as inexplicable and unjust as they may seem, are part of the nature of the universe. So he cries out, in the persona of Job: What is the Almighty that we should serve Him? What will we gain by praying to Him?

And yet the very same Job bows his head and confesses: "Yea, though [God] slay me, Yet will I trust in Him" (13:15).

Dear friends: where can we find faith like that? And is it worth the search? What will we gain by praying to a God who will not save an innocent baby? Who needs a God who presides over a Holocaust?

Do you know why I prefer the God who allows that innocent baby to be dashed on the rocks? Because *if I cannot depend on the absolute immutability of the laws of nature, as established by God, then I can depend on nothing.* Either there is a law of gravity or there is not. If a

183

baby falls one hundred feet to jagged rocks below, that baby will die. No matter how innocent, no matter how beautiful, that baby *must* die. Because if he does *not* die, then the law of gravity has been suspended. And if one of the basic laws of physics that govern the operation of our universe can be suspended occasionally, in response to a plea for mercy, then we can depend on nothing.

When Albert Einstein said, "I want to know how God created this world . . . I want to know [God's] thoughts," what he was teaching us was that *the more we understand the inexorable and ineluctable workings of this world created by God, the more we will understand God.* The more that we understand God, the more we will be able to live lives in the image of God. The more that we lead our lives in the image of God, demonstrating through our deeds that we do, in fact, have a spark of divinity within us, the more we can improve this o-so-imperfect world of ours. That is what our rabbis meant when they taught that we human beings are partners with God in the ongoing work of creation.

Let's spend just a minute on the painful question of where God was during the Holocaust. Why, I am asked so very often, couldn't God at least have saved the innocent little children? Over one million Jewish children were the pure and innocent victims of the Nazi reign of terror during our lifetimes. I was an innocent child during those very years when the crematoria of Auschwitz and Treblinka were belching forth the acrid smoke that was the last trace of so many innocent children. If my grandparents had not decided to leave Eastern Europe thirty years earlier, I would have been there with my cousins. And so too, many of you. And so, where was God?

The answer, dear friends, is that God was there, mourning and comforting. No, God could not put an end to the Holocaust, not because God lacks that power and certainly not because the forces of evil are greater than the forces of good. No. God could not end the Holocaust because that Nazi bloodbath was a product of the human will. Human beings hated and envied and feared, and the result was the Holocaust. *If God had intervened, that intervention would have required the suspension of human free will.*

Here, again, we come to one of those laws that govern the workings of our universe. God created humanity with the gift of free choice. God will not make us behave. God will not save us, like an indulgent parent, when our ill-considered acts spawn painful, even tragic, consequences. Cause and effect; sow evil and reap evil. Practice hate and envy and fear, and society will be corrupted. For God to intervene in this process would mean to take from us that gift that makes us human.

God sets before us life and death, blessing and curse, and God begs us, "Choose life!" And if we choose death? Then God can only suffer along with the innocent and comfort the mourners. God will not take back from us that awesome gift of free choice, even if we decide to allow a million people to starve in Somalia, even if we decide to allow the Bosnians and Serbians to wipe each other out, even if we decide to destroy the world in a nuclear holocaust.

It is not God who is today polluting our atmosphere; it is we human beings. But it is God who has decreed that if the water that we drink and the air that we breathe are filled with noxious gases and bacteria and viruses, then we will have cancer and AIDS and epidemic diseases.

It is not God who foments crime, poverty, and drug dependence in this incomparably rich land of ours; it is we human beings. But it is God who has decreed that if a society imports slaves and proceeds to rape them and beat them and exploit them and, even after emancipating them, subjects them to ceaseless indignity, then there will be urban jungles, and innocents will be caught in the cross fire. As Hosea put it, "They who sow the wind shall reap the whirlwind" (8:7). In the world as God created it, there is no effect without a cause. If we, having been clearly warned, go on depleting the ozone layer, then cancers will multiply. That is God's law: cause and effect.

I am reminded of a cartoon that I saw in a Methodist publication. Two friends are sitting under a tree and staring off into the distance, when suddenly one of them says, "Sometimes I'd like to ask God why He allows poverty, famine, and injustice when He could do something about it." His friend asks, "So what's stopping you." He answers, "I'm afraid God might ask me the same question."

If you are with me thus far, if you agree with me that there is a God, that this God is, in the words of the prayer that we read just half an hour ago, ". . . great, mighty, and awesome . . . God supreme," and if this all-powerful God, because of the laws that He established for this universe, will not intervene, even to save an innocent and beautiful little baby, then my final question: What do we need with such a God? Of what use is a God who will not save us from ourselves? Why this great religious pageant that we call the High Holy Days with its tens of thousands of words, all addressed to God?

Just a few weeks ago the prophetic reading for Shabbat morning was taken from the book of Isaiah. The scene: Jerusalem in flames; thousands of Jews killed by the Babylonian armies; and the remnant led off into distant exile. An all-powerful God, the people thought, could have prevented this monumental tragedy. And so the prophet, speaking for the people, cries out: "Adonai has forsaken me; Adonai has forgotten me."

Then we hear the voice of God. I hear that voice as if crooning a lullaby—gently, softly, with a stifled sob, God says,

> Can a woman forget her baby,
> Or disown the child of her womb?
> Though she might forget,
> I could never forget you.
> See, I have engraved you
> On the palms of my hands.
> (Isaiah 49:14–16)

That is the way that I picture the God whom I love, with the image of every human being engraved on the palms of His hands, as it were. When I needed comfort, just one month ago, I heard the voice of God, again through the prophecy of Isaiah, crooning gently to me, "Anochi Anochi Hu Menachemchem—It is I, truly I, who am your Comforter (Isaiah 51:12).

And as I cried, I felt that God cried also—and so I was comforted.

I want to close with two brief scenes out of the amazing mind of Elie Wiesel, one scene from his earliest novel, *Night*, and the second from his most recent novel, *The Forgotten*. In *Night* Wiesel tells about the hanging of an innocent boy in Auschwitz with the prisoners forced to stand facing the gallows to watch. The boy stands silent on a chair with the noose around his neck, and then the Nazi guard kicks over the chair.

The boy is so light, from months of hunger, that his weight does not kill him immediately. For more than half an hour he struggles between life and death. Then Wiesel, forced along with the other prisoners to watch the slow agony of this pitiful boy, hears a man behind him asking, "Where is God now?" "And," Wiesel writes, "I heard a voice within me answer him, 'Where is He? Here He is—He is hanging on this gallows.' "

God was there in the concentration camps, suffering with the sufferers, hanging on the gallows with the victims, suffocating in the gas chambers, and stealing bread for the sick. It was because God was there that some were able to survive. It was because God was there that some were able to hug and kiss their wives and husbands and children as the gas seeped in around them. It was because God was there—a palpable presence to many—that some were able to face their final moments with nobility, knowing that they had defeated death. It was because the young Elie Wiesel felt God hanging on the gallows next to that little boy that he is able today, after seeing his entire civilization annihilated, to believe in God, to question God, and to cry with God.

It is precisely because of His infinite mercy that God is able to restrain Himself from intervening to save us from our human follies, to save us from ourselves. For God to intervene—to miraculously excise the cancer or calm the hurricane or fill the grain silos or replace the ozone—for God to interject Himself to compensate for our human inadequacy would be to infantalize us, to make us puppets, dancing and dangling pathetically at the divine whim. That is not God's way.

God gave us an irrevocable gift—free will. Free will is the crown of our humanity; it is the divine gift which we celebrate during these High Holy Days as we evaluate the past and look prayerfully to the future. Humbly I thank God for that infinite patience that enables Him to see us make mistake after mistake—often mistakes of tragic and horrendous proportions—and yet not revoke that gift which makes us human.

For God to take away our free will, that, dear friends, would be the Ultimate Holocaust—millions of mindless and meaningless creatures, prancing and posturing on their hind legs, subject to the whim of an all-powerful but capricious deity. No, that is not my God. My God allows me to err, and then, when I am wounded, my God sits with me on the low mourning stool, and I am comforted.

Now that second Wiesel story that I promised you. World War II is raging, and the German forces are in retreat as the Russians advance across the Ukraine. Wiesel's hero, Elchanan, is in a Jewish partisan band that captures a Ukrainian village. There they find a pathetic little group of Jewish boys, emaciated and ravenous, who have escaped from the retreating Germans.

Elchanan asks, "What did the Germans do to you?" It seems that the Germans had locked them in a barn, without food, for about a week. Some had gone mad, and others had died of hunger and thirst.

As the boys are devouring the food that these Jewish partisans give them, one of the partisan leaders, Itzik, decides to so something for the boys. After they eat, he suddenly says, "Come on, kids. Follow me." Wiesel continues:

> He led them to a cabin at the edge of the village where six German prisoners were being held. He turned to one of the boys, handed over his submachine gun and said gently, almost tenderly, "Fire, boy. Fire at the whole lot!"
>
> The boy trembled. He looked at the weapon, examined his own hand, seemed to hold a debate with an invisible presence and finally said, "I don't know how." "Don't worry," Itzik said, "I'll show you." The boy lowered his eyes and said, "No."
>
> Itzik turned to another. The same answer. A third. Still the same answer. Itzik clapped them all on the shoulder and said, "All right, all right, I understand. Later on you'll know how."
>
> God of Israel, Elchanan thought, watch these, Your children, and be proud. (The Forgotten, pp. 127–128)

"Watch these, Your children, and be proud!"

Sometimes, dear friends, God is proud of us. Sometimes we are kind when our baser instincts tell us to be cruel. Sometimes we are gentle when we could be ruthless. Sometimes we are loving when we could be harsh. And God is proud. If we have faith, then we know that God is proud, and life becomes sweet. As Rabbi Mendl of Kotzk taught, "God dwells wherever we let Him in."

Dear friends, try, try during these next ten days to let God in. Life can be so sweet when we know that there is a God who loves us, who urges to join Him in the task of creating a better world, and a God whose patience, no matter what, is infinite. This is my God, whom I glorify, The God of my Father, whom I exalt.

Yitgadal v'yitkadash sh'mei rabba . . .

Amen.

W. GUNTHER PLAUT

Taking a Chance on God

On Rosh Hoshanah I spoke to you about my idea that being a Jew is an improbable proposition, and that existence in ordinary terms cannot be explained. The only explanation is the presence of God and our belief in a Supreme Being, a being that has some relationship to us. I admit that I cannot prove what I said. Faith is not a mathematical formulation, it's not an equation that can be resolved with x and y and z. Rather, it is taking a chance, making a commitment with regard to something that you cannot verify in the ordinary way. And so I told you that I would speak about that very aspect this morning.

Let me begin by saying something about taking chances. As I started thinking about the subject in preparation for my sermon this morning,

Rabbi W. Gunther Plaut completed law school in Germany when Hitler came to power, was disbarred, and turned to the rabbinate. Studying in Berlin and then at Hebrew Union College, Rabbi Plaut was ordained in 1939. He was Senior Scholar at Holy Blossom Temple in Toronto, to which he has served since 1978. In addition, he has served as President of the Canadian Jewish Congress and the Central Conference of American Rabbis. Rabbi Plant is the author of *The Torah: A Modern Commentary* and *The Haftorah Commentary*.

it suddenly became clear to me that in my own life I have been taking and continue to take more chances than I thought I was. In fact, life is one big series of taking chances.

Usually, we think of chances as being something we like to avoid unless the odds are in our favour. We think of gambling in Las Vegas—or at least some of you may be thinking in such terms—but taking a chance goes much further than that. Just let me give you a few examples.

When you cross a street, you take a chance that nobody will run through the red light and dispatch you into the next world. When you ride on an airplane or even a subway, you take a chance, it may be very small, but I don't believe you ever think much about it. You young people, when you make a friend in school, you take a gamble, for that friend may change your life for good or for bad or, perhaps, not at all; but the likelihood is that the friend *will* have some influence on the way you grow, think, and you react. Anybody who gets married takes a chance. Those of you in the congregation who have enjoyed a good marriage know that you took a chance, and it worked out all right. Those of you who have not been so fortunate know the opposite.

There are some here this morning who are contemplating going to university. Perhaps you want to enroll in medical school or in law school. You are going to have years of hard work ahead of you and in the end you have no guarantee that you're going to like being a doctor or lawyer or whatever. An increasing number of you will change your professions and occupations at least once or even twice during your lifetime. I know I did!

I was born in Germany and eventually decided to go to law school and I finished it. I was unaware that I was taking a chance when I enrolled, but it turned out I did. Hitler came along and said, "You can't be a lawyer," and that was the end of that! So I came to a new country which I had never seen, the language of which I did not speak very well, and where I knew nobody. I took a chance on a new life in the rabbinical school in Cincinnati—about which I knew nothing—and I became a rabbi. I had no idea what being a rabbi was like, or if in fact whether I would like being one. So you see, this little segment of my own personal life which can be duplicated by yours is one long series of taking chances.

That leads to my main observation, which is that we take our chance on practically everything a hundred times a day, but all too many of us don't want to take a chance on *believing in God*. To me that makes very little sense. Most adults admit that they know very few things for sure, and especially in reference to God. But children in the sixth and seventh grades already "know" that there is no God, and they're certain and ride happily into the future and that certainty. What they really say is, "This is one chance I don't want to take."

How about listening not to them but to others and their experiences, who have taken a chance on God and found that it is a wonderful, elevating, and enlarging experience. One does not have to be Orthodox to do this, believe me. One doesn't even have to be Jewish to do it. Turn on the radio or television and you hear about born-again Christians. Who are these people anyway—are they all freaks? Most of them are just ordinary people like you and me. What they have been doing is saying, "I've lived my life up to this point and I am not really satisfied. I'm going to take a chance on God." They, of course, put it in Christian terms, and I'm asking you to put it into Jewish terms. It's as simple as that, and Yom Kippur is a wonderful day to challenge you to do it.

Think of God as parent. You exist only because of your parents. The world exists only because of God. And so does the Jewish people, and in the end, so do you.

My challenge to you is to make a start. Take a chance on believing that there is something greater than you and your understanding of the world and even greater than science. Perhaps the order that surrounds us came into existence with a great Big Bang, but however it happened, I believe it was no accident. Rather, it was the result of something else. The Torah says, "God began to create." I believe that. I don't know *how* it was, I will never know, but then I'm just human and my knowledge of things beyond me is very limited. I take a chance on God. I have found it enlarging and satisfying, a kind of recourse that makes my life richer.

Some of you will say, "Rabbi, what about the Holocaust? If there is a God, how could God permit such ghastly crimes, especially against a people who believe that they have been chosen by that very God to testify to the Divine Presence?"

I've spoken on this subject on a variety of occasions and, this morning, I will only hint at my answer. We have been given free will by God to shape a good deal of our lives and our future. We can use this free will for good and for evil, and when we use it for evil, it is *our* doing and not God's. God, I believe, sustains the world and has given its creatures free will to do what they please. God, so to speak, stands by to energize us, to give us extra strength and power. But God will not prevent us from doing the wrong thing.

I generally do not pray in order to obtain things for myself. In answer to the occasional jibe from my friends on the golf course, who claim that I receive special help, I lay the matter to rest by saying, "She is not a golfer." In fact, I don't know what God really is; I only know that God exists and is the ground on which I stand and from whom I obtain my energy.

Here in our lovely synagogue everything is quiet except for my voice. Are you aware that this quiet space about us is actually filled with sound and music? For, if we had a little radio or television set in our pockets, we could easily tune in and hear and see it all. It's real, but we need to tune in.

That's the way I feel it is with God. God is here, right now, with all of us, but we find it hard to tune in. Yes, we do say the prayers, and it helps, but we haven't really charged our batteries enough to make our prayers work. We come here like strangers. The batteries are uncharged and perhaps even dead; yet we act as if it doesn't make any difference that we haven't charged them for a year. You would know how to do it with a pocket radio, and you don't seem to know how to do it with your life.

All I can tell you is, take a chance, be open and think in these terms not only once or twice a year but as part of everyday existence. I begin my day with prayer and end it with prayer.

I say a prayer every time before I eat and not just on Friday night when our ritual is more elaborate. I thank God for a bowl of soup, a piece of bread. I'll look at the sky and marvel, and I am happy that I am able to see that I am alive and can relate to God.

When I pray, I feel larger. I draw on the Divine Resource that is present all about me. Yes, I do say selfish prayers from time to time, it's in our nature for us to do this. Yet I know that the answer may not be forthcoming and may be a deep silence only. But, my parents too used to say "no" quite a few times to me and it didn't make them any less real to me nor did I love them any the less for it.

There is both good and evil in this world and both are, so to speak, tolerated by God. Our tradition has one way of expressing the ever-present Divine Being in relation to our suffering. It says that God weeps with us, because the things that we decide to do with our lives are out of God's hands. I'd rather have God as a partner. God offers help—I say, I'll take it.

That is what our people did when they had a unique religious experience. They took a chance on God, and that's why we're still here.

Our life is filled with taking chances, one after the other, minute after minute. Today you have come here to synagogue and while you are here, take a chance on God. Think about this for the rest of the day; it will be the best you'll ever do. It's a chance that I guarantee will pay off. You will enlarge your spirit, calm your soul, and connect you in a new way to your people, your family and yourself. Start by saying "Yes" to belief and from there go on to asking: "What does my new partner want me to do—as a person and as a Jew. Do it! Take a chance!

SALLY J. PRIESAND

Looking Backward and Ahead

As the twentieth anniversary of my ordination approaches, I am honored to have this opportunity to share some reflections with you. I am particularly pleased that the occasion is Founders' Day because I sense in my life a special link with the two men we remember now, those architects of Reform Judaism whose ideas shaped our movement and whose vision created our College-Institute. The reasons for this affinity are two in number. First, I suspect I am the only person privileged to serve as rabbi at both the Isaac M. Wise Temple in Cincinnati and the Stephen Wise Free Synagogue in New York. These two congregations, brought into being by our founders and existing today as monuments to their memory, contributed to my growth as a rabbi, teaching me important lessons about human nature and preparing me for the future.

Rabbi Sally J. Priesand, America's first female rabbi, was ordained in 1972 by Hebrew Union College-Jewish Institute of Religion. Rabbi Priesand's committment to all things Jewish is reflected in her many organizational affiliations. She is a member of the Board of Trustees of the Jewish Federation of Greater Monmouth County, the author of *Judaism and the New Woman*, and the recipient of numerous awards and honors.

My second reason for feeling connected to our founders is that early on in my career I discovered that both of them were wise enough to understand the need for equality and to encourage full participation on the part of women in the secular world as well as the religious community. You may recall that Isaac Mayer Wise championed the right of women to have both a voice and a vote in congregational life. This is what he said: ". . . the principle of justice and the law of God inherent in every human being demand that woman be admitted to membership in the congregation and be given equal rights with man; that her religious feelings be allowed scope for the sacred cause of Israel. We are ready to appear before any congregation in behalf of any woman wishing to become a member thereof and to plead her cause."

Stephen Wise shared this commitment and applied it to the larger community. In 1915 he wrote, "The woman's movement rests upon the cardinal truth that, inasmuch as life is a sacred thing and personality inviolable, woman ought to be as free as is man to determine the content of life for herself. Woman must not have life marked out for her by custom or convention or expediency. . . . She must make and shape her own life, and she must no longer be expected to live in terms of relativity, in terms of dependence, in terms of complement."

In addition, in 1919 Stephen Wise wrote the following letter to a young woman in his congregation, "If you are really in earnest and wish to study for the ministry there is no reason why you should not. The fact that no woman has served as rabbi is no reason why no woman should so serve. If you were my child, as in a sense you are, and felt you wished to enter the ministry, I should urge you to go on and prepare yourself with the conviction that opportunities for service would come to one eager to serve and possessed of the determination as you are to serve God and Israel through your vocation." When I read these words, I rather like to think that Isaac Mayer Wise and Stephen Wise would take pleasure in knowing that their vision has found fulfillment in our day and time.

Standing here before you now, on the threshold of an important anniversary in my life and in the life of our Movement, I feel privileged to have participated in this pioneering effort, the complete ramifications of which remain as yet unknown. At the same time, I am well aware that the accomplishment is not mine alone. By a quirk of history I was first, and since that time, many others have followed in my footsteps. I share this anniversary with all of them and express my gratitude for their creativity which so often energizes and inspires me.

Our tradition enjoins that we honor those from whom we learn. On this occasion, three deserve special mention. Nelson Glueck (ז״ל) dreamed the dream, and though he did not live to see it realized, he has earned our undying respect and gratitude for having laid the foundations that made possible the ordination of women. Fred Gottschalk, committed to the cause of equality, fulfilled the promise and today presides over a College-Institute that welcomes both women and men who seek to dedicate their lives in service to God and the Jewish people. Edward E. Klein (ז״ל), hand-picked successor to Stephen Wise, took pride in knowing that he was our Movement's first equal opportunities employer. He taught me how to be a rabbi, and even today I see reflected in my rabbinate his spirit and the legacy he left behind.

It sounds corny to say that I love being a rabbi, but the truth is that I do and I can't imagine doing anything else. In what other profession does one have the opportunity to touch the lives of other people in ways that are real and significant and often unknown? The satisfaction I experience is due in large measure to the support and encouragement I have received from family and friends ever since that day nearly three decades ago when I announced that I wanted to be a rabbi, and most especially, the love and affection that my congregation showers on me. Every day I thank God for the privilege of being associated with Monmouth Reform Temple. Our creative partnership these last eleven years has enriched my life in ways I never dreamed possible.

Among the many lessons my congregants have taught me, three are foremost in my mind today. I think of them now because I see reflected in them the gifts that feminism has given to all of us over the past twenty years. First, we have gained a broader understanding that the rabbi's primary task is to help other Jews become more responsible for their own Jewishness. In today's language, that's called empowerment, and nothing in my rabbinate gives me greater joy than to see my congregants study Torah, observe mitzvot, and do Judaism for themselves. The Jew-by-choice who comes to the bima for the first time to light Shabbat candles, family members gathered at the cemetery to conduct an unveiling ceremony for one of their beloved, the adult Hebrew student who sits in the sanctuary and proudly follows with her finger the words of the prayerbook, the engineer entrusted with the challenge of preparing a D'var Torah, the retiree who undertakes the mitzvah of *bikur cholim*, the young adult who blows shofar, parents and children participating together in the task of *tikun olam*—that's empowerment, and that remains our primary goal: to foster education, to promote observance, to encourage participation, to inspire commitment, to create a feeling of family—Not to be surrogate Jews, but to move away from the twin towers of hierarchy and power toward new opportunities for networking and partnership. It is not our responsibility to be Jewish for the sake of the congregation but to suggest ways in which all of us can be Jewish together. That idea is not unique to feminism, but the women's movement has served as catalyst, encouraging us to rethink previous models of leadership in which the rabbi maintained complete control and did everything for members of the congregation.

The second area in which we see the impact of feminism is that of theology. Like most of you, I too grew up with the image of God as King, omnipotent and clearly male. My congregation has given me the opportunity, through experience and study, discussion and experimentation, to discover new models of divinity, to know that God embodies characteristics both masculine and feminine, to fashion for myself and hopefully for them, a meaningful theology which has been a source of strength, particularly in those moments of difficulty that are part of every life. Together we have opened our hearts and our lives to greater spirituality. We are learning to talk to God and *with* God rather than *about* God, to enjoy that intimacy that comes when addressing God as "you." As a result, every member of our Temple family, man and woman, young and old, parent and child, has the freedom to imagine God in any way he or she finds meaningful and comforting. The process has been enriching, and the possibilities for future growth are endless.

The third lesson I have learned from my congregation is this: success doesn't mean bigger. Twenty years ago, I thought the ultimate goal was to become rabbi of a large congregation; indeed, as the first woman to be ordained I thought it was my obligation. Our society and our Movement teach us in so many different ways that bigger is better, and within the context of the rabbinate, that if you don't continue to move up through the category system, you have somehow failed. Fortunately, for my own well-being, my congregation taught me to reject that notion.

Life is not measured by wealth or power, material possessions or fame. Life is counted in terms of goodness and growth. Someone once said that our purpose in living is not to get ahead of other people, but to get ahead of ourselves, always to play a better game of life. That's what success is all about. Have we done our best? Are we continuing to grow? Are we affected more deeply today by love and beauty and joy than we were yesterday? Are we more sensitive and compassionate toward others? Have we learned to overcome our fears and accept our failures? Have we triumphed over selfishness and bitterness, cruelty and hatred? Do we count our blessings in such a way that we make our blessings count? That's what success is. In the words of Albert Schweitzer: "The great secret of success is to go through life as a person who never gets used up. Grow into your ideals so that life can never rob you of them."

These then are the lessons I have learned as I look back over the past twenty years. Empowerment is healthy for the Jewish people. Our renewed interest in theology makes us spiritually alive and thus better able to be whole persons. And success doesn't mean bigger. As I look ahead, I am well aware that our journey is only just beginning. Twenty years is but a speck in the life of the Jewish people, and much remains to be done. For guidance in that task, let us look to the words of our Torah which remains our tree of life.

This week's *parasha* describes for us the ritual of consecration. Moses marks the lobe of Aaron's right ear with blood, and the thumb of his right hand and the toe of his right foot. Of all the limbs and organs of the human body, we sense a purpose in the choice of these three. With the ear, we listen. With the hand, we embrace. With the foot, we move forward. Can the role of those who wish to lead be any clearer? Listen to the voices of women as well as men, be sensitive to both, and understand that our Movement is enriched when we open ourselves to the needs and experiences of all our members. Embrace one another in the spirit of equality, knowing that every human being is a piece of priceless mosaic in the design of God's universe. Each one of us has a unique contribution to make, and Reform Judaism will be stronger if we continue to offer the hand of welcome to women as well as men, whether it be in congregational life, in positions of national leadership, or on the faculty of our College-Institute. And finally, move forward together, providing new opportunities, encouraging growth, and creating options—all in the spirit of our founders who refused to stand still in the face of challenge. We are called by them to continue to re-form and refashion our Movement, knowing that ultimately what we do, or fail to do, will be the legacy we leave behind.

I conclude with the words of Stephen Wise: "When nice and refined and timid people say to you: Remember to be like everybody else, don't attempt anything new, don't run the risk of seeming peculiar, don't dream of venturing upon novel courses whether in things great or small, remember that there is a possible invasion of the soul's integrity that no person need endure. To the counsels of the timorous fling back the command to the brave—always do what you are afraid to do."

EMANUEL RACKMAN

Children of Three or Eight

In the literature of the Bible and in the literature of the Talmud, we are assured that whenever we want to return to God, the road is open. However, in a few instances, penitence is of no avail. Thus, for example, if a man should say, "I will sin and on every Day of Atonement I will confess my wrongdoing and obtain forgiveness," he is not forgiven. Penitence involves genuine remorse and a firm resolve not to repeat the same transgression. Consequently, any conduct which reveals the absence of genuine remorse vitiates the possibility of atonement.

In still another instance, penitence is of no avail. We are told in Deuteronomy that the day will come when the Jewish people will suffer great hardship and they will understand that all the evil was visited upon them because they had forsaken God. Yet, though they will recognize that it is the hand of God that bears down heavily upon them, this

Rabbi Emanuel Rackman is an Orthodox rabbi and author. He serves as a faculty member at Yeshiva University, CUNY, and is President of Bar Ilan University. Rabbi Rackman is a member of the Executive Jewish Agency, and is a World War II chaplain.

recognition will not help them. On that day, God will hide His face from them and not come to their relief. Now, why isn't their recognition of God as the one who is meting out their punishment adequate as penitence? Are they not thus acknowledging that their worship of false gods and their adoration of pagan practices have brought them to the brink of disaster? Isn't this awareness of the bankruptcy of idolatry enough to open the road to God's forgiveness? Why should God nonetheless hide His face from His people?

To this question, the great Chasam Sofer makes reply which has much meaning for us in our own day. The Chasam Sofer tells us that for Jews the recognition of God's might and power is not enough. The mere fact that a Jew is ready to acknowledge that God exists does not constitute penitence. For Jews, the true road to penitence is described in an earlier chapter of Deuteronomy in which it is said that after all their tragedies, the day will come when Jews will want to return unto God, and they will return. However, it shall be by *hearkening unto His voice.* On such a day, it could be said that they will have practiced penitence. Simply to admit that God is, simply to concede that He exists, is not religion. For us, religion begins when one is ready not only to acknowledge God's existence, but also to fulfill His Will and practice in our daily lives. That is why it will never be enough for a Jew merely to allege that God is King, or that it was because of God's anger that disasters had befallen him. He will have to take one additional step. He will have to open his heart to God's Word and fulfill God's Will.

Friends, it is this message that I want to communicate to you on this Sabbath of Penitence, for when we hear much discussion in our day about a religious revival, it is important that we understand what we mean by religion. True, the day has come when more and more people are willing to admit that there is a God. There are countless scientists who, because of their own research into nature, because of their own inquiries into the universe, have reached some kind of dead end which impels them to admit that there is a Creator. They must concede as a hypothesis that there is a force behind all forces and a designer underlying all designs. All of the theological arguments which were discarded a century or two ago by philosophers are being restored to popular discourse. They are being given a new dress, so that day after day we read of new books containing the admissions of prominent and renowned scientists that their agnosticism or atheism of an earlier day is no longer intellectually respectable. However, that does not make the scientists religious. It may be gratifying to many pseudo-intellectuals to learn that scientists, too, are willing to concede that there is a God. It may even give some religious people an assurance that they crave that they are not being old fashioned when they believe in a God, since scientists, too, make the concession. Yet, this is not religion in any mature sense of the term.

Certainly we Jews who first brought to the world the conception of one Creator are grateful to the scientists for confirming that which we knew four thousand years ago. However, if we stop there, we are being disloyal to our heritage. We are only inviting that which was described in the Book of Deuteronomy as God's hiding of His face from us. To be religious, one must go further. If one does not go further, then our conception of God is so primitive that we indeed regard Him as some kind of prima donna who wants us to be aware that He exists and seeks no more of us. Yet, it is precisely that kind of religion that is prompting many to believe that there is a religious revival in the world. It is that kind of religion that is making many believe that we are on the threshold of a new era in religious living. This is nonsense. I need but cite a few illustrations.

We know that throughout the country there are hundreds of thousands of people who are members of fraternal orders—Elks, Masons, Pythians—everyone of which is dedicated to the cause of brotherhood. Every member must also admit that he believes in the existence of the Supreme Being, otherwise he could not take the oath of initiation. Yet, it is also well known that in all of these fraternal orders there is an appalling lack of brotherhood. Some of these fraternal orders have lodges which will not admit Jews or Negroes. Often, Jews and Negroes must organize lodges of their own. That every member believes in God means nothing more than that all give lip service to the Creator. However, to what extent has their belief altered their lives and prompted them to recognize their own hypocrisy within the halls of their own lodges?

Take, for example, the entire problem of desegregation in the South. How can a person who really respects religion feel when he reads the statistics that there are more so-called religious people opposing desegregation than irreligious people? How can one feel when one discovers that psychologists who studied the situation report that among churchgoers there is a higher percentage of people who believe in the inequality of man than among those who are unchurched? Can one really regard this kind of churchgoing as churchgoing that is religious in character? Or is this the kind of churchgoing which involves only recognition of the fact that there is a God, plus a weekly perfunctory visit to a place to symbolize that one acknowledges His existence, without permitting that belief to challenge any of the prejudices or habits or attitudes which we have learned to cherish?

Take still another situation. We in this great metropolitan area were given the spectacle these past few months of hundreds of thousands of people going to Madison Square Garden for a religious revival. They sought the inspiration of a great preacher who would bring them God's salvation, and many were converted. Many were moved to admit that they know there is a God who forgives their sins. That was all. Yet, you know the tragic instance of one man who after having been saved, committed murder within twenty-four hours after conversion. Perhaps his being saved was a prelude to the crime, or perhaps it gave him the strength that he needed to consummate the crime that he had planned. This may be an abnormal instance, but at least it makes us realize the extent to which religion can be meaningless when it is equated with nothing more than the belief in God, the profession that He exists.

However, for us Jews the mere recognition of God's existence is not of great consequence. What is important is the performance of His Will. This insight has been captured in a few sentences written recently by one of the greatest psychologists of our day, Erich Fromm. Erich Fromm would have us understand that the conception of contemporary man with regard to religion is like that of a three-year-old child to his father. The child of three cries for the father when he needs him, but otherwise the child is quite self-sufficient when he can continue to play. Contemporary man's attitude to religion is exactly that. We cry for God when we need him, but otherwise we are quite self-sufficient, and as we do what we want to do, we ignore Him and His teachings. If we would rather be like men of truly religious cultures, we would try to be like children, who are at least of the age of eight and need their father as a helper but who also feel that the time has come for them to adopt the father's teachings and principles in their lives. That is religion on a mature level—the extent to which man, *because* he believes in God wants to change his life that it may be consonant with God's Will.

That is what the Chasam Sofer sought to teach us. *Tshuvah*, "penitence," does not mean being a child of three, but at least growing to being a child of eight. To practice penitence is at least to move up from one who simply recognizes God as a helper and otherwise is quite ready to ignore Him, to one who wants to change one's life because one believes in God.

That, friends, is the challenge that I must articulate on this Sabbath of penitence. How long will all of us continue to be children of three instead of growing up to be children of eight? How long will we think that we are religious simply because we admit that there is a God? When will we recognize that we haven't begun to be religious until we make some change in our lives, until we abandon some habit, until we alter some attitude, until we do something that we haven't done before, or stop doing something which we had been doing theretofore? Not until then have we really proved that for us the belief in God is something more than mere recognition that He is, but actually a commitment that will change our lives in one way or another.

There is a very charming story about a man who drove up to the synagogue one morning, and as he drove up, he noticed that the people were beginning to leave. He was somewhat disturbed, for he realized that he had come too late. He addressed the first person that he met and asked the simple question, "Is the service all done?" However, he was amazed at the reply that he received. The answer was not in the affirmative. The answer was, "No, no, not at all. The service is all *read*; we first start the *doing* now."

That, friends, is an important point to remember. To come to the Synagogue and experience the sense of belonging to God is one thing, but that is not yet *doing* the service. That is not yet being religious. The real service—real religion—begins when we have left the synagogue, when we meet with our fellowman, when we meet with the members of our families, when we establish our homes and conduct our business or our profession. It is there that we do the service that God wills us to do and that is the challenge that I leave with you on the Sabbath of Penitence.

To what extent will we only read services and not practice them? To what extent will we continue to be children of three rather than children of eight or ten in our outlook on religion?

Most of us are parents, and we feel peeved when our own children regard us as individuals from whom they need only take. We re-sent mature children who do not understand that parents would also like to have their wishes respected in the different areas in which parents and children have interests in common. How long will we continue to treat the Father of all mankind in that same shabby fashion? How long will we continue to call upon Him when we need something, and when the need is satisfied feel that there need be no further contact? We owe it to ourselves to consider what our relationship to God shall be. If it is no more than a relationship between a three-year-old child who wants things, then contemporary man will have to concede that his religious experience and motivation are infantile. If, however, God will help us to act at least as eight-or ten-year-old children, who are aware of the fact that there should be a reciprocal relationship between parents and children and that it is important for children to reckon with the will of their parents, then contemporary man will begin to think of reckoning with the Will of God and do the things every day of his life which have no purpose other than to indicate that he is submitting himself to the Will of God.

With such thoughts, we could not help but become more observant. We could not help but add things into our home which are done only because we feel that we want God's Will to prevail and to enrich our lives, and as we do these things we will fathom God's Will more and more, and our lives will be enriched in more directions than we could possibly visualize. This should be our prayer and our goal on the Sabbath of Penitence.

JACK RIEMER

Four Phrases to Live By

I must tell you that every year when I come back to the *Machsor*, after having been away for it for a year, I am *reimpressed* with how powerful and how accurate a document it is.

Some of the new prayers that I wrote 5 or 10 years ago are outdated already. But these prayers which were written two thousand years ago are still fresh and still on target.

I must tell you that of all the prayers in the *Machsor* the one that seems to me to be the most accurate and the most insightful is the *Al Het*.

This list of forty-four sins, two for every letter of the Hebrew alphabet, hits me and hurts me every time that I say it because it is true. What amazes me about this list is that, even though it was written many

Rabbi Jack Riemer was ordained at The Jewish Theological Seminary, and has served several conservative congregations. He was the founder of the National Rabbinic Network, and is the spiritual leader of Congregation Beth Tikvah in West Boca, Florida. Rabbi Riemer is author and editor of several books and conducts sermon seminars for rabbis. He has also composed several prayers that have been published in prayer books.

centuries ago, I can't think of a single serious sin that we do that is not on the list! I can't think of a single sin that is on the list that we don't do. It is an accurate mirror of the human situation. It is an accurate x-ray of the human psyche, is it not?

It says that we are gluttons. Aren't we? It says that we brood. Don't we? It says that we gossip and lust and that we are proud and arrogant, and inquisitive. It says that we drink too much, and that we give too little. It says that we are too competitive, and that we are too conformist. Is there a single sin on this list that any of us can deny? I can't think of any.

If you look at the list carefully, you will notice one thing more about them. More than a third of the sins on the list are sins of speech: For the sin that we have committed before You by gossip, for the sin that we have committed before You by slander, for the sin that we have committed before You by talebearing, for the sin that we have committed before You by boasting, etc., etc., etc. More than a third of the *al hets* are sins of speech.

Why? Because that is the part of the body with which we sin the most, isn't it? I don't think that I have hurt anyone with my fists even once during this past year. I don't think that I have hurt anyone with my foot even once during this past year. But I am sure that I have hurt many people with my tongue. Isn't that true of you as well?

So the *machzor* is right in reminding us that the tongue is a powerful and a dangerous weapon. And that therefore we must be careful in how we use it, and we must atone for how we abuse it.

Yet I would suggest that there is one sin that is missing from the *Al Het*, that there is one sin that ought to be included in this list. If I had my way. If I were the editor of the *machzor*, there is one sin that I think should be added to the *Al Hets* because I think that there is one sin that we all commit that is at least as harmful, at least as destructive, as any of the sins of speech. The sin that I would add to the list of the *Al Hets* is the *sin of silence*.

The sin of silence is usually understood in a political sense. We usually think of it in connection with keeping quiet while evil is being done in our society. It is a phrase that is used, for example, in connection with the Holocaust or in connection with the plight of Bosnia or some cause like that. It is usually taken to refer to people who sit on the sidelines and don't speak out as they should when evil is being done. But that is *not* what I have in mind today. That is an important sin to talk about, there is no denying that. There is an obligation on every human being to speak out when he sees injustice being done. But that is not what I have in mind today. What I have in mind today is the much more insidious, the much more widespread, and the much more destructive sin of silence that goes on within our homes and within our lives. What I have in mind today are the many homes in which husband and wife sit side by side before the television set for hours and never say a word.

What I have in mind today are the many homes in which kids come back from a date and the parents say, "What did you do?" and the kids say "Nothing." And the parents say, "Who did you see?" And the kids say, "No one." And the parents say, "What is new?" And the kids say, "Not much."

What I have in mind today is the invisible iron curtain that separates so many us from each other as we go through life. For that kind of silence can warp and mar and strain and stain and spoil and hurt the growth of a soul. That kind of silence can hurt and harm at least as much as angry words can and maybe more.

Divorce statistics are easy to compile; we have all seen the figures. God only knows how many homes there are in which people stay legally married while being emotionally divorced? God only knows how many homes there are in which people are officially married and yet have so little that they can communicate to each other. For these homes we have no statistics available, and yet we know that there are many, perhaps as many as the homes that are officially broken up. These are marriages that are just as dead as those that have been officially dissolved and buried. For a home in which people do not speak, or in which they can only talk about trivia, is a cell or a hell or a motel or a catering station or something else, but it is not a home! Do you remember the old limerick that we used to sing when we were kids?

> Sticks and stones
> may break my bones,
> but words
> will never hurt me!

You know something? It's not true! Now that I am older, I realize that song is inaccurate. Words *can* hurt, even more than sticks and stones. And silence can hurt even more than words. So let me offer you what I think is a more accurate version, one that I learned from Rabbi Sidney Greenberg:

> Sticks and stones are hard on bones.
> If aimed with angry art,
> And words can sting, like anything,
> But silence breaks the heart.

Silence breaks the heart. Silence hurts a thousand times more than sticks or stones or even angry words. Therefore the sin that we ought to face up to on this holy day (And I mean *we* for it is my sin at least as much as yours)—the sin that we ought to face up to on this holy day, the sin with which we hurt each other perhaps more than any other, is the sin of silence.

So let me make four specific suggestions. I think that if you want to measure the worthwhileness of your life, I think that if you want to measure the amount of help and health that you have given to others during this past year, I think that if you want a program by which you can learn how to become more of a *mentsch* in this coming year, you can do so in this simple way: resolve that in this coming year you will learn to say these four phrases more often than you have in the past: Thank you, I love you, How are you? and What do you need?

These are four simple phrases. And yet I tell you that you cannot overemphasize the difference that they can make in our lives and in the lives of the people with whom we live.

I don't care how big your vocabulary is, or how many languages you know. If you can't say these four phrases then you are emotionally crippled. If you can't ever say any of these four phrases then you impoverish the lives of those with whom you live.

"Thank you. I love you. How are you? What do you need? What can I do for you?" are phrases that have the power to transform lives and to give power and purpose, dignity and zest, spirit, value, and purpose to the people around us.

When was the last time you said thank you to your wife for a meal? Do you take it for granted that you are entitled to a good meal whenever you come home? Do you take it for granted that the meal is supposed to be good? Or do you take time to say: Thank you. I noticed what you did for me. I appreciate it. If you do, the meal will taste better—to you and to her.

Why does a Jew begin the day with *Modeh Ani?* Why does a Jew
end a meal with Birkat Hamazon? Because to live and not say thank
you is a perversion. To eat and not say thank you is vulgar!

Just as we must say thank you to God, so must we say thank you
to those with whom we live, and through whom we live.

So it is with these other three phrases: "I love you." There is nothing unmanly about saying that. On the contrary, it is the manly, or at
least if not the manly, it is the *mentschlich* thing to do.

I am not sure about this. I didn't see them all, but I suspect that
in all of his long film career, in all of the more than seventy films that
he made, John Wayne, *alev hashalom,* probably never once said, "I need
you" or "I love you." It would have seemed unmanly or lacking in
macho if he did. But still, it may not be the manly thing to do, as some
cultures understand manly, but it is certainly the *mentschlich* thing to
do. If it is a choice between being manly and being *mentschlich,* it is
much more important to be a *mentsch.*

It is a *mitzvah* of the highest importance to say "how are you?"—
To really say it, and then to listen to the answer, and not just say it in
a perfunctory manner with half a head, while your mind is on something else.

It is a *mitzvah* of the highest order to say to someone whom you
love, "What do you need? What can I do to help you?"

If we said that often enough to our children, if we said it and meant
it when we said it, then perhaps there would not be such a wall and
such a gap between us. Then perhaps when we asked, "Where did you
go?" They wouldn't say, "Nowhere." And when we asked, "What did
you do?" They wouldn't say, "Nothing."

Let me finish with two stories, two stories that mean a great deal
to me, two stories that I hope will touch you as much as they do me.
The first comes from the Russian writer, Turgényev. I read it years
ago and it has stayed with me ever since. Turgenyev writes, "I was once
walking in the street when a beggar stopped me. He was a frail old
man, with inflamed eyes, blue chapped lips, filthy rough rags, and dis-
gusting sores. Oh how poverty had disfigured this repulsive creature!
He stretched out to me his red, swollen, filthy hand and whimpered
for alms. I reached into my pocket, but no wallet, no coins, no money
did I find. I had left them all at home. The beggar waited, and his
outstretched hand twitched and trembled slightly. Embarrassed and
confused I seized his hand and pressed it and I said 'Brother, don't be

angry with me! I am sorry but I have nothing to give you. I left my wallet at home, brother.' The beggar raised his bloodshot eyes to mine. His blue lips smiled and he returned the pressure of my fingers. 'Never mind,' he stammered. 'Thank you, thank you for this, for this too was a gift. No one ever called me brother before.'"

I love that story, and I hope that you do too, for it makes the point that a kind word is also a gift, a real gift, that you can make a person's day brighter and his life more worthwhile with a word.

The second story that I want to tell you is, beyond question, the most powerful story that I have heard in many a year. I heard it from a man in Harrisburg. Usually, when someone comes over to me and says that they have a story for me I wince, for it is either a story that my great-great-grandfather would have found old, or else it is usually a story that I can't tell on the pulpit. But this story was different. It is a story that has haunted me since I first heard it.

The rabbi there officiated at a funeral, and when the service was over, the mourner would not leave the grave. The rabbi tried to lead the man away but he wouldn't go. The rabbi said, "The service is over now, you have to leave." But the man shook him off and said, "You don't understand. I loved my wife." The rabbi said, "I am sure you did, but the service is over now. You have to leave." The man shook him off again and said, "You don't understand. I loved my wife." The rabbi said, "I am sure that you did, but still, the service is over. You have to leave." The man shook him off again and said, "But you don't understand. I loved my wife, *and once I almost told her.*"

Can you imagine what pain there must be? Can you imagine what shame there must be, if you have to stand at a grave and bid farewell and realize then what you didn't say when you could have, when you should have, when there was still time? Can you imagine having to live the rest of your life with the knowledge that you loved someone, and that once you almost told her?

Let none of us ever have to live with that kind of regret in our hearts. Let none of us hold back the words of love, the words that could help and heal. Let none of us keep them choked up and bottled up inside where they can do no good, until it is too late.

My friends, if you remember nothing else from all of the hundreds of words that you hear on this pulpit during these Holy Days, if you remember nothing else from all of the thousands of words that you have prayed from this prayer book on these Holy Days, I ask you to remember these four phrases, to remember them and to say them, not just once, but many times during this coming year, not just today when it is cute and funny to say them, but all during this coming year: Thank you, I love you, How are you? and What do you need?

I ask you to say them to your wife or to your husband. I ask you to say them to your son or to your daughter. I ask you to say them to your mother or to your father. I ask you to say them to your God, and to your people, who have given you so much, and who need you so much. Say them and mean them. Say them and hear them many times in this coming year. For if you do, then it will be a good year, a holy year, and a blessed year for all of us and for the whole house of Israel. *Lishona tova tikoseyvu.* God bless you all.

JACOB PHILIP RUDIN

The View from
a Hospital Window

My first word is one of profound appreciation to this congregation which is here for worship on this Sabbath Eve. I am anything but insensitive to the implication of this large gathering and I want to express my gratitude for the friendship which it implies. It is a friendship and an affection which I most warmly reciprocate.

I want, further, to acknowledge the debt of thanks which I owe the members of this congregation for the innumerable attentions shown me during the weeks and months of my illness. There were literally over five hundred messages which came to me—messages which I cherished, but which it was manifestly impossible for me to acknowledge individually and personally. But the messages made a difference, and I want to say "thank you" to all of you for them.

One final word of appreciation—this one to Rabbi Henry Cohen who so magnificently stepped into the breach and so competently and

Rabbi Jacob Philip Rudin received his ordination at the Jewish Institute of Religion. He is president of Central Conference of American Rabbis in Great Neck, New York, and president of Synagogue Council of America. Rabbi Rudin has authored several volumes, and is active in civil rights and interfaith relations.

215

effectively assumed full responsibility for the rabbinical duties of this large and active congregation. He did all the preaching; he did all the teaching; he served the congregation in hours of joy and hours of sorrow. We are fortunate to have him with us. One of my private blessings was the comforting knowledge that rabbinical affairs were in his hands and I didn't have to worry.

During these past weeks I had imagined how it would be to stand before you again and to tell you how much I appreciated all that you had done. But none of my anticipation was commensurate with this reality. It is good beyond expression to be back home in our Temple in the midst of this congregation which I love so dearly. What I have to say isn't so much a sermon as it is a series of private observations which I want to share with you.

Illness is always an important experience in a person's life; and serious illness involving operations and hospitals is a towering experience indeed. This would be a magnificent opportunity, tailor-made, to talk about my operation to hundreds of people all too polite to walk out on my recital, to take twenty minutes to talk uninterruptedly. Don't think it is a temptation easily resisted. I do so with extreme reluctance, believe me. But I'll say nothing about an elaborate kidney operation, so very skillfully performed by an exceptional surgeon in a fine hospital. Names supplied on request.

I want to talk about some things that became clear to me as a result of that operation and the tremendous experience which it was for me.

It all happened very, very suddenly, literally without any advance warning. On November 18 last, at 2:45, I was delivering a talk on Federation from a radio station in Hempstead. Some four hours later I was checked into the hospital and was in the operating room for the first of the preliminary investigations which led finally to the operation itself the next week.

This happened to me! Hardly sick a day in my life! Me? In a hospital, having an operation? It couldn't be! Other people had operations. Hospitals were for somebody else. Operations weren't for me; and I didn't need hospitals. Then suddenly my private world had been tuned upside down and the operation was my operation and the bed being reserved in the hospital was for me. One never knows how a day will end from the way it begins. Just as I never dreamed that November 18 would end for me in the operating room of a hospital.

216

One never knows, indeed, how many days remain. Nor how much strength is left.

So I relearned the simplest—and the hardest—lesson that life has to teach. Don't waste the precious now. Don't wait for the tomorrow that may not ever come. Don't put off the kindly deed, the letter someone is waiting for, the visit that will bring comfort. Don't withhold the gift you can give today. Don't say, "When I have leisure, I will study. Perchance thou wilt have no leisure."

These were the words that were in my heart. But there was another side to this coin of thought which I was fingering there in the hospital. Sure! Don't waste the *now*, nor the opportunities which today affords. There is an urgency about life. Time is always running out. Health is shadowed by illness. Life is barely ever more than a step ahead of death. I saw it myself! It had happened to me.

It is reasonable when one has been frightened in this sudden way to want to grab hold of life again by a new set of handles. Have fun today! Let tomorrow worry about tomorrow.

That makes sense. If we aren't sure of tomorrow and if there is a kidney operation maybe waiting for us, then why not? Why not enjoy yourself? And by "enjoy yourself" we mean, of course, good times, parties, fun, no slave to one's job, no candidate, any more, for ulcers.

"So that's what I'll do!" one says to one's self. "I won't kill myself on my job. Why try to get two days work done in one? I'll take it easy. There will be plenty left for the fellow who follows me. I won't shirk my responsibilities, of course. But I'll stop knocking myself out. I'll enjoy myself. I'll have my fun today."

Then the view from a hospital window began to teach me something. I came into the hospital in the comparatively mild days of late November. (I remember I was wearing only a top coat when I went in.) A month later, when I came out, it was winter; and I had seen the change from the hospital window.

Imperceptibly the season transformed itself. The golden sun had taken on a hard, burnished look and it shone without much warmth, almost as though from the surface alone, without tapping the inner fires that flamed at its core. The grass was silvered with frost, snow had occasionally fallen, and there were patches of ice where rain had been trapped. If one opened the window more than a crack, winter blustered its way into the room.

It all suited a postoperative mood. The weather outside was proper background to one's aches and pains, one's preoccupation with bodily needs, with pills, injections, medicine. My new convictions kept drifting through my mind: Remember now what you are going to do. Enjoy yourself! Have fun today. Tomorrow may never come. Or if it does, it will be a winter's tomorrow and cold, and it will probably bring snow.

Now a view from a hospital window, properly considered, doesn't begin outside the room, but starts inside the room. Once this was manifest to me, the view changed. Inside the room, along the window-sill, were ranged flowers which kind friends sent to me. For a time, I might be looking out upon the winter world through the vivid beauty of roses; on another day upon a landscape framed in the lush, exotic loveliness of birds of paradise or the unassuming freshness of asters or the quiet charm of gladioli. Maybe there was winter outside, but it was winter bordered by the inner beauty of color and fragrance that was the promise of spring to come.

The snow and the flowers were part of the same view. The view was saying to me: Why so hot, little man? Why so frightened? Why so frantic about enjoying yourself? The view was saying, "There is always plenty of time, when winter is never seen by itself, but always part of the spring that will be born and of the fall that prepared its way; when one's life isn't seen isolated and alone. There is always plenty of time when one's life is linked through the winter of pain and sorrow with others in the springtime of hope, and the summer of fulfillment with the harvest of the autumn years."

The view from the window said, "Steady! Today isn't by itself. The winter passes and even in its dreariest days there are roses on the windowsill somewhere. There are roses in the seasons of humanity not less than in the seasons of nature's world."

I learned this, too, in the view from my hospital window. Right-angled, a wing of the hospital abutted the section in which my room was. From my window I could look across at the long rows of windows that patterned the adjoining wall. At night when sleep was elusive, I would lie there and look over at the soft, steady light of the lamp on the desk of a floor nurse, a kind of eternal light of the human spirit, of the meaning of compassion and pity and healing. The dark was never too dark to dim its gleam. Indeed, it was the darkness that the lamp subdued.

There were other windows, windows looking out from laboratories, from an x-ray room, from an examining room. The view from my hospital window broadened as by magic and it embraced all the hospitals everywhere and all the laboratories and all the patient work carried on quietly, in dedication, by doctors, researchers, scientists, and technicians—the slow, arduous, undramatic, unremitting warfare against disease and illness.

My view took in the skilled hands of surgeons, the healing of the physicians, the reassuring fingers of nurses. It goes on all the time, like the seasons, like fall into winter. It goes on, the endless task of all these nameless ones who labor that people be kept alive, and that man's mind and heart and spirit may be ultimate victor over the mysteries which now hold us victim.

There is a community of pain in the world and a community in suffering. All the hospitals around the world are testimony of this truth—from the most modern institution in a great city to the simple outpost of Dr. Albert Schweitzer in Lambarene in equatorial Africa. There is universal affliction of sickness and disease. But by the same token there is a fellowship of service. There are the selfless men and women who attack sickness and disease on every front, who push back the frontiers of ignorance, who put mankind before self and the needs of people before their own aggrandizement.

Now the view told me that the words, "Have fun," by themselves are foolish words; and that fear of tomorrow is a foolish fear; and that selfish living, doing only what one wants to do or is required to do, is a foolish way to live.

Dr. Lister did not do only what he was required to do; nor Pasteur, nor Florence Nightingale, nor the Curies, nor Dr. Salk. Nor can any of us do only what we want to do and are required to do. We owe a debt to tomorrow—to the roses yet to bloom against another winter's snow.

We cannot live alone, nor can we live frightened, nor can we live in desperation. We live today at the best that we are today. We do today what is given into our hand today: the kindly word, the visit, the compassionate deed. We let our spirits touch the lives about us, husbands, wives, children, friends, strangers. We see today as an opportunity. We see tomorrow as a bright and shining possibility. We see life as a continuous dynamism, as an endless stream. We are part of that stream. We enrich it with our years.

Humankind is a single family and who serves one of its members serves them all. The truth is that the view from my hospital window was the world; and I, obscure, unimportant and of not much value, was the beneficiary of all that the world had learned, so that I might be kept alive.

Should I not be grateful? Should I not be bound to take the roses of the spirit outside and help transform mankind's winter world into a shining and everlastingly loveliness?

I think that we must. We have no right to receive and not be willing to give. We cannot let anybody's view from his hospital window look out on a landscape which is without people—nay, more, on a landscape which is without us.

In the silent procession of the generations, perhaps someone is waiting desperately for the sight of us, our hand raised in friendly salute, our lips speaking words of fellowship and cheer.

Not less than doctor or scientist or teacher, each of us, in his own way, adds his life to the view from the hospital window. May God grant that it is for good. May we help make the view a better view. It is never later than you think when people stretch out their hands, when God and man are partners in bringing roses to the winter view from the hospital window.

JACOB J. SCHACTER

Was There Nothing Worth Fighting For?

A Yom Kippur Sermon

If Israel is nothing else (and surely it is) Israel is a passionate country. I am consistently struck by the power of the passions that swirl about even matters of simple everyday life, let alone those relating to the economy, foreign policy, the religious character of the state, and more. Everyone, very definitely, has an opinion—right and left, religious and secular, Ashkenazim and Sephardim, sabra and new immigrant.

But never, I believe, has the power of passion been expressed more forcefully than it has been in the course of the emotional, bitter, and harsh debate currently taking place over the peace process. On this issue, feelings, emotions, and passions are running at an all-time high.

At the White House signing in September, 1993, the late Prime Minister Yizhak Rabin spoke with exceptional eloquence:

Rabbi Jacob J. Schacter is rabbi of The Jewish Center in New York City and editor of *The Torah u-Madda Journal*. He earned his Ph.D. from Harvard University and was ordained at Mesivta Torah Vodaath. Rabbi Schacter is adjunct Assistant Professor of Judaic Studies at Stern College, and is the author and editor of several volumes, articles, and reviews. Rabbi Schacter was recently appointed as Fellow in the Department of New Eastern Languages at Harvard.

We have come from Jerusalem, the ancient land and eternal capital of the Jewish people. We have come from an anguished and grieving land. We have come from a people, a home, a family that has not known a single year, not a single month, in which mothers have not wept for their sons. We have come to try and put an end to the hostilities so that our children, our children's children, will no longer experience the painful cost of war, violence, and terror. We have come to secure their lives and to ease the soul and the painful memories of the past—to hope and pray for peace. We say to you [the Palestinians] today, in a loud and a clear voice: enough of blood and tears. Enough.

On the other side of the aisle, as it were, there is equal eloquence, power, and passion. Peace, of course, claim its proponents, but not at such a high price. We are endangering the security of the State; we are putting hundreds of thousands of Jews at risk. This direction will not bring peace to the State, they argue, it will bring only further death, danger, and insecurity.

In Israel, passions run high about almost anything. But what about us? What about American Jewry? What are *we* passionate about? What do *we* really care about? What is it that engages *us*, deeply and intensely, to the very core of *our* beings?

I find the power of passion projected in an interesting detail in the ancient Yom Kippur ritual. The highlight of the Yom Kippur service in the Temple (featured in the Torah reading of that day and in the traditional Musaf service) was, without any question, the entrance and hopefully safe exit of the High Priest into and out of the Holy of Holies. Once a year, there took place a convergence between the holiest person (the High Priest), the holiest place (the Holy of Holies), and the holiest time (the day of Yom Kippur). For a brief moment, the High Priest entered this place which was off limits even to him the entire year and prayed there on behalf of the Jewish people. His concentration had to be perfect, his involvement total, and the intensity of his devotion all encompassing. One slip, God forbid, and God could take his life. And so, when the High Priest emerged safely from this holiest of places, you can imagine how relieved he and the members of his family surely were. Then, culminating his Temple Service on this great day, the High Priest recited a beautiful and meaningful prayer:

May it be thy will, Lord our God and God of our fathers, that the forthcoming year shall be for thy people, the house of Israel, a year of abundant prosperity; a year of generous decrees declared by thee; a year of grain, wine, and oil; a year of attainment and success; a year of meeting in thy sanctuary; a year of enjoyable living; a year of dew, rain, and warmth; a year of delicious fruits; a year of atonement for all our iniquities; a year wherein thou wilt bless our food and drink; a year of business transactions; a year of attending our sanctuary; a year of plenty and delight; a year wherein thou wilt bless our offspring and the fruit of our land; a year wherein thou wilt bless our coming and going; a year wherein thou wilt save our community; a year wherein thou wilt be merciful toward us; a year of peace and serenity; a year wherein thou wilt let us make joyous pilgrimages to our country; a year wherein thou wilt open thy goodly treasury for us; a year wherein thy people, the house of Israel, will not be in need of one another's aid nor the support of another people, for thou wilt bless the products of their own hands (Philip Birnbaum, *High Holiday Prayer Book* New York: [Hebrew Publishing Co.] 1951, 826).

It is a beautiful prayer because it is a real prayer, a direct prayer. It covers all the bases—personal and communal, physical and spiritual. "A year of delicious fruits" is immediately followed by "a year of atonement for all our iniquities." It touches all of a human being's possible needs.

But there is something missing from our text, one particular detail found both in the Babylonian Talmud (*Yoma* 53b) and Jerusalem Talmud (*Yoma* 5:3) versions of this prayer: In the Babylonian Talmud, "The prayer of the travellers should not enter before you," or in the Jerusalem Talmud's version, "Do not be swayed by the prayer of the travellers."

The issue is a very simple one. Travellers on the road want to get home safely but, in ancient times faced a serious threat from rain—and traveller was unprotected, roads would wash away, etc. As a result, the traveller would pray for no rain. But the community as a whole needed rain; crops had to grow, food had to be produced, the harvest needed to take place. So the High Priest prayed to God: Don't be influenced by the traveller's prayer for no rain; send it anyway, to a hungry and needy world.

But I have three questions. First of all, is this so important that it was included in both Talmuds' version of this prayer? Is this on the same level as the request for "abundant prosperity," "generous decrees," "enjoyable living," or "atonement for all our iniquities?" In the

223

Babylonian Talmud's version, this is the final, culminating prayer! Does it not seem so out of proportion to all the rest?

Second, are we to assume that a just God, who obviously recognizes the need for communal rain, will listen to a few lonely individuals on a road somewhere to the detriment of the vast overwhelming majority of Jews? Why would He even consider withholding rain from the many for the sake of just a few?

Finally, if this was such an issue, why didn't the High Priest simply issue a proclamation announcing that travellers are not allowed to pray for no rain? Simply prohibit the traveller from uttering such a prayer and all the problems will be solved!

We focus on a small, seemingly insignificant detail but herein lies a crucially important message for us during these difficult times. How does prayer work, anytime? Does God need our prayers? Does God not know what we need, and will our prayers make a difference if He decides not to grant us our desires? How do we understand the notion of the efficacy of prayer in general?

It seems to me that in order for prayer to be effective, it is crucial that we fulfill one essential condition described by the rabbis in the Talmud (*Berakhot* 32a). The Bible records that after the sin of the golden calf, Moses prayed to God on behalf of the Jewish people, but the Talmud elaborates on *how* he prayed:

> R. Ababu said: Were it not explicitly written, it would be impossible to say such a thing. This teaches that Moses took hold of the Holy One, blessed be He, like a man who seizes his fellow by his coat and said to Him: "Master of the Universe, I will not let You go until You forgive and pardon them."

Moses grabbed God by the lapels, as it were, and said, "God, you *must* forgive them! I am holding on here for dear life and not letting go until you forgive them."

The basic principle is that prayer requires passion. You have to want what you want, and you have to want it with passion.

The traveller who prays for no rain undoubtedly prays with passion. He is very concerned about arriving home safely and, as a result, expresses himself with real feeling. This kind of a prayer—addressed to God by one who prays for what he or she *really needs*—cannot be arbitrarily outlawed. The High Priest could not possibly proclaim a decree against such a prayer. A genuine instinctive expression of real inner need cannot be externally controlled. So the High Priest is afraid that if the traveller is passionate enough, if he grabs onto God's lapels, as it were, firmly enough, then God might respond to his entreaty even if it means overriding the needs of the community. The power of passion knows no bounds. So the holiest man includes a most important component to his most joyous prayer upon safely exiting from the holiest place on the holiest day—a prayer that the community's prayer be *even more* passionate, that *all* Jews pray to God always with seriousness, with solemnity, with passion. Don't listen to the traveller's prayer, he asks. May the prayers of the community be even more passionate.

We need more passion in our lives, not just in prayer but in all aspects of our lives. What *are* we passionate about? What *do* we really care about? What *is it* that engages us deeply and intensely, to the core of our beings? Unfortunately, not terribly much.

A number of years ago, my father, Rabbi Herschel Schacter, told me a story about the early years of Communism when many religious Jews became caught up in the ideals of that movement and rejected their own tradition; when thousands of yeshiva boys closed their Gemaras drawn by the utopian promise of this new society. Once, a number of Hasidim were sitting with their Rebbe and, in a sad and despondent mood, asked him, "Rebbe, tell us. Why is it that the Communists are so successful and we are on the defensive? After all, what we have is *emes* (truth) and what they have is *sheker* (falsehood)?" Said the Rebbe, "Yes, my children, you are right. We have *emes* and they have *sheker*. But there is also another significant difference between us. You see, they fight for their *sheker* with *emes* while we fight for our *emes* with *sheker*. They fight for their falsehood, but they do so with conviction, with feeling, with passion, convinced of the certainty of their position. We, on the other hand, fight for our truth, but we do so halfheartedly, in a matter of fact way, in a haphazard and perfunctory manner. We have the *emes*, no doubt about it, but in order to win the battle we need to fight for the *emes* with *emes*."

Indeed, we do fight for so many causes.

We are concerned about Israel, of course. But how concerned are we really? How much are we really deeply invested in the fate and future of Israel? How often do we visit and tangibly express our connection and commitment? How much do we give in support of Israel?

We continue to be concerned about Jews in the former Soviet Union as the scepter of Communism continues to threaten Jewish life in those countries. But how concerned are we really? How active have we been to strengthen Jewish life in the former Soviet Union? How much have we done to insure the ability of the Jews there to leave, whether to Israel or to other countries in the free world?

We are concerned with the rising threats of assimilation and intermarriage that gnaw away at the vibrancy and vitality of Jewish life in this country. Of course we are. But how concerned are we really? How much of an active role have we taken to stem the tide of apathy and ignorance that characterizes so much of American Jewry?

Our religious lives are a source of concern for us. But how concerned are we really? Regardless of our religious orientation, we consider those to the left of us as "lazy" (they really observe nothing), those to the right of us as "crazy" (they clearly are fanatics and extremists) and have trouble acknowledging that we ourselves are not much more than "hazy," not really committed to our observance. Is this a way to insure our future, to perpetuate our values to our children? Do we merely pay lip serve to Torah observance or are we genuinely committed to it—with passion?

We are committed to our synagogue. Of course we are. But how committed are we really? Do we do all we can to insure that it be the strong religious and moral voice in the community that we know it must be?

Surely we love our families—our spouses, our parents, our children. Of course we do. But how passionate is that love? How many other things somehow manage to intrude into the middle of that love? How much time do we spend involved in activities that do not give us an opportunity to appropriately express that love?

We are now at the juncture of the Yom Kippur service immediately prior to *Yizkor*. What do we remember most about our loved ones who are no longer with us? I would venture to say that only secondarily is it their wisdom, their intellect, or their teachings. I have no doubt that primarily it is their feelings—their love, their emotion, their passions. *That* is what made the greatest impact on us and it is *this* which will make the greatest impact on others—on God, our children, on our community.

In one of his novels, the late Alan Paton has one of his characters say: "When I shall ascend to heaven, which I certainly intend to do, I will be asked, 'Where are your wounds?' When I will say, 'I haven't any,' I will be asked, 'Was there nothing worth fighting for,' and that is a question that I do not want to have to answer."

Confronted by such a question today, on this Yom Kippur, what would *our* answer be?

ALEXANDER M. SCHINDLER

Lessons of the Holocaust

Jewish custom prescribes that Holocaust Remembrance day be marked in the month of April, for it was in April that the Jews of the Warsaw ghetto rose up against their oppressors with empty hands facing guns and tanks, the most lethal weapons of war.

Come to think of it, though, this is a most unlikely time to mark so somber and melancholy an occasion. After all, April is the first full month of spring, and spring is the time "when the air is calm and pleasant," so Milton wrote, "and it were an injury and sullenness against nature not to go out and see her riches and partake in her rejoicing."

As individuals, we can well do that. We can go out into the public gardens and rejoice, roll up our sleeves to feel a little springtime

---

Rabbi Alexander M. Schindler was born in Munich and fled from Nazi Germany with his family at age 12. A ski trooper in WWII, he earned both the Purple Heart and Bronze Star for bravery in action. Rabbi Schindler is a graduate of CCNY, and was ordained by Hebrew Union College—Jewish Institute of Religion. He serves as Assistant Rabbi of Temple Emanuel in Worcester, Massachusetts, president of Union of American Hebrew Congregations, founding editor of *Dimensions*, and is editor of *CCAR Journal*.

warmth; but as Jews, rolled-up sleeves all too quickly remind us of those numbers tattooed on the arms of death camp inmates.

As individuals we can rejoice in April showers and breathtaking rainbows; but as Jews, we cannot hear of "showers" without shuddering, nor view a rainbow without thinking of the Nazi killers who shattered its radiance, who took its colors and pinned them to our hearts: yellow for Jews, red for Communists, brown for gypsies, pink for gays, and on and on through the spectrum of murdered souls.

As individuals we can hearken to the Song of Solomon "arise . . . my fair one, come away!" But as Jews, we are mired in agonizing memories and cannot come away. We cannot see a meadow without thinking of mass graves. We cannot see a dancing butterfly without recalling the poem of a 12-year-old Jewish girl inmate of Theresienstadt who said of her captivity that she "never saw another butterfly."

Oh, would that we *could* forget. But quick forgetting is not the realty of a people who lost one third of their number in half a decade; who lost one and one-half million of their children in that time, innocent, guiltless all! Quick healing is not the reality of a people for whom nature itself was defiled by the Nazi murderers who sowed bones instead of seeds in the month of April!

And so we remember . . . memories continue to hurt and haunt us. They still make us stagger. The pavement sinks under the feet, the walls spin around, the world reels. We cannot stop it even if we would. We cannot pluck the remembrance of all this carnage from us, its anguish pierced too deep. The bitterness has eaten into our sinews, dissolved our flesh into festering sores, reduced the very spirit of our lives to sparkless, blackened ashes.

Our response to all these aching memories is silence. It must be that, it always will be that—a silence. For our speech has been stifled by darkness and our suffering is of a kind that has no tongue. Our martyrology is one long stillness, an endless silent scream reaching to the heavens where God was silent too.

Yet we must speak, for we are the spokesmen of the dead. It is our duty to testify in their behalf. Ever to remind the world that it was not God, but brutal men who brought darkness to the human soul.

Those who lived through and outlived this evil do not need to speak; the yellow badge is burned on their flesh for all to see. But their ranks are thinning; the generations come and go. Memory fades. People forget. There are those who have determined to wipe its slate, to make it seem as if these things had never been.

But these things *have* been. They really happened. Millions of God's children perished through the cruelty of the aggressor, victims of demonic hate; the aged and young, the learned and unlettered; all driven in multitudes along the road of pain and pitiless death.

So we must speak—and meet, and write—however faltering our tongue and unavailing speech. And we begin this task as did our forebears, with words hallowed by centuries of our martyrdom: "*Yitqadal veyitkadash sh'mey rabba . . . ,*" "*Magnified and Sanctified be the name of God.*" It has been ordained that this prayer be repeated six million times. People must never forget why this is so.

Are there any lessons to be gleaned from all this sorrow and sadness?

In a way I find it loathsome even to ask such a question, to speak of the "lessons" of genocide, for to do so is to attribute purpose to acts that were grotesquely purposeless, acts of naked savagery, of twisted paranoia and grim bureaucratic inhumaneness. Yet it is that very purposelessness, that monstrous human capacity to butcher without need, to wade through rivers of blood without so much as a redeeming sense of destination or direction, which impels us to seek explanation, to scour us yet again with stinging memories.

Therefore we infer certain lessons from the suffering we have endured, and by so doing, we convert the mystery of suffering into a revelation.

First and foremost we have learned to resist, at earliest warning, any and all threats to our community, to our people. "If I am not for myself," taught the Hebrew sage Hillel, "who will be for me?"

Wherever there is a single Jew in danger, in whatever country or continent or the remotest corner of our far-flung world, there are we determined to find him, to reach out to him, offering our hand, our heart, our life. Never more will it be said that we had eyes but did not see, that we had ears but did not hear, that we had mouths but that we failed to speak.

"Never will we allow this to happen again!" This is the vital force which propelled the creation of the modern Jewish state, and which impels the Jews of the world to do everything humanly possible to secure its safety. This is the vital force which spurred the Israelis to legendary acts of heroism like Entebbe or to the recent rescue, over one short weekend, of nearly 15,000 endangered Ethiopian Jews. And remember, this was the first time in human history when blacks were taken from one continent to another not in chains but in love. "Never again!" has become our motto, though that motto was stained by a racist in our own midst.

I suppose we Jews are overly sensitive, even paranoid, on the subject of our safety. Yet where will we find reassurance?

How can we feel at ease when recent studies report a global rise in anti-Semitism; denials of the Holocaust; the refurbished iconization of erstwhile Hitler puppets such as Antonescu in Romania and Tito in Slovakia; the proliferation of neo-facist parties and extremist right-wing groups in many places, four hundred of them in the CIS alone; Jewish cemeteries desecrated; synagogues defaced; acts of violence, even murder, several such incidents recorded every single day now, and all this only one generation after Auschwitz.

How can we feel secure when a recent poll showed that over thirty percent of the Germans of today believe that Jews and not the Nazis are largely to blame for the holocaust, that the victims and not the murderers are guilty after all.

How are our fears allayed when even in our own country anti-Semitic incidents have seen an alarming rise during the year just past . . . when a David Duke who wears a swastika as a halo if not a breastplate, nonetheless gathers a majority of the white votes in Louisiana's senatorial election; or when a Pat Buchanan, whom even Bill Buckley has assessed to have indulged in anti-Semitic rhetoric, stumps our economically troubled America inciting passions of xenophobia and selfishness, and yet nets one-third of the Republican Primary vote.

Nor are our fears allayed by the trauma of having the public classrooms and college campuses become a combat zone for competing interests battling over multi-culturalism, by having the Martin Luther Kings and Bayard Rustins supplanted by purveyors of hate like Sharpton and Jeffries; or by the fact that our country's failure to fully implement the civil rights revolution, particularly in the economic sphere, is producing an explosive African/American nihilism, with no small portion of anti-Semitism for fuel.

No, alas, our wounds are not merely of another era. Our wounds bleed anew. So we are not likely to forget the first lesson of the Holocaust: "If I am not for myself, who will be for me?" We intend to deny

Hitler a posthumous victory. We are, and we will continue to be. Survival: it is the best defense, the sole revenge, the only worthy response to those who seek our destruction.

There is a second truth which emerges from the experience of our anguish, and it is this: that we are not alone to have been afflicted, that other peoples too have suffered grievous wrong; that we are bound to one another, all humans are, in an unbroken unity of pain.

We cannot deny this reality. True, the Holocaust is *sui generis*, unprecedented and unmatched in its evil. Nonetheless, it is but one of the many man-made roads that have led into the abyss of human iniquity. Our age has many pathways sinking into this hell: the archipelagos of Stalin's Russia, napalm-scorched Vietnam, death squads in Latin America, and perhaps most damning of all, the pathway of hunger, of neglect and apathy, upon which forty thousand more corpses are strewn every single day of our lives.

I have been told that an international human rights association has determined that since the end of World War II, there have been eleven other instances of race extermination which can properly be labeled as genocide. Think of the horrors of Cambodia, of Indochina's killing fields. Think of Afghanistan and Ethiopia—and on and on. Numerous indeed are the roads that lead into the hell of human depravity.

A Yiddish proverb encapsulates this truth: *"A velt brent brider nit nor unzer shtetl."* An entire world is aflame, not just *our* villages. What is needed, therefore, is a bucket brigade to save the world, and not just to douse the blazing roofs of our own hamlets.

This second lesson is infinitely more difficult to internalize than is the first. When a people is beset by fear, the likely consequence is a reactive isolationism, and it is precisely this malady that has afflicted too many of our fellow Jews. "We are surrounded by enemies," they say, "so what's the use? Let's dig in our own garden. Let's go it alone. No one else will fend for us."

But this simply is not so. We did not achieve our freedoms alone. We broke out of the ghetto walls only because many other enlightened forces in Europe amplified and fought to realize our demands for equal status. We would not have achieved the high state we presently enjoy here in this land were it not for the Bill of Rights, which was neither crafted nor realized by Jews. The State of Israel would not have been established had not a majority of the world's peoples recognized the moral rightness of our cause.

Separatism is bad for Jews. We need allies to prevail. But we will not find and retain them if we care only for ourselves.

The Chasidic master, Moshe Leb Sassover taught:

> A peasant helped me to understand the true meaning of love. I overheard him at an inn talking to his companion. He asked his friend, "Do you love me, Ivan?" And Ivan replied, "Of course I do." And then the peasant asked, "And do you know what hurts me, Ivan?" "No," replied he. "How can I possibly know that?" "Well," concluded the peasant, "if you do not know what hurts me how can you say that you love me?"

If we do not feel the pain of *others*, they will not feel *our* pain. If we stand aloof from *their* causes and concerns, we can scarcely expect them to stand at *our* side and we will not survive without the help of others.

Far more important than this consideration of an enlightened self-interest is the awareness of our solemn duty as Jews to care not just for our fellow Jews, but for all of human kind.

Even thus we read in Scripture: "It is too light a thing that thou shouldst be my servant to raise up the tribes of Jacob and to restore the offspring of Israel I will also give thee for a light unto the nations. That my salvation may be unto the ends of the earth."

We Jews are not just another ethnic group or another pressure bloc. Our survival in the past has been for a higher purpose, and our survival must continue to have meaning today.

Al Vorspan once cleverly and movingly wrote,

> If, in order to survive I must become a bald-headed Meir Kahane, . . . if, in order to survive I must kiss the world good-bye and separate myself from humankind, . . . if I must emulate the violence, the callousness, the bigotry and narrowness of my opponents, then survival is not worth the candle for me.

All this is true not just for Jews, but for all groupings in our society and indeed for all the peoples of the earth. None of us lives alone. We interact with others, depend on others always. The Jewish sage Hillel may have counselled, "If I am not for myself, who will be for me?" But then he quickly added, "But if I am only for myself, what am I?"

We simply dare not define our group identities in parochial terms alone. Was it not that very nearsightedness and the arrogance that it

234

bred that led Germany to its feverish fantasies of a master race? Was it not precisely this parochialism run amok that led dictatorships to their barbaric sense of "national security"?

The philosopher George Santayana taught, "When you believe in absurdities, you can commit atrocities." Surely, the commonest absurdity that human beings have believed is that of the superiority of individuals or groups over others. Surely, it is that absurdity which has led us into a century of savagery. Surely, that selfsame absurdity now threatens to turn the whole globe into the charnel houses of Auschwitz.

Our survival depends upon our ability to develop an alternative understanding; the understanding that we are, each of us and all of us, like the sons and daughters of Noah emerging from the ark on Mount Ararat. We are, each of us and all of us, anxiously scanning the sky for the rainbow sign, the reassurance that a life of peace and growth and meaning can be ours. We are, each of us and all of us, confronting the *challenge* of God's rainbow; a challenge to recognize and act upon the awareness of our common humanity, to work together to ease the suffering of all peoples, to open the eyes of the blind, to bind the wounds of the afflicted, to loosen the fetters of the bound wherever they might be imprisoned.

For what is the rainbow after all? It is every color of the earth combined into one great spectrum. It is mist, invisible, until light and liquid fashion it into visible, iridescent shape—an arch that binds the world from horizon to horizon. It is a metaphor made physical. It is the earth's arbor. It is the arch of God.

All peoples of the earth are witness to what happens when the rainbow buckles and pieces of the sky collapse. All of us are primary color bands in the spectrum of suffering humanity.

We must, therefore, hold our heads high, wear our colors, speak our languages, let ourselves be seen by all.

When the gaze of humanity is upon is, we must bid them look back in time and see the monstrosities that give birth to our modernity.

We must bid them to look into their own hearts and see the internal bleeding that is draining us of our very humanity.

We must bid them look at one another, whatever be their nationality or color or creed, and say, "You are the bone of my bone, the flesh of my flesh, for one God has created us all."

The universal and the particular are inextricably intertwined within us; we dare not deny the claims of either. If we repudiate our particular heritage for the sake of a greater humanity, we will inevitably betray humanity in the end. But if we repudiate humanity and serve only ourselves, we will betray those ideas and ideals which alone give meaning to our people's survival.

This, then, is the twofold truth forged on the anvil of Jewish suffering, these the thoughts that stir within us as we recall with loving remembrance our martyrs, all those who perished through the cruelty of the oppressor. Not punished for any individual guilt, but indiscriminately, men and women, the aged and the young, the learned and the simple were driven in multitudes along the road of pain and pitiless death. They lie in nameless graves. Their places of everlasting sleep are not known to us. Yet we will not forget them. We take them into our hearts and give them a place beside the treasured memories of our own beloved.

May their remembrance give us the strength to turn from death to life, to love where others hate, to hope where others despair, to bring beauty to chaos and reason to the madness of our days. In a word, to speed the fulfillment of that promise of lasting life made by God to humankind when He arched His wondrous rainbow over Noah's ark in the springtime of human history.

236

HAROLD M. SCHULWEIS

Shall We Talk Politics?

Let's talk politics! Or do we argue that politics and Judaism have nothing to do with each other? Does Judaism have any bearing on our political sensibilities or do we leave political conscience to the Christian Coalition and content ourselves by venting our anger at Jerry Falwell, Pat Robertson, Rush Limbaugh, and Ralph Reed? Do we fulfill our political responsibility simply by demonizing the Christian Coalition?

And where is the Jewish coalition? Where is the Jewish voice heard in the social and moral policies in the land in which we live? Or do we cede such matters to partisan political parties? Cleanse it from the sacred precincts of the synagogue.

Rabbi Harold M. Schulweis received his B.A. from Yeshiva College, his M.A. from NYU, ordination from the Jewish Theological Seminary, and his Th.D. from Pacific School of Religion. Prominent editor, college professor, and innovator of many groundbreaking programs promoting Jewish life and eithic and moral causes, Rabbi Schulweis is a prolific author, prominent lecturer, and recipient of many prestigious awards from both Jewish and non-Jewish organizations. Since 1970, he has served as rabbi of Congregation Valley Beth Shalom in Encino, CA.

There are voices who ask, "What has spirituality to do with politics?" After all, the synagogue is a place of prayer. What does the liturgical life of a Jew have to do with his political life? Jewish piety should be concerned with ritual life, with the study of Torah, with the practice of Sabbath and festivals, prayers, and *kashruth*, and synagogue attendance. There is a proper division between the sanctuary and the polling booth, between the sacred and the secular, between the holy and the profane.

"Stick to your last, rabbi. Teach Torah. Teach rabbinic tradition. Tend to your own vineyard."

But I do. As I search the Bible, the prophets, the writings, the Talmud, there is one thing about Jewish tradition that is abundantly clear. In Judaism, you cannot segregate God. There is no *mechitzah* between heaven and earth. In the Torah there is no wall of separation between sanctuary and society; no boundaries between morality and polity. Here rationalists and mystics alike agree there is no place devoid of God. So rabbinic tradition declares that whenever you pray in an enclosed area, there must be a window open to the world. Pray with your eyes onto the market place. There is in Judaism no separation between stars and bread. No Jewish prophet ever declared, "Render unto Caesar that which is Caesar's and unto God that which is God's."

The Jewish prophets are not concerned with the celestial universe of angels or of paradise or of hell. The prophets are passionately concerned with power and powerlessness: about the widow, the orphan, the corruption of judges, the oppression of rulers, swindlers in business transactions, public and private deceit.

The Jewish prophet is political. The Jewish prophet is engaged in a constant struggle against spiritual isolationism, against those who would use the temple as a hideout, as an escape from the world of weights and scales, against those who put their trust in the security of the sanctuary, against the hypocrites who shout, "*Heychal Adonai, heychal Adonai, heychal Adonai.* "This is the sanctuary of the Lord, this is the sanctuary, this is the sanctuary of the Lord." Here behind the Temple walls we are safe. Here we can declare a moral holiday. Here we can burn incense and sacrifice rams and bring wine oblations and camouflage the dust and deceit of the marketplace.

The prophets taunt moral segregation. "Hear this you who trample upon the needy and bring the poor of the land to an end . . . you who deal deceitfully with false balance and buy the poor for silver and the needy for a pair of sandals. Will you steal, murder, swear falsely, oppress the weak and stand before Me in My sanctuary and cry, "*Nitzalnu*," we are saved, we are saved?

The prophet is political and God is preeminently political. The God of Judaism is not a Creator who has resigned from the world, an absentee Landlord. God is not only the God of nature. God is the Lord of history. God is preeminently political.

Here is how the Bible defines God (Deuteronomy 10:18), "He executes justice for the fatherless and the widow and loves the stranger in giving him food and raiment. Therefore, you shall love the stranger for you were strangers in the land of Egypt."

There can be no apartheid between the spiritual and the political life. Far from being strange bedfellows, Judaism and the political conscience are united in a holy covenant. There is a moral convenant between God and Israel. With these words do we bind the leather thongs of the tefillin around our fingers each morning. God says to us, "I betroth you unto Me, through righteousness, justice, loving kindness, and mercy." Judaism and political conscience are covenantal bedfellows.

But now the question deepens. Is Judaism liberal or conservative? Does Judaism condone capitalism or socialism? Does Judaism protect the propertied or defend the poor? Is Judaism inherently liberal or conservative? Is God a republican, a democrat, or a libertarian? Or is He like Ross Perot and Colin Powell—undeclared.

Last month I sent you in the mail two advertisements published in the *New York Times*, one with the banner "*Mazel Tov* Newt" that argues that the Republican contract reflects "the eternal values of Judaism." The advertisement was signed by rabbis and laymen. Alongside, I included a later advertisement, this one protesting the conservative one and listing other rabbis and laymen claiming that "the core political commitment" of Judaism is inherently liberal and that the contract contradicts the covenant.

I sent you that literature for a reason, to illustrate that both equations of Judaism with liberalism or Judaism with conservatism are equally misleading. They manipulate the integrity of Judaism so as to canonize their parochial, partisan political positions. They engage in "gerrymandering" of the Torah by carving up the Bible and the tradition into quote bites favorable to their politics.

Does Judaism defend the poor? Of course. Deuteronomy 15:4, "There shall be no poor among you." But equally Leviticus 19:15 asserts, "You shall not favor the poor nor show deference to the rich but you shall judge your kinsmen fairly."

The synagogue has a sacred opportunity to rescue the integrity of the Jewish tradition from political split-thinking where things are assigned column left or column right. The synagogue can introduce a measure of spiritual wholeness into the schizoidal politics that splits issues and candidates into bleeding heart Democrats or sclerotic Republicans.

"A neo-Conservative," Irving Kristol writes, "is a liberal who has been mugged" and the liberal retorts with his own joke widely circulated in this political year. "A seriously ill person is asked by his surgeon, 'Which would you prefer? A heart transplant from a healthy young twenty-five year-old being or an octogenarian republican?' The answer 'Of course I'll take the heart of the old republican because *I know for sure it has never been used.*'"

So the caricatures persist, "Anyone under the age of thirty who is not a liberal has no heart. Anyone above the age thirty who is not a conservative has no brains." Nonsense. Which political party and which chronological age has a monopoly on mind and who on the emotions?

When I urge the synagogue to place social and political concerns onto the Jewish agenda, I mean that a serious synagogue such as ours can help rescue political discourse from the polarizing mentality of "Crossfire" or "The Capital Gang" in which Michael Kingsley is pitted against John Sununu, and Bob Novak screams at Mark Shields, a meretricious contest whose victory goes to the most voluble, volatile, and voracious. That's not dialogue, that's not political thinking, that's not discourse. That is F.C.C. licensing of libel and slander.

One reaction to partisan polarization is to stay away from the polls—just don't vote, "a plague on both your houses." But that cynicism throws the precious baby of social concern out with the dirty water of vulgarized political partisanship. Isolation from the issues of social policy signals to young and old that the synagogue has nothing to say about the way we govern our citizens.

Jewish conscience and the political life are inextricably bound. It does not mean that Judaism or the synagogue can tell you how to decide about NAFTA or GATT, or the closing of military bases, or the forms that affirmative action should take, or whether Medicare is to be saved, and how taxes should be lowered or raised, or how the budget is to be reduced.

No Jewish book and no Jewish sacred text will tell you what political, economic, or military means should be used. Torah is not a book of political strategies or economic means. Torah is a book of social ends.

Judaism does not have a party platform. It provides a spiritual and moral foundation for political decisions. Judaism is a way of thinking, a way of hearing that offers moral perspective on living.

Let me put it personally. How do I as a religious Jew take my political stance? As a Jew I hear with a third ear. Beneath the liberal-conservative rhetoric on contract and covenant, family values and entitlement, and the role of government and of society, I hear with a unique Jewish historical and theological ear the depths of a more basic controversy with theological roots. Let me illustrate.

At the turn of the century there emerged in the Western world a deeply influential political philosophy called Social Darwinism, At its head were celebrated philosophers, Herbert Spencer in England and William Graham Sumner in the United States. They were called Social Darwinists because they used Darwin's evolutionary theory of "natural selection" and "the survival of the fittest" to justify their political philosophy.

Herbert Spencer, in his *Social Statics* published in 1897 not long after Darwin's *Descent of Man* (1871), argued that government ought not to interfere with human society. Learn from the ways of nature. In nature the weak, the afflicted, those of low ability are naturally weeded out and should be. Spencer and Summer argued—come on and open your eyes to the wisdom of nature.

What happens to a sow who has a runt in its litter? She eats it.

What happens to a mutational baby chick? The mother hen pecks it to death.

What happens to wolves who go on a hunt? The injured and slow among them are soon abandoned.

But what do we do? We do our utmost to check the natural process of elimination with artificial governmental intervention. To quote Darwin's *Descent of Man*, "We build asylums for the imbeciles, the maimed, the sick; we institute poor laws, our medical men exert their utmost skill to save the life of everyone to the last moment. No one who has attended to the breeding of domestic animals will doubt that this must be highly injurious to the race of man." Thomas Malthus in his essay on population disapproved of the relief for the poor because war, disease, and poverty are natural antidotes to the rapid explosion of the population. When you tamper by governmental interference with the laws of nature, with "the survival of the fittest" and "natural selection," you drain our economy, exhaust our energy, and you are left with an effete, decadent civilization.

The Social Darwinist, Herbert Spencer, offers a case history of Margaret, "a gutter child," supported by welfare. Margaret proves to be "a prolific mother of a prolific race." Margaret herself, ignorant, indolent, incompetent was supported by public welfare. The records of the court of New York show that two hundred of Margaret's descendants were idiots, imbeciles, drunkards, lunatics, paupers, prostitutes. So Spencer concludes, "Was it kindness or cruelty which generation after generation enabled these to multiply and become an increasing curse to the society around us?" Society's so-called altruism only increases positive misery and prevents positive happiness. We would all be better off if Margaret died. Why keep her alive?

Now the truth of this interpretation of Darwin I leave to you. Whether it is fair to Darwin, many scholars will deny. But right or wrong, I hear with my Jewish third ear. For me the underlying issue is not statistical, not biological, but theological. It has to do with a Jewish way of understanding and responding to nature, human nature, and social character. All around us today in different guises we witness the resurrected theology of Spencer and Summer. Social Darwinism reborn—a resurgence of thinking rooted in the belief that the survival of the fittest should be applied to our social relations and social policy. That the losers of society should "sink or swim."

Much older than Social Darwinism, with my third Jewish ear I hear an echo of a major Biblical controversy. It is the ancient Jewish struggle against pagan pantheism, against the paganism that equates might with right, against the paganism that worships the power of nature. Might is right. That power theology the Bible calls *idolatry.* Idolatry deifies nature. Whatever nature does, nature gets and should get. Pantheism means nature is God and God is nature. The idolatry of paganism declares *"imitate nature."*

Don't we Jews believe in nature?

- Of course the Jewish tradition recognizes nature as God's creation. That is what Rosh Hashanah is all about, the celebration of the creation of nature. But our tradition has insisted that

242

while nature comes from God, nature is not God. Nature is morally neutral. Nature is morally indifferent to earthquake, tornado, hurricane, monsoon. Nature is amoral. The strong devour the weak. You see it in every documentary on nature: in the contest of the lions and the lambs, the leopards and the antelopes, the venomous scorpion and the fleeing deer.

- Of course Judaism recognizes the instinctual behavior of men and women, of lust and of aggressiveness and inquisitiveness. But Judaism does not sanctify natural impulse. It places control, constraints, limits on our animal passions.
- Of course Judaism recognizes that the human being is created along with the animals of Genesis, tigers, lions, and vultures. But Judaism insists that we are more than animals. We are more than beasts. We are more than fangs and claws and teeth. We are more than biology. We are human beings. We are not created to imitate nature. We are created to imitate God.

Survival of the fittest? Who is the most fit: the bully, the tyrant, the mailed fist, those with the sharpest teeth, the hardest nails, the longest elbows? Judaism repudiates that fitness. The Jewish and moral spiritual revolution declares we humans are mandated to emulate God. "As God clothes the naked—clothe the naked, as God visits the sick—visit the sick, as God buries the dead—bury the dead, as God comforts the mourners—comfort the mourners." The Jewish model to be imitated by human beings is the God of compassion, not nature "Red in tooth and claw." Survival? Survival without compassion is suicidal. Survival without compassion is murder and compassion is the soul of Judaism. Rachmonis is derived from the Hebrew word *rechem* which means "womb", the lifeblood of civilization. In Greek the womb is called *hystera*, the root of "hysteria"; in Hebrew the womb is called compassion.

All around me human beings are afflicted. Millions of lives are lived in fear and trembling. Something is demanded of me! Hunger is real. So we fast to remind ourselves. What am I? Who am I? The Jewish answer to that search for my identity? The Jewish answer is *tshuvah*, "response."

I respond, therefore I am. I am moved, therefore I am. I care, therefore I am. As a Jew, I must not remain immobilized. Carved in the marrow of my Jewish bones is the ethical demand, "You shall not stand on your brothers' blood." I cannot turn aside, avert my eyes. I cannot throw the weak to the wolves and declare, "That is the will of nature."

This is not liberalism or Libertarian or Conservatism. This is the soul of Jewish *mentschlicheitism*—this is the heart of Jewish theology, the soul of Jewish belief.

What does Jewish theology have to do with political life? What does the Jewish thought have to do with politics? What you believe makes all the difference in the world. Beliefs have consequences. Ideas have consequences. Theories about nature have consequences. Let me illustrate.

I mentioned William Graham Sumner, one of the most influential of American social Darwinists in the late nineteenth century. In the name of social science a hundred years ago, he and other intellectuals agitated for closing the gates of immigration to America. These intellectuals proclaimed that the new immigrants who were coming here from Italy, Hungary, and Russia did not come with the old Anglo-Saxon frontier virtues of native stock. They did not have the qualities of those we wanted. One hundred years ago they argued that the wave of new immigrants were polluting society. Most notably the Jews. Listen to the sounds. Jews come as "beaten men from beaten breeds . . . moral cripples, their souls warped and dwarfed by iron circumstances . . . too cowardly to engage in violent crimes they concentrate on shrewdness." Only the natural selective breeding of individuals will protect a nation's good racial traits and prevent a nation's collapse. In the early part of the twentieth century Sir Frances Galton and other geneticists warned against "the mongrelization of America." They all had academic titles. But we were not born yesterday. We Jews have learned from the scientists with Ph.D.'s who experimented on innocent men, women, and children. Science without conscience is not culture. Science without conscience is murder.

My Jewish antenna picks up today's talk of the Bell curve of eugenics, the foreboding insinuations that identify races and nationalities that are genetically inferior. I have heard those voices before. I carry millennial memories in my bones. As a Jew I was not born yesterday.

When today I hear the denigration of the new wave of immigrants in the 90s, that they bring with them crimes, violence, the worst features of society. When I hear the myth of the golden past, "How come they can't be like our immigrant grandparents and parents?" Hold on. My third ear arrests me. Did I forget? Did we forget what was said about our fathers and mothers? The report of the New York Police Commissioner, Theodore Bingham, announced in the "North American Review of Criminality" that half the crimes in New York were committed by Russian Jewish immigrants. Listen to Commissioner Bingham (1908), "Jews are fire bugs, burglars, pick pockets, and robbers when they had the courage." "The most expert of all street thieves are the Hebrew boys under sixteen." Police Commissioner Bingham was not alone. High officials joined in his declaration that "the Jewish propensity for criminality" required the formation of a special detective force. All the ghosts of Fagin and Shylock took on human apparitions of immigrants.

The Reverend A. E. Patton, a respected Protestant leader, summarized the national revulsion toward the huddled wretched masses. "For a real American to visit Ellis Island and look upon the Jewish hordes, ignorant of all patriotism, vermin-infested, stealthy and furtive in manner, too lazy to enter into real labor, too cowardly to face frontier life, too lazy to work, too filthy to adopt ideals of cleanliness from the start . . ." These leaders, officials in high place, were not speaking about Hispanics or Puerto Ricans or Haitians or African Americans, they were speaking about us, our people.

When I hear in the land today the mounting chorus of xenophobia, left, right, center—the fear and hatred of the stranger—from all sides spouting that these new immigrant people come to our shores, drain our money, increase our taxes, fill our streets with crime; that they are inassimilable, that they do not speak our language, my third ear resonates.

How about my Zayde and Bubbe? I think about my Yiddish-speaking, inassimilable *bubbe* and *zayde* from Tchechenova and Nashelsk who came to these shores at the turn of the century and lived on Rivington and Houston streets, and in Brooklyn and Bronx for the rest of their lives only talked Yiddish. For years, I insisted to the teacher of P.S. 89 that my "Christian" name was Hersehel.

Listen with your third ear. In 1890 Senator Henry Cabot Lodge sponsored a bill to exclude all males over sixteen unable to read or write English "in the language of their native or resident country." The target was Jews like zayde and bubbe, whose principle dialect was Yiddish, who read and wrote in Yiddish. But Yiddish clearly was not "the language of their native or resident country."

"Remember the immigrant, for you were immigrants on Ellis Island."

When I see Haitians or Cubans turned back in their vessels of refuge I say good—who needs them? Then my Jewish memory bites me. Did I forget that in 1939 a bipartisan proposal by Republican Edith Rogers and Democrat Robert Wagner sought to permit 20,000 refugee children to enter the United States on a two-year plan in 1939. The bill provided that the children would be card for by private agencies or individuals. Not a single child would become a ward of the public. Who could possibly find it in his heart to refuse to rescue children in 1939? In 1939, the bipartisan Wagner–Rogers bill Republican and Democrat was defeated in the Senate Immigration Committee. The arguments were the same as we hear today. Labor was opposed to it, nativists were opposed to it, politicians who read the polls were opposed to it. Have I so soon forgotten? Have I grown so deaf to the parallels? Have I grown so blind to the analogies, to the horrifying similarities from my own blood and flesh?

When I hear and see on talk shows and in newspapers the mounting sentiment against the immigrant, I can't get out of my head the 930 Jewish passengers on the boat from the hellish harbor of Hamburg, Germany, to the haven of Havana. I can't get out of my head the magnificent anti-Nazi German Gustaf Schroder, the captain of the St. Louis who treated his passengers as honored guests and who when his boat with its passengers was denied entry into Havana, deliberately steamed his ship off the Florida coast of the United States hoping for rescue, only to be escorted by the U. S. Coast Guard, forced to leave American territorial waters and to return to the crematories of Europe. The passengers aboard the St. Louis formed a committee to prevent suicide.

I listen with my third ear. Even during World War II, only ten percent of those who could have legally been admitted as refugees to the United States were admitted. Seventy-eight percent of Americans in the polls refused to allow refugees to enter. Xenophobia, fear of the stranger, resonates in my Jewish ears.

And it's not directed against illegal immigration. That's a smoke screen. Today in Congress there are an unprecedented number of immigration-related bills calling for all kinds of restrictions to deny social services and educational opportunities to immigrants legally residing in the United States. And more than eighty-five percent of newcomers reside in the United States legally.

Do I have to resort to the argument that according to the Urban institute, immigrants and refugees pay 30 billion dollars a year more in taxes than they consume in services? So it's profitable, Okay. People are running for their lives. Today Congress ponders a proposal to cut refugees numbers from 110,000 to 50,000. As Republican Howard Berman said, "If this law had been in place in the 1930s my mother would have gone to the concentration camp." Where would my parents be?

You ask how does Jewish faith and Jewish experience affect my political life? It does not tell me how to vote or even for which proposition to vote but it won't let me forget the moral factors that I must consider beyond those of economic self-interest. Judaism, Jewish history is my moral gadfly. It forms my conscience. It informs my soul before I vote and remains with me after the vote. After the vote!

For the day after the vote, Jewish conscience stays on and whispers in my third ear, "Now that you have done what you have done and for good reasons as well, what now?" Sure, it is important to limit immigration. Sure, it is important not to practice reverse discrimination. Sure, it is important not to have quotas. Sure, it is important to build more prisons and to have more policemen. But after I pull the lever am I exempted from political responsibility?

What do I say about the submerged community? Should I practice toward them a so-called benign neglect? Do I mean to create a permanent underclass in our society? Sure I'm for work force.

Poor mothers with children under the age of five should be back to work! Who will take care of children cut off aid to families with dependent children? But both George Will and Pat Moynihan give up the image of children sleeping and freezing on subway grates! Yesterday the Senate voted to give the Pentagon $7.5 billion more than the Pentagon requested. Who speaks for the poor?

Infant deaths among African Americans are twice as high the white race. Maternal deaths are three times as high among African Americans as among whites. Do I turn now to the wisdom of the Social Darwinists and turn women and children back to the dark laws of the jungle? Let Margaret die, and her children too? Do I act like the sow, the chicken, the wolf?

Why should I give them food stamps and breakfasts for school children? Why should we give them free breakfasts? Where is the responsibility of their parents? Should we feed their children and create a paternalistic culture of dependence?

Then with my third ear I hear the testimony of a staff member from the Minnesota Food Share Program who tried to explain the problem of hunger to an elementary school class. He asks the kids, "How many of you ate breakfast that morning?" When only a few of them raised their hands, he continued, "How many of you skipped breakfast this morning because you don't like breakfast?" Lots of hands went up. Then, "How many of you skipped breakfast because you didn't have time for it?" Many other hands went up. "How many of you skipped breakfast because your family just doesn't usually eat breakfast?" A few more hands were raised. He noticed a small boy in the middle of the classroom whose hand had never gone up. He thought that the boy hadn't understood his questions. So he asked him, "And why, son, didn't you eat breakfast this morning?" The boy replied, "It wasn't my turn."

Too bad son. But not out of my taxes. The issue is not the *L* or *C* word, it's the *R* word. Not liberal or conservative but *rachmones*. In Yiddish and Hebrew *rachmones*—compassion. The prayer we will recite at *Yizkor* addresses God as *El Mole Rachamin*. Jewish compassion is not an aesthetic feeling. Jewish compassion means to act, it means to intervene in nature, it means to transform the jungle of civilization.

A word to the young so that you will understand the resonances in the Jewish third ear.

Let me speak to the youngest among you, to my children and grandchildren who did not know your immigrant ancestors or the Depression. Our immigrant grandparents may not have spoken English when they came to these shores yet they brought with them a legacy of social institutions dating back to Mishnaic and medieval times, organizations with Hebrew names: societies to protect the poor, societies for free burial, homes for the aged, charities to clothe the naked, to provide for women who need support to get married, charities to provide *matzah* and wine for the poor for Passover, homes that cared for orphans and societies that buried the indigent without charge. That was accepted as the duty and responsibility of the entire society. That was intervention by community.

They spoke broken English and with Yiddish dialects. But with what a moral literacy they spoke.

Whether Jews vote for one party or another is truly not my concern. I am concerned with the moral legacy of my ancestors. I am concerned with the health of the Jewish heart. I fear the petrification of the compassionate society that threatens to grind down our Jewish sensibility. I fear in the so-called political realism that dries the tear ducts and thickens the heart. Children, you were Bar/Bat, don't forget your *Haftorah*; it came from the prophets, those nonpartisan disturbers of social indifference, those spiritual politicians who knew that to believe in God is to care about God's special children: the poor, the homeless, the widow, the stranger.

Children, don't forget your *Haftorah*—not the *trope* but the soul. The true goal is not to learn the *Haftorah* by heart. It is to take the *Haftorah* to heart. The heart of Judaism is the heart. The prophet, the greatest and most unique spiritual hero Judaism has admonished against "hardness of heart," "stubbornness of heart," "stiffness of heart," "the uncircumcision of heart."

Children, what I fear is not the "others" outside us. I fear the enemy within. I fear that we will grow accustomed to placards of the hungry and jobless, that we learn cleverly to avert our eyes, and shrewdly speed up our cars so that we are not forced to see them at the intersection.

I fear that we learn how deftly to step over the homeless bodies on the street so that we do not trip. I fear that we will see more emergency rooms shut down, more clinics shut down and rationalize with calculative intelligence the balance of budget. What I fear is we will cut the budget out of the hides of the powerless.

Children, be smart but not cruel—the brain is vital but don't let it kill the heart.

Children, better be accused of having a bleeding heart than having a frozen soul. Children, don't let the jungle take over. "Seek justice, undo oppression. Defend the fatherless. Plead for the widow" (Isaiah 1:17). God bless us and our children with strong and good hearts.

ISMAR SCHORSCH

The Sword and the Book

On July 3, 1994, the town of Esslingen (near Stuttgart) commemorated
the fiftieth anniversary of the death of my grandfather, Theodor
Rothschild, in Theresienstadt. I delivered the following address in
German for the occasion.

When my sister and I visited Esslingen briefly in July, 1977, we
came unannounced. It was our first visit since we had fled Germany in
December, 1938. We made our way to the building which had once
housed the well-known Jewish boarding school run by our grandfather
for forty years and our great grandfather for twenty-six. It had been
plundered by Nazi zealots on November 10, 1938, and closed for the
last time at the end of August, 1939, just before Hitler invaded Poland.

My sister recognized the stately house instantly, because it was basically unchanged from the place she had roamed as a young girl on

---

Rabbi Ismar Schorsch was born in Germany in 1925 and came to the U.S. in
his youth. He received his B.A. from Ursinus College in Massachusetts, his Ph.D. from
Columbia University, and was ordained at the Jewish Theological Seminary. Jewish
historian scholar, author, and military chaplain, Rabbi Schorsch is currently the sixth
chancellor of the Jewish Theological Seminary, where he is professor of Jewish History.

summer vacation. My own memories, those of a three year old, had long evaporated. When no one answered the door, we made our way inside and slowly walked around without ever meeting a soul. Indeed, the building was still a school, now run by the state, clean, bright, and airy. What saddened us to no end was the obliteration of the institution's Jewish past. Its public spaces held no trace of any photographs, plaque, or memorial to make the students aware that this school had not always been what it presently was.

I relate this visit to underscore how much has changed for the better. Not long after, a number of local residents mounted an arduous campaign to rename the school after its prominent last Jewish director, that culminated in victory in November, 1983. Inside, the walls of the school now recount the history and fate of the Jewish school which was founded in 1841, and a trove of documents and pictures are assembled in the director's office to instruct any curious student or visitor who might wish to know still more. Today, the city of Esslingen has chosen to commemorate the fiftieth anniversary of my grandfather's death in Theresienstadt because he was unwilling to abandon his children while his school was still permitted to stay open by the Nazis.

I do not make light of these gestures. They are reflective of a groundswell across Germany during the last fifteen years for reconciliation, often spearheaded by the younger generation. While the past cannot be undone, it can be mastered through honesty, understanding, and contrition. These are the sentiments which motivate many hundreds of university students every year to take courses in Jewish studies, even to the extent of learning Hebrew and spending a year at the Hebrew University in Jerusalem. These are the sentiments which mount major Jewish exhibitions such as the one in Berlin in the winter of 1991–92 and minor ones in local communities. These are the sentiments which prompt many towns and cities to bring back at their expense former Jewish residents for a visit, to erect monuments to memorialize what was destroyed, and to care for Jewish cemeteries. The media prefer to focus on the outbursts of extremists; they utterly fail to note how deep and diversified and mainstream has become the German effort to confront the Holocaust and turn its grizzly lesson into a force for good. Surely, Germany has done far more in this regard than any other modern nation guilty of genocide. It is critical for Jews to recognize and celebrate that the Germany of 1994 is not the Germany of 1944.

Theodor Rothschild was a teacher and author, a lover of books and a transmitter of culture. In his school he had created two libraries, one for the children and one for the teachers. Reading aloud in small groups was part of the culture of the place. He personified the love of learning and addiction to books which has long marked Jews as the people of the book. In Judaism sacred works are not discarded but buried, as if they were human. And indeed they are, because it is the written word that makes us most human.

When the Nazi mob plundered his school on the afternoon of November 10, 1938, they assaulted civilization itself. Besides brutalizing its teachers, they took out the Torah scroll from its synagogue and the books from its libraries and torched them in a public bonfire in the courtyard. In Esslingen they wildly reenacted the bonfires of Jewish books lit across Nazi Germany on May 10, 1933, by university students bent on cleansing the German spirit. In Berlin, Goebbels had blessed the violence with a personal appearance and announced the end "of a period of excessive Jewish intellectualism (*Zeitalters eines uberspitzten Judischen Intellektualismus*)." In the flames he professed to see the spiritual foundation of the Weimar Republic reduced to ashes.

The spectacle of torching Jewish books brings to mind the luminous line written by the young Heine on the burning of the Koran by the Spanish grand inquisitor, "That was merely a prologue. There where books are burned, people will also be burned in the end." What Heine caught in this unforgettable epigram is that books are not a mere symbol but the very essence of civilization. To burn books is to repudiate the instinct renunciation, sublimation, and rationality that separate the jungle from civilization. It is, to move from Heine to Freud, the revolt of civilization's discontents ever ready to rip off the constraints vital to producing culture. Once unleashed, the repressed urges of the Id move quickly from pyres of books to mass murder, from Kristallnacht to the Final Solution.

As Freud already intuited, Judaism epitomized the triumph of spirit over the sense and intellect over instincts. Goebbels was not wrong, Judaism did revere the mind. Long before, a Palestinian rabbi of the second century had imagined that the book and the sword once descended from heaven locked together in eternal combat. With its devotion to study and religious practice, Judaism called for self-conquest rather than the conquest of others and literacy rather than license. Even when vanquished and forced into exile, Jews did not become homeless. The sacred written text became their portable homeland. They persisted in spinning webs of words which transported them to tranquil realms of lasting meaning and inured them to the harsh conditions outside. They based their Shabbat liturgy on the annual reading of the Torah, the Five Books of Moses, and marked the passage of time by their location in the text. Above all, Jews grew into masters of textual analysis, putting a premium on slow, reflective reading with commentary as the quintessential mode of Jewish literary expression.

Moreover, it is this cerebral religious tradition which uniquely prepared Jews to embrace modernity, even before emancipation freed them from their shackles. Barely out of the ghetto, Moses Mendelssohn and Heine became masters and models of German prose and poetry. By 1886–1887, Jewish students represented ten percent of all students studying at Prussian universities, and by 1912, eight and a half percent of all students at institutions of higher learning in the Russian Empire where Jews had still not been emancipated. Nor can there be any doubt that the extraordinary achievement of a new nation like Israel to govern itself effectively and democratically owes much to the affinity of Jews for education. The first official act of the Zionist movement in Palestine in 1918 after having received the Balfour Declaration a year before was to lay the cornerstone for the Hebrew University on Mt. Scopus. Today Israel publishes annually more books per capita than any country in the world except Iceland, in a language that a century ago was barely living.

When the Nazis came to power in 1933, German Jewry took up the pen in a heroic five-year struggle of spiritual resistance. They published books to nourish the mind and comfort the soul, such as the daring *Schocken Bucherei*, a series of nearly one hundred titles, both old and new, drawn from the entire range of Jewish creativity and printed in inexpensive pocket-size editions. Beginning with the lyrical prophecies of Second Isaiah in the gritty Buber-Rosenzweig translation, the series included German renditions of talmudic and midrashic texts, medieval Hebrew poetry and modern Yiddish literature, as well as works of Jewish history written long ago and in the 1930s.

The shattering of emancipation also prompted my grandfather to take refuge in the world of the spirit. Along with two other Jewish educators, he published in 1936 a splendid anthology of modern Jewish poetry whose title *Need and Hope (Not und Hofnung)* indicated its purpose. Its contents covered broad topics: Jewish history, days of holiness, the land of Israel, and resistance to oppression. In the forward, the authors stressed the solace to be found in the poetry evoked by earlier experiences of persecution. "If prejudice and persecution have accompanied us throughout the millennia, so have our poets and singers, faithful companions who illuminated our pain in their works." The Nazis regarded the pathos and power of the book as subversive and immediately confiscated the entire edition.

The medieval history of the Jews in Esslingen also offers remarkable testimony on the bookish nature of Judaism. It is the place of origin of the oldest Hebrew manuscript from Germany with a recorded date. Just a few decades after Jews had settled in Esslingen, Qalonimos ben Yehudah notes in a postscript (colophon) to his *mahzor* (prayerbook) for the fall festivals of Rosh Hashanah, Yom Kippur, and Sukkot that he completed his work on the Hebrew date of 28 Tevet 5050, that is, January 12, 1290. An illuminated manuscript with decorations typical of thirteenth century Ashkenazic (German) manuscripts, the fragmented *mahzor* of Kolonyomos has just recently been reunited. Evelyn M. Cohen, a young and sensitive Jewish art historian dramatically recognized that the incomplete section in the Bibliotheca Rosenthaliana in Amsterdam derives from the same patrimony as the truncated one preserved in the library of my own institution, the Jewish Theological Seminary. Moreover, on the basis of the Esslingen *mahzor*, scholars are beginning to identify other medieval Hebrew manuscripts as originating in Esslingen, making it an important transmitter of Jewish culture.

In Theresienstadt, two books served to fortify the faith, good humor, and indomitable will of Helene Rothschild, Theodor's only sister. Like her, they came through the horror of this "model" camp and are today among my most treasured possessions. The first is a pocket-size traditional prayerbook for weekdays and Sabbath with Hebrew text and German translation. The inside cover bears the inscription of her name. What else makes this *siddur* uncommon is the fact that according to its title page, it was printed in Frankfurt am Main (Rodelheim) in 1939, long after any hope which German Jews might still have harbored for an accommodation with the Nazis had vanished. It must surely be among the last Jewish works printed in Nazi Germany. To me, it has always symbolized the flicker of eternal light in the midst of total darkness, the book which in this instance denied the sword its victory.

255

The second spiritual bulwark of Tante Helene, as we knew her, was an equally small and slender volume of prayers in German for Jewish women for all occasions. Edited by Fanny Neuda a century earlier and reprinted many times, this particular edition of *Stunden der Andacht (Moments of Meditation)* was published in Prague in 1873. It was intended to bring edification and solace to women who could not read Hebrew. On the inside front cover there is a list of some seventeen first names of family members, including my mother's, with the birthday of each one alongside. More poignant still, on the back inside cover is recorded the day of death of Tante Helene's two brothers, who died in Theresienstadt in rapid order after the bitter winter of 1944. Karl died on June 2 and Theodor on July 11 (actually July 10). In each instance the Hebrew date is given. The women endured adversity better: Theodor's sister, wife, and sister-in-law survived. One can only imagine the comfort they drew from sending their anguish aloft in the sacred vessels of these two fragile links to eternity.

In every generation, civilization hangs by a thread. Neither culture nor morality are imprinted in the genes; every child must be socialized afresh. As a teacher, Theodor Rothschild protected that which makes us most human. His being was filled with compassion for children, with love for the forms and values of Judaism, and with wonder at the marvels and mysteries of nature. I knew him only through the person of my father, who came to Esslingen at a tender age from a broken home, and for whom my grandfather became a lifelong model. For both of them the immediacy of God's presence was a daily reality experienced in the countless miracles of the ordinary. I am convinced that my father's doctoral dissertation at Tubingen on *"The Teachability of Religion" (Die Lehrbarkeit der Religion)* came right out of my grandfather's school, where Judaism was lived and learned unself-consciously. Its pattern of daily prayer and sacred days determined the rhythm of the school. My father went on to become the rabbi that my grandfather, as a gifted teacher and genuine religious personality, had always been, even without the title.

Theodor had two daughters, my aunt Berta and my mother Fanny. My aunt and her husband left Germany in August, 1938, to resettle in the United States, and my family followed in December, 1938. I still have the many letters that Theodor wrote to his children in the two years before Pearl Harbor. Obviously self-censored and laced with family matters, they nevertheless convey the robustness of his unbroken spirit. By December 8, 1938, nearly a month after his school had been closed for the first time, he had come to realize how misguided had been his belief that by not applying for a visa number from the American consulate, the Nazis would allow the school to remain open. "That we did not permit ourselves to get a number is an act of neglect that we can never make good. We must simply adjust to it and hope that the many numbers ahead of our own will be quickly disposed of." It is heartrending to follow in this correspondence from the world of insanity the interminable delays and dashed hopes that marked the tireless efforts of our families, without financial resources, to secure the emigration of Theodor and his wife, Ina. As late as November 4, 1941, he wrote with renewed optimism about soon getting an American visa, after a telegram from us that held out the prospect of passage to Cuba.

He used the time to deepen his knowledge of Hebrew and master English. On September 5, he declared proudly from Esslingen, "In English I have come so far that I can read and understand quite well simple stories, which gives me great joy. By the time we get to you, we will surely understand some English and even be able to speak a bit." At the time he was teaching twenty-six hours a week, including math and geometry, the only teacher well enough to carry such a heavy load.

Once removed to Stuttgart, he continued to teach, conduct religious services, and serve on the executive committee (*Der Oberrat*) of the organized Jewish community. On November 27, 1941, in one of his last letters, he admitted, "It is right now very tough. He who visits this upon us, also gives us the strength to bear it. Particularly unpleasant for us is that we needed to vacate our apartment and have still not found another. But also in this instance we hope for a solution. All this means that we approach our holidays in low spirits. But I don't want to be disheartening and will offer in the services as much comfort and strength as I possibly can." Ina and Theodor finally found a one-room apartment which required sharing a common kitchen and bathroom with four other families.

In Theresienstadt, spiritual nourishment sustained his declining physical strength. He never missed a chance to hear a lecture. After the war, Ina reported to us that he used every free minute for study. "A Czech doctor studied Hebrew with him. English books cluttered his workplace. It was well known that anything to read would give him the greatest joy." It is true that he finally succumbed to the brute force of the sword, but only after prolonged spiritual resistance. Less than a year later, Hitler's vaunted thousand-year Reich was to fall after a twelve year reign of terror. Theodor Rothschild's inspiring legacy of humanity in the face of inhumanity personifies the very essence of Judaism and the secret to its extraordinary survival.

How Shall
We Measure Life?

Each year marks the passing of time and the passing of time brings to
us reflections, somber and earnest, touching life, its meaning, its goal,
and all its strange vicissitudes. One question among many emerges from
these reflections. How shall we measure life? By what rule shall we
gauge it? Shall we measure life by time? Shall we say that he who lives

Rabbi Abba Hillel Silver was born in 1893 and immigrated to the United States
in 1902. He studied at Yeshiva Etz Chaim where he helped establish the first Zionist
Youth Organization in the U.S. He received his A.B. at the University of Cincinnati
and his D.D. from Hebrew Union College. In 1917 he became rabbi of the Temple
Tifereth Israel in Cleveland where he served until his death in 1963. Rabbi Silver
emulated the prophets in the fight against evil in the name of God, defended the people
of Israel in a non-Jewish world, organized the non-sectarian anti-Nazi League to cham-
pion human rights and boycott German goods, and formed the American Zionist
Emergency Council. Rabbi Silver was the one who announced to the United Nations
that Israel had declared itself an independent state. He was an eloquent and impassioned orator who authored important books on Judaism and published volumes of
his sermons and addresses.

longest lives best? Assuredly, there are few people who really believe that length of days is life's highest prize. We all wish to live long enough to carry through our life's program, and to see, if only in part, the fruits of our labor. But we would never conceive of ourselves as having lived splendidly simply because we had lived to be seventy or eighty years old. The size of the canvas does not determine the value of the painting, nor does the number of our years determine the worth of our life. "It is possible," said the Roman sage Seneca, "or rather usual, for a man who has lived long to have lived too little."

If we are to think of life only in terms of time, we are likely to be saddened by the prospect as we grow older. For on the sunny side of the hill of life, on the upgrade, time brings with it joy and eager anticipation, but on the shadowy side of the hill, on the downgrade, time brings with it, often as not, sadness and disillusionment and the thought of the certain and ineluctable end. In our youthful years time means the burgeoning of our hopes, the relish of novel experiences, the glow of ambition. In our aging years, time means the ripening of all things unto harvest, the ingathering, the retarded tempo, the reduced powers and hopes bounded by ever narrowing rings.

It is true that time teaches us wisdom. Time softens sorrows, subdues passions, and oftentimes brings peace to the restless soul. But time also wears all things down, robs us of the rich zest of living, teaches us what we cannot do, and brings us at last, spent and wearied, to the gates of death.

What does human life amount to after all, when taken as time? It is amazingly insignificant. The whole life of man is less than a second in the cosmic calendar, less than a point on the chart of time. Our life is just a moment's continuation of that life which was in our ancestors and further back through unnumbered generations in the animal, in the protoplasm, in the unicellular organism, in the sun-heat and the flaming, leaping seas of hydrogen. Our individual life is but an imperceptible vibration in that infinite throb of cosmic life. How can it be measured at all? It is so infinitesimal. What meaning has the flurried eddy of a man's threescore years and ten, when one comprehends the immeasurable sweep of the tides of time? "A thousand years are in Thy sight but as yesterday, and as a watch in the night." Nay, ten thousand thousand years are in Thy sight but as yesterday! Perhaps a thousand million years passed before the first invertebrate evolved out of the lowest form of life. Another five hundred thousand years possibly elapsed before the first vertebrate and the first mammal appeared, and incalculably long cycles of time before man emerged from the man-ape. Against this background of stupendous epochs—eras which even our imagination cannot encompass—what is man's puny life of three-score years and ten?

How then shall we measure human life? Shall we measure it in terms of possessions? Is that man to be credited with having lived most who has accumulated most? Shall we say, "Behold, this man got the most out of life. Witness his wealth. This man got the least out of life. Witness his poverty." Is this the true gauge of life? Few of us would really consent to this. When we wish to speak kindly of someone who has departed from the world of the living, do we say of him, "He lived superbly as proved by the money which he accumulated?" If we were to write our own epitaph, I dare say that this would be the last thing we would think of for our final eulogy.

For few of us are really beguiled in our judgments touching the relationship between wealth and life's real values. Most of us who strive after material success do so not because we regard it as life's highest good and the true criterion of life's worth. Rather do we seek it in order to acquire by means of it other, and to us more valuable, ends: security, independence, power, the respect of our fellow men, and a chance to play a role in the world.

Some people, to be sure, do think of wealth as life's greatest good. In their estimation, life is summed up in beautiful houses and rich appointments, in costly raiment and glittering jewels, in many servants, in much luxury and ease. The wise man only pities them. The wise man does not underestimate the need for material things in providing himself and his family with the indispensable requirements of civilized living. He is not an ascetic and he does not make a virtue of want and privation. But he does not confuse that which is necessary with that which is ultimate. He sees things in their proper perspective—as means to an end, as aids in removing some of the obstacles in the way of life's advancement. He knows too, as Socrates knew, "how many things there are in the world for which he has no use." How many are the things he can get along without, how frequently the superabundance of things becomes a burden and a drag, and how often wealth makes us slaves more abject than ever poverty makes us. Man does not require much to be happy. It is in his passionate striving after the excessive that the root of his unhappiness lies.

The great Russian, Tolstoi, illustrates this truth in one of his legends called "How Much Land Does a Man Need?"

Pakhom was a muzhik, a peasant who was not rich but who had enough. He was satisfied. But one day he visited a richer relative in the city, and envy made him dissatisfied. His few acres were no longer enough. He wanted more. So with his savings of a hundred rubles, with selling a colt and half his bees, with putting his son out as a laborer, and with borrowing, he succeeded in buying some more acres. He sowed his land and prospered. He was happy. He thought he knew now how much land a man needs.

But soon the rumor spread that people were moving to new places, down the Volga, where there were rich, fertile acres free for the asking. Pakhom reasoned, "Why remain here in straitened circumstances? I can sell my house and land and with the money I can buy many more acres down there in the Volga region, and together with the free land which I will obtain there I would have a real establishment." And so he did. He settled in the new place and again he prospered on an even larger scale. Now he knew how much land a man needs.

But again glamorous rumors reached him of land most good and nourishing in the territory of the wandering Bashkirs which could be had for a song—thousands of acres of it. Pakhom was fascinated by the prospect. So he again gathered up all of his available capital and traveled five hundred versts to the land of the Bashkirs. He was well received and he was told that he could have all the land he wanted. The price was one thousand rubles a day—all the land that a man could go around in a day was his for one thousand rubles. There was but one stipulation. If he did not come back within the day to the place from which he started, his money was lost.

Pakhom was delighted. He knew that with his sturdy peasant legs he could cover a good deal of land in a day—in fact all the land a man needed.

Early at dawn he arose, and with the Bashkirs watching him, he set out upon the steppes. He walked about a mile, halted, and dug a little pit and piled turf in it to show where he had passed, and then went on. He quickened his pace. He stopped and dug other pits. It began to grow warm but still he kept on in a straight line. It was too early as yet to turn around. He saw in front of him beautiful black soil covered with lush, green grass. No, he could not forego that. So he continued in a straight line. The farther he went, the better the land became. He began to feel weary. He thought of turning—but no, he must not miss this land. "Endure it for an hour," he said to himself, "and you have a whole lifetime to live." But the sun was now high in the heaven. So he turned sharply to the left and went on a long distance again in a straight line. He knew that he should be turning again to the left—but the land was so rich and the soil so moist and fertile. He walked on and then he turned the second corner. When he started on the third side he knew that he must hasten his pace. The sun was already far down in the west. He must now hurry back to the starting point, which was now a full ten miles away. But his legs began to fail him. He felt a desire to rest, but he dared not. His money was at stake. The sun was sinking lower and lower. He took to the double-quick. He threw away his blouse, his boots, his flask. He hurried on, weary and staggering. His breath began to fail him. His mouth was parched. His heart was like a mill beating. He was afraid of dropping dead, and yet he could not stop. He ran and ran. He was getting nearer. Now he could see the starting point. The Bashkirs were waiting. Pakhom exerted his last energies. He threw himself forward with his body, reached out his arms to the starting point, and collapsed. A stream of blood poured out of his mouth and he lay dead. A Bashkir took a hoe, dug a grave, made it just long enough, from head to foot, seven feet, and buried him.

And this was all the land the man needed.

What then is the true measure of life? Not time. Not things. Is it happiness? Shall we say that the man who has been most happy is the one who has gotten most out of life? But then what do we understand by happiness? Shall we say that it is contentment, ease of mind, a sense of general satisfaction with one's self and with life? Then the least enterprising among men, the most stolid and unimaginative, the vegetative temperaments, the meagre souls would have to be accounted the most happy. For these, as a rule, are the most complacent and satisfied. But are we truly inclined to concede this? Shall we say that those whose souls are tuned to a higher pitch, more vibrant and sensitive, the pendulum of whose life swings to greater heights and to lower depths—the artist, the prophet, the dreamer, the thinker, the leader of men—shall we say that their lives are less blessed and weigh less in the scale of being? Do we not rather see in these lives, shot through as they frequently are with fury and despair, flung into revolt, hurled against the brute might of circumstance, and yet reaching up tortured and bleeding for the divine gift of truth and beauty, do we not see in them the very acme and perfection of human existence? When you think of the great men of the earth, "when you call to remembrance the great and the good through whom God hath wrought great glory": Moses, Jeremiah, Jesus, Michelangelo, Dante, Spinoza, Shelley, Lincoln. Do you think of them as happy? Clearly there is no visible relationship between magnificent living and happiness.

The ancient Stoics drew a sharp line of distinction between pleasure, which they called *voluptas*, and happiness, which they called *gaudium*. The distinction is readily apparent. Pleasure is a physical, bodily enjoyment borrowed from without, induced by physical things, by food or drink or play or passion. It is a moment's or an hour's stimulation, followed by sharp reactions. The more it is indulged in, the longer are the periods of reaction, ennui, and depression. Happiness, they held, is an intellectual enjoyment, rising from within, "from our own store." It springs "from the knowledge that we possess the virtues—that we are brave and just and true." Such happiness, which to us seems to be a rather stern and cheerless happiness, they held to be unbroken and continuous. But this Stoic definition makes no allowance for the accidents of fortune, for the sorrows which crowd in even upon the brave and the just and the true, "for the arrow that flieth by day and the pestilence that walketh in darkness," for the evils which come unsought, unheralded, and unwelcome, and which turn even the *gaudium*, the justly merited serenity of men, into bitterness and despair. It is not ours to order "tomorrow's bloom or blight." It is not ours to decree that among the wheat there shall be no tares. Nor does this definition take into account the fact that the very men who most aspire to be brave in a world of moral fear, to be just in a world of oppression and exploitation, to be true in a world of deception and falsehood are the very ones who most often taste the bitter dregs of defeat and disillusion, and who most often experience the feeling of the utter emptiness and uselessness of all their efforts.

No, happiness is not always within our ordering, nor is it ever continuous, nor can it summarize the profoundest meaning of life.

How then are we to measure life? By success? Shall we say that he who has achieved what he set out to achieve has derived the most out of life? Then those with the lowliest ambitions, whose life aims are the most ordinary and commonplace, would have to be adjudged victors by this test. For it is they who succeed most. The man whose ambition is high, who links his destiny to a soaring vision, who brushes aside the petty gains near at hand for the distant goal is not likely to succeed. His hope outdistances him. His arms cannot embrace what his soul descries. Ofttimes such men have nothing to show for their labor but the labor itself, nothing to show for their sacrifices but the sacrifices themselves—and the heartaches.

There is an Indian fable which bears out this thought of ours. An Indian chieftain once commanded his three sons to climb a certain steep and difficult mountain and to bring back some object from the highest point which they reached in their climb. Toward sundown the three sons returned. One had climbed halfway up the hard and dangerous slope and brought back a cluster of rare flowers which he had found there. The second had gone farther and brought back specimens of rare stones which he had discovered there. The third, the youngest and the bravest of the three, had by his pluck and daring climbed to the very top, but he had found nothing there to bring back with him. The crest of the mountain was above the timber line so that nothing grew there, and it was one solid rock from which he could abstract nothing. "Father," he said, "I have brought nothing back. I have nothing to show for my labors. But from the heights which I reached I caught sight of the sea! . . . I caught sight of the sea!"

No, success is no more a true measure of life than it is a true index of character. There are men who are great in the arena of thought and character and helpless in the arena of action.

How then, shall we measure life, our life? Not by time, not by things, not by happiness, not by success. By what? Why, by growth! Growth! Mind and soul growth! How much have we grown since yesterday, since yestermonth, since yesteryear? By how much have we bettered our yesterday's best? Are we able to find beauty today where a while ago we could see none? Are we more reverent of truth today than yesterday? Do we love more truly now because we have learned to understand more profoundly? Do human sorrow and human joy and all the sweet, sad music of humanity stir us more deeply now because we have attuned our souls more accurately? Were there any fears which darkened our days in the past, any hates or bitterness, any selfishness or self-deceptions which we have now sloughed off and cast aside? If so, we have grown and we have lived.

Man's true life does not take place in time or space but in the secret processes of growth. All life is growth. The splendor and miracle of the universe are growth, unfoldment, becoming—the life-seed passing through the dark mysterious stations of death and resurrection until it breaks forth into the breathless glory of flower and fruit. "And the earth brought forth grass, herb yielding seed after its kind, and tree bearing fruit, wherein is the seed thereof, after its kind; and God saw that it was good." This was the supreme miracle of creation. Everything is a growing and a becoming. Nothing is done. Nothing is ended. Stars grow. Planets grow. Worlds grow. Throughout all creation is an unceasing, throbbing life which manifests itself endlessly in endless variety.

To live is to feel continuously the teem and thrust of expanding life within one's soul, the thrill of new ideas, the throb of new purposes, the stir of revelation and new insight. Some plants live longer than others, some are hardier than others, some are more colorful and fragrant than others, some bear fruit while others do not, but there is one ineffable glory which they all share—they grow. They fulfill their destiny. Some men live longer than others, are richer, happier, more successful. That is interesting but not important, not the crucial test. The real test is growth. Do they grow? Are they fulfilling their heroic destiny of endless spiritual and mental inflorescence?

This measure of life is a hard measure, for it does not preclude pain and suffering. All birth and all growth in sentient creatures are attended by pain. This is the law of the physical world. It is also the law of the spiritual world. No one can attain to the compensations of maturity, to the satisfactions of abundant life, physical or spiritual, without these growing pains. We must be ready to pay the price.

If, then my friend, you have made of your life a developing romance, a legend of budding and blossoms; if you have made your past fruitful and your present a seedbed for future growth; if you are striving sunward even though it be through pain and struggle; if every year an added measure of mind- and soul-ripening comes to you: keener perceptions, finer discriminations, sounder judgments, deeper loyalties; if you feel that you are growing, then you are alive, and the greatness and the glory of life are yours, and you are to be called blessed among the children of men.

BARUCH SILVERSTEIN

God's Prayers

The famous theologian, Solomon Schechter, once made a brilliant observation about the multiplicity of prayer books published annually in America. "Years ago," he humorously remarked, "when all Jews prayed regularly, one *Siddur* was sufficient. Now, when so few retain this practice, we are treated to so many different kinds of prayer books."

Whether we agree with this observation or not, it certainly does not apply to the High Holy Days. On these days most American Jews do pray. On Rosh Hashanah and Yom Kippur the synagogues are crowded with serious worshippers. The High Holy Day prayer book

Rabbi Baruch Silverstein was born in Poland in 1914 and came to the U.S. at the age of 15. He received his B.S. from CCNY in 1936, was ordained at the Jewish Theological Seminary in 1940 and was granted a doctorate of Hebrew Literature at the Jewish Theological Seminary in 1950. He served as a Chaplain in World War II and Rabbi of Temple Emanu-El of Boro Park in Brooklyn from 1946 until his retirement in 1985. He taught Homiletics at the Jewish Theological Seminary, was President of the New York Board of Rabbis from 1978–1980, and served as President of Brooklyn's Zionist Region. Rabbi Silverstein published two books of his sermons as well as articles that appeared in "Congress Weekly" and "The Torch."

is more fortunate than its two companions: the Sabbath and Daily Prayer Book. The *Machzor* is a familial and well-rehearsed volume. Its pathways are well-trodden roads and its stopovers are well-known landmarks.

The prayerful mood of the High Holy Days extends also to those of us who are not so well acquainted with the ritual and order of Services. Once we cross over the threshold of the synagogue, we are gripped with a mystical craving to pray and to communicate with God. Unfamiliar with the art of communal prayer, we grope to express our sentiments in whatever means available to us. Unable to participate intelligently in the congregational ritual, we attempt to articulate our supplication in impromptu and halting ways of our own. On these Days of Awe we feel a strong compulsion to join our fellow Jews in prayer even though we have not been trained how to pray. Overwhelmed by the sanctity of the day and the crowded emotions of our souls, we are tempted to whisper silently, "Oh God, teach me how to pray. Put the proper words in my mouth."

The compulsive urge to pray has been frequently dramatized in Jewish literature. Our folklore is filled with many imaginative stories which describe the strange methods used by inarticulate worshipers in their attempts to communicate with God. There is the famed shepherd boy who, unable to withstand any longer his involuntary silence on Kol Nidre night in the synagogue, placed his fingers expertly in his mouth and emitted a loud and shrill whistle. The saintly rabbi smiled understandingly while many of the congregants stared angrily. There is the story of the farmer who became so annoyed at himself for not being able to decipher the strange letters of the prayer book that he tossed the volume out through the open window of the synagogue. Directing both his aim and eyes heavenward, he asked God to select the appropriate prayers from the prayer book and to apply it to his credit. There is the fascinating account of the villager who sat in the synagogue all day and repeatedly enumerated the letters of the Hebrew alphabet in their proper order. At the conclusion of each sequence, he asked God to arrange the letters into words and the words into paragraphs and to compose the prayers which he was unable to read from the printed pages.

But it is not only the untrained worshiper who needs guidance on the High Holy Days. All of us are in need of assistance. All of us search for clues as to how to articulate our prayers properly on Rosh

Hashanah. On these days we desire to clothe our supplications with greater intensity. On the High Holy Days we wish to go beyond the prescribed prayers of the printed ritual and to compose original meditations and supplementary prayers. On these sacred days we should like to offer prayers which transcend individual welfare and personal blessings. If possible, we should like to give vent to the deeper craving of becoming a blessing unto others. True to the spirit of the Days of Awe, we should like to pray not only for *B'racha* (blessing) but for *He-Yay B'racha* (*being* a blessing).

Such prayers, however, are not easily articulated. Such supplications present difficulties even to the habitual worshiper. Such meditations cannot be easily transformed into words. Some measure of assistance is needed. Instruction and guidance would be most welcome. Direction and inspiration are definitely called for.

Where shall we turn for help? To whom should we turn for guidance? We could, of course, turn for inspiration to our patriarchs and prophets, kings and poets, scholars and mystics, whose dialogues with God have been recorded for posterity in our sacred literature. But on this sacred day of Rosh Hashanah, we should like if at all possible to aspire for even higher standards and to emulate even greater models. If only God prayed! How we would like to repeat His prayers! If only the Master of the Universe employed such means of communications, how we would love to emulate His example! If only the Almighty articulated His Divine meditations, what a perfect model this would present to us!

But you will ask, "Does God pray? Is the Almighty also in need of help and inspiration?" Well, strange as it may seem, this is precisely the contention of the rabbis of the Talmud. Contrary to all our conceptions of the Deity, our ancient teachers maintain that God also prays. In a striking passage in the tractate *B'rchot* we find the following statement, "Said Rabbi Yohanan in the name of Rabbi Yosi: The Holy One, blessed be He resorts to prayer. How do we know it? Because it is written: And I shall bring them to My Holy mountain and I shall make them rejoice in My house of Prayer. Note, that the Biblical prayer deliberately states My house of Prayer and not Their house of prayer. From this we deduce that God also prays."

Having established biblical confirmation for this unusual contention, the rabbis, in the same passage, proceed to ask the next logical question, "What kind of prayers does God offer?" The answer consists of three specific prayers, which are surprisingly ordinary, homespun, and unsophisticated. Indeed, these supplications are so unpretentious and so human as to arouse a sense of disappointment and even disbelief. You and I would hardly associate such simple prayers with the Lord of the Universe. But obviously, our sages felt that these are most sensitive and vulnerable areas where even the Divine Master encounters occasional obstacles and difficulties. If the Holy One, Blessed be He, is in need of prayers in these areas, how much more so we, frail and erratic human beings?

The first prayer mentioned by the rabbis, consists of a simple request for success in controlling periodic outbursts of anger. "May it be My will," the Almighty prays, "to resist wrath and rage. May My compassion conquer My anger."

A most unusual prayer! If God does pray—an admission largely beyond our human conception—we would expect Him to offer more momentous and more sophisticated prayers. Yet we can readily see why this particular supplication should receive Divine preference. On more than one occasion, God's wrath resulted in such catastrophic destructiveness that He was filled with regret and remorse. Observing the ruin wrought by the waters of the flood, the Master of the Universe exclaimed, "I have placed the rainbow upon the horizon as a sign between Me and the earth that never again will a flood destroy the world." Immediately after the sin of the Golden Calf, Moses pleaded with God to subdue "His wrath against His people" and to recall the severe decree. The Biblical chapter describing this sorrowful incident concludes with the following meaningful sentence: "And the Lord repented over the evil that He contemplated to do."

Fortunately, we human beings are not capable of so much destructiveness. The harmful effects of fits of anger, however, must not be minimized. It brings pain and anguish, sorrow and distress, torment and grief. Momentary loss of temper is capable of provoking widespread an lingering harm and is invariably accompanied by remorse and regret. "Anger in the home," the Talmud warns, "is like a worm in a plant." It is a persistent despoiler. It corrodes and demoralizes. It spreads fear and alienates friends. It destroys not only the object of our rage but also our own personalities. A moment of anger may ruin a reputation which was earned over years and decades.

Judaism has always displayed a special sensitivity to this malady. The author of the Biblical Book of Ecclesiastes maintains "anger rests only in the lap of the foolish." In the Talmud we read, "A man who is quick to lose his temper—if he is wise, his wisdom is taken away from him; if he occupies an exalted position, it is decreed in the Heavens that he be demoted to a lower status." Hillel and Shamai were two of the greatest Mishnaic scholars, but Shamai remains relatively unknown because he was a *Kapdan*, subject to fits of anger. According to the Ethics of the Fathers, the outstanding characteristic of a Chassid is "hard to anger and easy to appease."

Our tradition's irritation with outbursts of anger is fully corroborated by our own personal observations. Do not such explosions invariably result in deep regret and painful remorse? What would we not do if we could only rescind and annul the intemperate words? How we would love to recall that period of wrath? Once the moment of rage passes and tempers cool, we shamefully realize that we have suffered from temporary madness, and we brood over our inability to exercise a greater measure of self-discipline. It was Thomas Jefferson who once said, "When angry count to ten before you speak; when very angry, count to one hundred." A saintly rabbi once counseled his disciples never to express displeasure at the instant of initial reaction; it is much wiser to say, "Yesterday I was angry with you."

The rabbinic statement associating God with this particular prayer contains great symbolic significance. God Himself experiences deep regret over His occasional outbursts of anger, and He prays for added strength in His solemn resolve to exercise greater measures of self-control. We would do well to join Him in this absorbing meditation.

The second Divine prayer is also surprisingly human and elementary. "May sentiments of pity permeate My relationships with My children. May mercy and compassion predominate over My other emotions." The Almighty prays (and He invites our participation in this intimate petition) that when He sits in judgment over His creatures He should be motivated by inclinations of tenderness and pity. The Lord of the Universe prays (and He wants us to join Him) that loving kindness and sympathy may be His constant companions.

We would do well to heed this Heavenly advice. We would do well to emulate this prayer and to join in this celestial chorus. If the All Merciful periodically resorts to petitions for added measures of compassion, how much more so should we indulge in such supplications? The "quality of mercy" is the noblest attribute of human beings. Through it we rise to the highest potentialities of being "a little lower than the angels." By ascending to the "Seat of Mercy" we reveal the image of God within us. He is a success as a human being, whose heart is overflowing with pity and tenderness; he is a failure, who remains callous to human suffering. True greatness is judged not by the immensity of possessions but by the intensity of compassion. Great is he who opens his heart to the needs and the cries of his fellowman. Deserving of honor is he who voluntarily assumes the problems of his neighbors and whose soul overflows with tender mercy. Pity and compassion are the distinguishing marks of man. Without it we forfeit the privilege of being the highest rung of the ladder of creation, and we descend to the category of animal.

Judaism does not neglect a single opportunity in stressing the significance of the development of a compassionate heart. It is one of the magnificent obsessions of our religion. Judaism is a religion of *Rachamanut*. The Almighty is often referred to as the *Ha-Rachaman*, the All-Merciful or the All-Compassionate. In our liturgy, God is described as occupying the "seat of mercy." The mystical strains of the shofar are intended to remind the Judge of the Universe to transfer His heavenly seat from the "chair of justice" to the "chair of mercy." When our ancient teachers wish to express their affection for the Jewish people, they refer to them as "compassionate people, the children of compassionate ancestors." The expression "pity for the living" has become a refrain of the Jewish way of life. In multiple direct and blunt admonitions Judaism urges its adherents to cultivate the art of compassion, the most luminous attribute of the Divine and the most glorious characteristic of the religious personality.

The third prayer of the Almighty is very much similar to the last petition, but it contains undertones of even keener sensitivity. "May My judgments and decrees be based not on strict laws and justice, and may I always be inclined to give My children the benefit of the doubt." In simpler language, God prays that when He sits in judgment over us He will judge us upon the scale of tolerance and sympathy; that He will overlook some of our erratic actions; that He will resist the tendencies of reprisals and retaliations; that He will be patient with our faults and forgiving of our sins.

This particular prayer of God should be especially welcome to us. This unusual Divine petition should evoke within us feelings of relief and gratefulness. For if God chose to judge his creatures upon the scale of strict justice, none of us would emerge pure and innocent. "If Thou should insist on the depths of the law, who would remain righteous before Thee?" Who knows what evil judgments would be decreed against us if the principle of "measure for measure" were applied to us. If the Lord were not tolerant of our faults, our heavenly ledger would contain many unattractive entries.

This Divine prayer, however, contains a deeper implication. Its true purpose is serve as an example for human meditation and articulation. This prayer of God is intended as a model for emulation by us upon earth. The Divine meditation is a dramatic reminder to man to cultivate such dispositions and to apply them in our daily relationships with our fellowman.

That humanity is in urgent need of this quality is obvious to any objective observer. Our civilization is literally infected with an almost endless variety of mutual antagonisms. Our society is plagued with national, racial, religious, and economic friction. Daily contacts between man and man are marked by mutual suspicions and distrust. We judge our fellowman uncharitably, and we seldom grant him the "benefit of doubt." We misinterpret innocent mistakes as deliberate attempts at inflicting harm. We are intolerant of shortcomings. We are skeptical about our neighbor's motives. We are engaged in a constant search for hidden plots and schemes. We question true expressions of idealism and altruism. "What is the angle" has become a popular idiom of our society. The tactics of the competitive market have been carried over to our friendships, our organizations, and even our homes. While in the world of business such suspicions are partly understandable and perhaps unavoidable, they are utterly intolerable in the business of life and in the market of human relationships. Such attitudes negate whatever joy and happiness we may derive from life. Such inclinations transform life into a virtual battlefield and our fellowmen into lurking enemies.

The oft-repeated story of the delicate truce is very much in place at this point. After a prolonged controversy, the two partners agreed to appear before their rabbi on the eve of the Day of Atonement. The respected teacher impressed upon them the sacred importance of the season of forgiveness and succeeded in arranging a reconciliation. But the period of peace proved to be short-lived. Before leaving the rabbi's study, one of the former opponents extended his hand to his companion in a gesture of friendship and said, "I wish you everything that you wish me." To which his associate quickly retorted, "You see, rabbi, he is starting up again."

Mutual suspicion is destructive of life and whatever happiness it has in store for us. It is a vicious cycle from which it becomes increasingly more difficult to escape. For every expression of distrust brings in its train acts of retaliation which, in turn, result in more intense forms of antagonism. Thus the vicious cycle continues to spin around its axis with ever-greater force, with an ever-widening circumference and with ever-deeper harm to ourselves and our fellowman.

How significant, therefore, that humanity take to its heart this Divine meditation! What added measures of happiness life would release if this reflection became the guiding principle of human conduct! How important for all of us to repeat this prayer with special fervor and sincerity: "May we resist the inclination toward suspicion and mistrust; may we cultivate the capacity of mutual confidence and faith; may we judge our fellowman with the scale of sympathy and tolerance; may we be forgiving of our neighbors' errors and may we be deserving of their forgiveness; may we be blessed with the Divine attribute of granting others the 'benefit of doubt.' "

These, then, are the three prayers of God which we are invited to emulate. These are the Divine meditations which we are summoned to transform into human reflections. These are the additional petitions which should supplement our well-rehearsed prayers for life, health, prosperity, and happiness! At first glance, these prayers may appear optional and unrelated to our petitions for a Happy New Year. But they certainly contain the elements which will make the next year a happier one for those around us. If this is so, is there anyone who will deny that it will also become a happier year for ourselves?

To Hold
With Open Arms

There are texts in us, in our commonplace experiences, if only we are wise enough to discern them.

One such experience fell to my lot not so long ago. There was nothing dramatic about its setting nor unusual in its circumstances. Yet to me it was moment of discovery, almost of revelation.

Let me recount it very briefly, as befits a text. After a long illness, I was permitted for the first time to step out of doors. As I crossed the threshold, sunlight greeted me. This is my experience, all there is to it. Yet, so long as I live, I shall never forget that moment. It was mid-January, a time of cold and storm up north, but in Texas, where I happened to be, a season much like our spring. The sky overhead was very blue, very clear, and very, very high. A faint wind blew from

Rabbi Milton Steinberg obtained his A.B. at CCNY, his M.A. from Columbia University, and was ordained at the Jewish Theological Seminary. He served Conservative Congregations in both Indianapolis, Indiana, and New York City. He authored several books including one novel, *As a Driven Leaf.* This brilliant preacher and lecturer has also served on the editorial board of "The Reconstructionist."

off the western plains, cool and yet somehow tinged with warmth—like a dry, chilled wine. Everywhere in the firmament above me, in the great vault between earth and sky, on the pavements, the buildings—the golden glow of the sunlight. It touched me, too, with friendship, with warmth, with blessing. As I basked in its glory, there ran through my mind those wonder words of the prophet about the sun which some day shall rise with healing on its wings.

In that instant I looked about me to see whether anyone else showed on his face the joy, almost the beatitude, I felt. But no, there they walked, men and women and children, in the glory of a golden flood, and so far as I could detect, there was none to give it heed. Then I remembered how often I, too, had been indifferent to sunlight; how often, preoccupied with petty and sometimes mean concerns, I had disregarded it. I said to myself, how precious is the sunlight but, alas, how careless of it are men. How precious—how careless. This has been a refrain sounding in me ever since.

It rang in my spirit when I entered my own home again after months of absence, when I heard from a nearby room the excited voices of my children at play; when I looked once more on the dear faces of some of my friends; when I was able for the first time to speak again from my pulpit in the name of our faith and tradition, to join in worship of the God who gives us so much of which we are so careless.

A resolution crystallized within me. I said to myself that at the very first opportunity I would speak of this. I knew full well that it is a commonplace truth, that there is nothing clever about my private rediscovery of it, nothing ingenious about my way of putting it. But I was not interested in being original or clever or ingenious. I wanted only to remind my listeners, as I was reminded, to spend life wisely, not to squander it.

I wanted to say to the husbands and wives who love one another, "How precious is your lot in that it is one of love. Do not be, even for a moment, casual with your good fortune. Love one another while yet you may."

And to parents, "How precious is the gift of your children. Never, never be too busy for the wonder and miracle of them. They will be grown up soon enough and grown away, too."

We human beings, we frail reeds who are yet, as Pascal said, thinking reeds, feeling reeds, how precious are our endowments: minds to know, eyes to see, ears to listen, hearts to stir with pity, and to dream of justice and of a perfected world. How often are we indifferent to all these!

We who are Jews and Americans, heirs of two great traditions, how fortunate our lot in both, and how blind we are to our double good fortune.

This is what struggled in me for utterance as it struggled in Edna St. Vincent Millay when she cried out, "O world I cannot hold thee close enough."

I want to urge myself and all others to hold the world tight, to embrace life with all our hearts and all our souls and all our might. For it is precious, ineffably precious, and we are careless, wantonly careless of it.

And yet, when I first resolved to express all this, I knew that it was only a half-truth.

Could I have retained the sunlight no matter how hard I tried? Could I have prevented the sun from setting? Could I have kept even my own eyes from becoming satiated and bored with the glory of the day? That moment had to slip away. Had I tried to hold on to it, what would I have achieved? It would have gone from me in any case. I would have been left disconsolate, embittered, convinced that I had been cheated.

But it is not only the sunlight that must slip away; our youth goes also, our years, our children, our senses, our lives. This is the nature of things, an inevitability. The sooner we make our peace with it the better. Did I urge myself a moment ago to hold on? I would have done better, it now begins to appear, to have preached the opposite doctrine of letting go, the doctrine of Socrates who called life a *peisithanatos*—a persuader of death, a teacher of the art of relinquishing. It was the doctrine of Goethe who said, "*Entsagen sollst, du sollst entsagen*," "Thou shalt renounce." It was the doctrine of the ancient rabbis who despite their love of life said, He who would die let him hold on to life.

It is a sound doctrine.

First, because, as we have just seen, it makes peace with inevitability. The inevitable is something with which everyone should be at peace. Second, because nothing can be more grotesque and more undignified than a futile attempt to hold on.

Let us think of the men and women who cannot grow old gracefully because they cling too hard to a youth that is escaping them; of the parents who cannot let their children go free to live their own lives;

of the people who in times of general calamity have only themselves in mind.

What is it that drives people to such unseemly conduct, to such flagrant selfishness except the attitude which I have just commended—a vigorous holding on to life? Besides, are there not times when one ought to hold life cheap, as something to be lightly surrendered? In defense of one's country, for example, in the service of truth, justice, and mercy, in the advancement of mankind?

This, then, is the great truth of human existence. One must not hold life too precious. One must always be prepared to let it go.

Now we are indeed confused. First we learn that life is a privilege, cling to it! Then we are instructed: Thou shalt renounce!

A paradox and self-contradiction! But neither the paradox nor the contradiction are of my making. They are a law written into the scheme of things: that a man must hold his existence dear and cheap at the same time.

Is it not, then, an impossible assignment to which destiny has set us? It does not ask of us that we hold life dear at one moment and cheap at the next, but that we do both simultaneously. Now I can grasp something in my fist or let my hand lie open. I can clasp it to my breast or hold it at arm's length. I can embrace it, enfolding it in my arms, or let my arms hang loose. But how can I be expected to do both at once?

To which the answer is: With your body, of course not. But with your spirit, why not?

Is one not forever doing paradoxical and mutually contradictory things in his soul?

One wears his mind out in study and yet has more mind with which to study. One gives away his heart in love and yet has more heart to give away. One perishes out of pity for a suffering world and is the stronger therefor.

So, too, it is possible at one and the same time to hold on to life and let it go, provided . . . well, let me put it this way. We are involved in a tug of war: Here, on the left, is the necessity to renounce life and all it contains; here, on the right, the yearning to affirm it and its experiences. Between these two is a terrible tension, for they pull in opposite directions.

But suppose that here in the center I introduce a third force, one that lifts upward. My two irreconcilables now swing together, both pulling down against the new element. The harder they pull, the closer together they come.

God is the third element, that new force that resolves the terrible contradiction, the intolerable tension of life.

For this purpose it does not especially matter how we conceive God. I have been a great zealot for a mature idea of God. I have urged again and again that we think through our theology, not limping along on a child's notion of God as an old man in the sky. But for my immediate purpose, all of this is irrelevant. What is relevant is this: that so soon as a man believes in God, so soon indeed as he wills to believe in Him, the terrible strain is eased; nay, it disappears, and that for two reasons.

In the first place, because a new and higher purpose is introduced into life, the purpose of doing the will of God, to put it in Jewish terms, of performing the *mitzvoth*. This now becomes the reason for our existence. We are soldiers whose commander has stationed them at a post. How we like our assignment, whether we feel inclined to cling to it or to let it go is an irrelevant issue. Our hands are too busy with our duties to be either embracing the world or pushing it away.

That is why it is written: "Make thy will conform to His, then His will be thine, and all things will be as thou desirest."

But that, it might be urged, only evades the problem. By concentrating on duty we forget the conflicting drives within ourselves. The truth is, however, that, given God, the problem is solved not only be evasion but directly; that it is solved, curiously enough, by being made more intense. For, given God, everything becomes more precious, more to be loved and clung to, more embraceable; and yet at the same time easier to give up.

Given God, everything becomes more precious.

That sunshine in Dallas was not a chance effect, a lucky accident. It was an effect created by a great Artist, the Master Painter of Eternity. Because it came from God's brush it is more valuable even than I had at first conceived.

And the laughter of children, precious in itself, becomes infinitely more precious because the joy of the cosmos is in it.

And the sweetness of our friends' faces is dearer because these are fragments of an infinite sweetness.

All of life is the more treasurable because a great and Holy Spirit is in it.

And yet, it is easier for me to let go.

For these things are not and never have been mine. They belong to the Universe and the God who stands behind it. True, I have been privileged to enjoy them for an hour but they were always a loan due to be recalled.

And I let go of them the more easily because I know that as parts of the divine economy they will not be lost. The sunset, the bird's song, the baby's smile, the thunder of music, the surge of great poetry, the dreams of the heart, and my own being, dear to me as every man's is to him, all these I can well trust to Him who made them. There is poignancy and regret about giving them up, but no anxiety. When they slip from my hands they will pass to hands better, stronger, and wiser than mine.

This then is the insight which came to me as I stood some months ago in a blaze of sunlight: Life is dear, let us then hold it tight while we yet may; but we must hold it loosely also!

Only with God can we ease the intolerable tension of our existence. For only when He is given, can we hold life at once infinitely precious and yet as a thing lightly to be surrendered. Only because of Him is it made possible for us to clasp the world, but with relaxed hands, to embrace it, but with open arms.

SAUL TEPLITZ

America—Haven to the Oppressed

The entire history of America's emergence as a haven for the oppressed, particularly of the Jewish people, testifies to the prophetic role that Providence had destined the new Promised Land to play in the history of man's wanderings. The founding fathers of this country, who saw a parallel between the history of ancient Israel and their new Zion, established this nation on a base cemented with Hebraic mortar. The first United States sovereign seal, submitted to the Congress by Jefferson, Adams, and Franklin, portrayed the Egyptians engulfed in the Red Sea with Moses and the Israelites safe on the opposite shore. At one time, the Pilgrims seriously considered adopting Hebrew as their national language, and the early settlers gave Hebrew names to their children.

Rabbi Saul Teplitz received his B.A. from the University of Pittsburgh. He was both ordained and received his doctorate in Hebrew Literature from the Jewish Theological Seminary. He served several Conservative Congregations before retiring from the Congregation Sons of Israel in Woodmere, New York, in 1991. During his career, he served as President of the Rabbinical Assembly, Synagogue Council of America; occupied high office in several communal organizations; edited 12 volumes of "Best Jewish Sermons," and wrote numerous articles in major Anglo-Jewish periodicals.

The Torah portion of this Shabbat opens with God telling Abraham, "Lech Lecha—Go forth from your native land and from your father's house." It was surely difficult for Abraham to leave the household of his parents and his native land to go to places unknown. Abraham was the first Jew to go into Galut. One rabbinic commentator says, "*Avraham Avinu mekabel gzara zo lmalaya r'tzon adoshem.*"

The first Jew came to the Galut called America in the year 1654. But the basic saga of Jewish life in America began with the pogroms that were launched over hundred years ago in Russia in 1881 under the reign of Alexander III and his successor Nicholas.

Living conditions in Eastern Europe were deplorable for all peasant and proletarian groups, but for the Jews, they were intolerable. From 1881 to 1924 Jews came to America, first in the thousands and finally in the hundreds of thousands. By 1924, nearly three million Jews had made their way to America, settling mainly in the huge ghettos of New York, Philadelphia, Baltimore, Chicago, and other large cities of the East and Middle West. Often, the head of the family would come first, leaving his wife and children behind, until he had made enough money to bring them over and reunite the family. What resulted was their transplantation from the "shtetl" to the American ghettos.

The synagogues were often organized on a European community basis: the Polisher shul, the Litvisher shul, the Galitzaner shul. The Landmanschaften were the social agencies by which those who came over first could offer help to those who came later. They endured the wretchedness of the sweat shops or lived in the back part of their pathetic stores, driven on to any sacrifice to educate their children. Their goal was to enable their offspring to fit more easily into the American scene and to guarantee their own integration into the fabric of American life.

The passage of the Johnson Bill in 1924 ended unrestricted immigration thus stranding millions in European countries who could no longer escape from poverty or repression by flight to America. There were repeated incidents of anti-Semitism. In the 1920s, when President Lowell tried to restrict Jewish admission to Harvard, he claimed that fifty percent of all the students caught stealing from the Widener Library in the previous year were Jewish. When he was asked how many students stole books, he had to admit that there were only two.

Eddie Jacobson had served with Captain Harry Truman in World War I. Later he became his partner in an unprofitable haberdashery store in Kansas City. Bess Truman's family, the Wallows, were aristocracy and therefore never invited the Jacobsons to their home. Yet, Truman, who would not invite Jews into his living room in Missouri, met with Jacobson in the White House in 1948 when Jacobson managed to persuade Truman to meet with Chaim Weitzman. This resulted in America's recognition of the newly established State of Israel in 1948.

Michael Peschkowsky was born in Berlin in 1931 and came to the United States in 1939. He could barely speak a few words of English. He became Mike Nichols, a foremost writer in the American theater. Today, there are more Jews enrolled in Harvard Law School than any other ethnic group. Swarthmore, organized as a Quaker School, has more Jews than Quakers in attendance. Jews are abundantly represented in medicine, science, research, creative arts, and government service. Only a few years ago, there were two Jewish Senators and twelve Jewish members of the House of Representatives. Today there are ten Jewish Senators and a fluctuating higher count of Jewish Representatives, as well as state legislators.

Starting as a poor, proletarianized minority, bearing the onus of substantial discrimination and prejudice, Jews have economically attained living standards that would have astonished their grandparents. One recent study of groups in American life has called the ascent of the Jews "the greatest collective Horatio Alger story in American immigration history." With hard work and faith in individual achievement Jews have advanced from shtetl to steerage to slums and then to suburbs. Statistics indicate that in their income level, Jews have moved into first place, forging ahead of the Episcopalians, who had been the leaders for generations. In the 1983 Forbes magazine, there was a listing of the financial resources of Americas top four hundred richest citizens, each of whom had amassed $100 million. The clearly Jewish names and those active in philanthropy revealed close to twenty percent were Jewish.

At the beginning of the twentieth century, Israel Zangwill described America as a melting pot in which all groups would merge into a synthetic homogeneity. But that prediction soon outlived the reality. It was quickly realized that the flight from one's origins weakened America and thinned out its vitality. This great nation is not a melting pot but an orchestra in which each group adds its distinctive differences, its ancestral treasures to the symphony of our free society.

We, American Jews, have the privilege of living in two civilizations. English is our language but so is Hebrew. Jewish history is our background but so is the history of America. Lincoln and Jefferson are our heroes together with Moses, Akiba, and Maimonides. We sing American ballads as well as Chasidic and Israeli folk songs with equal ardor. We move from one civilization to another with such ease that we are scarcely aware of the change. The process is facilitated by the essential harmony of spirit between the two traditions. Both are expressions of democracy, emphasizing the worth of the individual and his right to freedom with a passionate devotion to the ideal of social justice.

Many years ago, the great Jewish philosopher Ahad Ha'am wrote an essay entitled, "Slavery in the Midst of Freedom," in which he declared that East European Jewry enjoyed spiritual freedom within the structure of political and economic bondage, while Jews living in the West were living in a condition of spiritual slavery within the context of political freedom.

I hope that Jewish historians of the future will write about the American Jewish community, describing it as living in a condition of *charut b'toch charut*, "spiritual freedom and devotion in the midst of physical liberty." May the promise that God made to Abraham be fulfilled for us "and you shall be a blessing and all the families of the earth shall bless themselves by you."

MORDECAI WAXMAN

Why Be Jewish?

If anti-Semitism does not compel you to be a Jew, whether you want
to be or not, and on the other hand, you have no strong belief in Jewish religious ideas or in Jewish religious behavior and you are young,
alive, and well in an America where today being a Jew is no bar to the
satisfaction of personal, economic, social, or cultural desires—why
should you work at being a Jew?

That is the issue which has recently produced a spate of books
and articles and symposia on why be Jewish as well as a strong concern about Jewish identity and Jewish continuity.

The alarm bell has been sounded for the Jewish community in
America by the growth of the rate of intermarriage from seven per-

Rabbi Mordecai Waxman was ordained at the Jewish Theological Seminary in
1941. He has served as Rabbi of Temple Israel in Great Neck, New York, since 1947.
Rabbi Waxman has edited "Tradition and Change," as well as the Rabbinical Assembly journal, "Conservative Judaism" from 1969–1974. He has also served as President
of the Rabbinical Assembly (1974–1976), President of the World Council of Synagogues
(1981-1985), and President of Synagogue Council of America (1983–1985). Rabbi
Waxman was also a Chaplain during World War II.

cent in 1965 to over fifty percent between 1985 and 1990 and it may be higher by now. Combined with belated marriages by Jews—from twenty-eight to thirty-two years of age and a low birth rate, this portends a major decline in American Jewish population, which has already gone down from being three and three tenth percent of the population in the 1930s to two and a half percent of the American population today.

The anomaly is that most American Jews are fixed in their Jewish identity and have no intention of changing it. They just don't feel that it ought to control their pattern of behavior or whom they marry and for great numbers, it has no meaning as a system of religious beliefs. They are the first Jewish generation which lives in a time and place in which being born Jewish is not destiny.

However, the existence of Israel where Jewishness is taken for granted, whether or not given traditional content, and where in-group marriages are taken for granted would seem to guarantee the ongoing existence of the Jewish people.

In Israel, the future of the Jewish people or some form of Judaism is automatic, but in America and in all Diaspora, neither Jews nor Judaism can be continued without major effort, commitment, and sacrifices. Therein lies our problem.

The sacrifices involved are making time for Jewish children and young people to pursue studies which don't appear on the records of their college applications and which teach such peculiar concepts as responsibility. It involves financial sacrifice to maintain synagogues and schools and the many agencies which maintain Jewish life in America. It involves concern with the welfare of Jewish people wherever they may be and a willingness to help them financially, politically, and personally. It involves setting aside the Sabbath as a special day with special modes of behavior and attitudes. It involves not only attention to the cholesterol content and the fat content and the caloric content of the food you eat, but also to what might be known as the *treif* content or alternatively, the kosher content. Above all, it requires a sacrifice of choice in whom you marry and how you raise your children and perhaps even of where you live. In short, you have to decide whether you are prepared to live under the sign of the *Mezzuzah*.

Our ancestors made these and far more drastic sacrifices because they lived in a closed and hostile society. We are perhaps the first generation who are living in an open society where anti-Semitism is presently at least quiescent. We are products of a society which is dedicated to enjoyment rather than sacrifice. Why then should we work at being Jews in America?

I would like to suggest and discuss three major reasons as answers to why be a Jew and why sacrifice to be one.

1. The first is the Jewish stories.
2. The second is the personal needs of people.
3. The third is the needs of the world.

1. Why work at being Jewish if you are an American Jew in an open society? One reason is the Jewish stories.

By stories I mean the great stories which have become the common heritage of Western man and which underlie civilization today.

The great stories of course are the Biblical stories capable of infinite interpretations. Thus only Adam and Eve were created so that no person can say, as the Talmud reminds us, that my ancestors are greater than yours. The Garden of Eden story is there to remind us that when everyone denies responsibility, the good world cannot endure. Cain and Abel are there to set the tone that we are indeed our brothers keepers and that spilled blood cries out from the ground. The Exodus is the shaping story for the idea of freedom. Sinai is there to remind us that the world cannot exist without a moral law and that there are moral imperatives which are superior to the vagaries of time and place and superior to the whim of different societies.

The great Jewish stories which set forth a situation and leave it to us to discover the moral speak to us in different tones and different times of our lives. But what is unique is the variety and richness of such stories which cover the range of civilized history, afford us the opportunity to pick among available pasts to speak to different situations.

Thus the rabbis of the second and third centuries who spoke to the needs of their generation dipped into the Bible to set as the Torah reading on Rosh Hashanah, which we say marks the birthday of the world, not the story of creation, but the story of Abraham and Issac. Faced as they were with the destruction of the Temple with the bloody conclusion of the Bar Kachba revolt against Rome in the second century, they chose to make the message of Rosh Hashanah, that Jews following the example of Abraham, do not abandon their faith in God even when God seems to demand the impossible in the sacrifice of Isaac.

The message of Abraham as the knight of faith as Kirkegard labels him, and the intervention of God to reward that faith by saving Isaac and thereby ensuring both the continuity of the time and the faith spoke to many generations. Generations of our ancestors lay upon the altar with upraised knives above them and maintained faith and secured survival. Here is one of the great stories then which spoke to generations. But in our times the knife did fall and Isaac was immolated on the altar.

Our time and generation has needed a new story which reminds us that we need not wait passively for God's intervention, but can bring salvation by our own actions. And so the great stories of our time center about the creation of the state of Israel, of the War of Independence, of the miracle of 1967, of the shofar blast of Rabbi Goren at the Western Wall which signaled the return of the Jewish people to Jerusalem, of the swearing in, in the early days of Israel, of army officers in the ruins of Masada, the last symbol of heroic resistance to the Romans in the war of the years 66-73 and of the oath taken that Masada would not fall again.

These stories interpreted and reinterpreted have been providing answers for a generation or more, but now they seem to be failing.

Yes, they still speak to the emotion and nostalgia of most Jews, but they have ceased to be decisive in guiding their behavior.

While the Biblical stories in their infinite meaning continue to speak to those who will listen, we, I believe, now need to speak to the human dilemma and to the complexities of life which now overwhelm a generation which no longer resonates to Tradition, Tradition of *Fiddler on the Roof*.

We do, for *there is another story*. And *we* are the story. The last fifty years have been one of the greatest periods in Jewish history, indeed, in some respects the greatest. The Holocaust was a greater enslavement than the slavery of Egypt. Far more Jews fought for freedom in World War II and in the Israeli Wars than the 600,000 men at arms of Joshua. We are of the generation which created the state of Israel and defended it and developed it.

Sitting here are men and women who came out of the concentration camps and the ghetto unbroken, to rebuild their lives in other lands and to achieve greatly. Here are others who were heroes of resistance. Sitting here are men and women who have fought in three or four wars for the survival of the state of Israel. *We are the story.*

288

Here are the men and women who have made American Jewry the most creative Diaspora community in history in every realm of Jewish and general culture. Yes we did not compose the Talmud, but we have given it life and application in a new land, in new circumstances, 1500 years after it was completed.

Here sit the children and the grandchildren who have inherited the efforts and the fruits of that generation.

We are the story. The question is will new generations continue the story and add to it.

2. It is worth working at being a Jew, secondly, because it offers answers to the deeply felt needs we all come to feel.

For many of us, our lives are filled in our youth with our professions and business, with success, with marriage, with buying a home, with raising a family. Then suddenly, all this is accomplished. The challenge is gone, the goals are achieved, and *what is left?* The prospect of retirement and of endless rounds of golf and endless restaurant meals.

There must be something more and *there is something* more. The Hebrew Poet Bialik caught the mood and the need in his poem.

And it shall come to pass when the days shall grow long
And every day shall be like yesterday and like the day before . . .
Then shall weariness lay hold of man and beast alike . . .
Then hunger shall appear
A hunger mighty and great before
Not hunger for bread or bard, but hunger for the Messiah.

Yes, there is a hunger and a deep need to feel that life has meaning beyond being an economic machine or a role player in the family. Our problem is that many of us are in the position of the two Zen monks lost in the desert who finally sink to the ground in sheer weariness. One says to the other, my brother is lost. The other, after meditating replies. No I am here. The *way* is lost.

It is precisely the *way* that is a central concept in Jewish life for that is what *Halachah* means, the way. We usually use the term as though it refers to Jewish law. But it is far more. It means the path to go on—and so to the seeker Judaism offers a way which embraces believing, behaving and belonging.

The Jewish way starts with belonging before believing. From the beginning anyone born into a Jewish family with the slightest sense of tradition is surrounded by, involved in ceremonies thousands of years old. They embrace birth and marriage and death. They make a boy and now a girl as they enter young adulthood study ancient texts and recite blessings which proclaim that Jews are a chosen people and that the Torah is God's gift to us. We are called to the Torah or commemorated in tombstones by Jewish names—Hebrew or Yiddish—as so and so, the son of so and so, and so back, in some cases, to the eighth generation.

To be born a Jew is then to be born into a community united by destiny and committed to a covenant of meaning which answers the hunger for worth and meaning which all of us share. The covenant may be ignored, rejected, or never understood or communicated, but it is what has distinguished the Jewish people throughout its history.

Paul Johnson who has written a perceptive view of Jewish history from the point of view of a non-Jew says that he embarked upon his study because it gave him the opportunity to study a people four thousand years old who have lived in all areas, penetrated and influenced all of them, to address the most intractable of all human questions. What are we on earth for?

"Is history meeting a series of events whose sum is meaningless? Is there no fundamental moral difference between the history of the human race and the history of ants? Or is there a providential plan of which we are, however humbly, the agents."

His answer is "no people has ever insisted more firmly than the Jews that history has a purpose and humanity a destiny."

In a world where national purpose has disappeared and grand visions of mankind have collapsed, Judaism offers to the searcher for meaning a community to which one comes by destiny or by choice, but which is united by a covenant of meaning that human history has significance and destiny.

The Jewish way teaches us to translate belonging into behaving.

The most notable example of that is that Jews belong to a four thousand-year-old community, which is scattered across the globe, yet takes seriously the statement "All Israelites are responsible for one another." This is, I suppose what is now meant by *Jewish identity*. Dedication to this principle has been translated in this century into the huge development of Jewish philanthropy which made possible the rescue and resettlement of survivors of the Holocaust, which helped create and maintain Israel, and which, in making the right of Russian Jews to leave an international issue, began the weakening of the Soviet

Union. But more remarkable still is the sense of peoplehood which enabled a scattered and persecuted community with no political center or power to gather together just one hundred years ago to propose to create a Jewish state in the ancestral land with a minuscule Jewish population and to succeed.

Behind all these events which are taken for granted by a younger generation was the principle which united an older generation, religious and nonreligious, the involved and even the marginal, in moments of great decision because they heard ancestral voices proclaiming *Kol Yisrael Arevin Zeh Ba-Zeh*, all Israelites are responsible for one another.

But, the gift of Judaism to the individual in our time is deeper and wider than philanthropy and a sense of mutual responsibility. Judaism offers a behavior pattern, an approach to life and society which is desperately needed in a world where the mundane, the profane, the material, and the progressive reduction of standards of morality and behavior is destroying our society.

The Jewish position is that the world and all actions must be seen from the point of view of *Kedushah*, of sanctity, and it calls for a return to the sacred.

The Jewish approach asks us to behave as though every ordinary action is sanctified. That is the thesis behind the injunction to recite one hundred blessings, *Brachot*, a day—blessings whose point is that the ordinary is extraordinary and therefore one is enjoined to pause a moment in an action and to utter a blessing. Thus we bless the actions of ingestion such as *Hamotzi* and all similar blessings, and also to give thanks for excretion and for the functioning of the body.

We give thanks for the functioning of the mind, for the ability to see, for the satisfaction of needs, for clothing, and for freedom. There is a blessing for beholding beauty, for encountering a person of wisdom, for meeting a ruler.

The sense that time itself can be sanctified, that every action from eating to sexual relations can be viewed and treated as sacred is the underlying premise for Judaism's view of the world. Therefore it makes every one of our actions and attitudes fraught with meaning, instead of being another trivial action.

Belonging and behaving may culminate in believing, but belief is something no one can command. It is often hard to believe that there is a God, since so many bizarre things happen in the world or to believe that God cares or that God is good.

Judaism has no formula for instant conversion to such belief. There are some who like Job can say, "Though he slay me, yet I trust in him." There are others like Jeremiah who wrestle with disbelief even while they believe. Jacob Glatstein, the Yiddish poet, has caught the dilemma and the need of the modern Jew when he writes:

> Who will dream you?
> Who will remember you?
> Who will *deny* you?
> Who will yearn after you then?
> Who *will flee you over a bridge of longing?*
> *Only to return again.*

Many in our generation have indeed fled, but there is a bridge of longing over which one may return. That is where the Jewish concept of *Teshuvah*, *"Return,"* comes in.

It is not based on instant conversion which is always suspect. It is rather based on a pattern of learning which supplements behaving and belonging.

There is a Jewish path for return over the bridge of longing once that longing is aroused and that is the path of study and learning, the immersion in the great texts in which the Jewish spirit has expressed itself.

Does it pay to work at being Jewish? To seek belonging, behaving, believing. Yes the reward is great. It makes you and your life and deeds important and prevents you from being trivial.

Third and last, does it pay to work at being Jewish? Yes, because the world needs Jews.

Winston Churchill once said, "Some people like Jews, some do not, but no thoughtful man can deny the fact that they are beyond question the most formidable and the most remarkable race which has ever appeared in the world."

Yes, there has been great Jewish talent and the twentieth century has in many respects been a Jewish century in the degree to which Jewish men and women of talent and of genius have shaped modern thought, science, and culture.

But the great contribution of the Jewish people has been to discover, to define, to refine, and to represent the organizing ideas of our civilization: the idea of equality before the law, the dignity of the human being, the sanctity of life, the democratic idea which emerges from the idea of man created in the image of God, and the notion not only that you should love your neighbor as yourself, but the stranger as yourself. All have their origins in the Bible and their implementation in Jewish life. To that one must add, among many other things, the Sabbath and the Jubilee year whose motto "proclaim liberty throughout the land" is inscribed on the Liberty Bell.

If much of this is now the common change of civilization, there are nonetheless even new elements which Jews are introducing into civilization and even old elements of which we are the standard bearers.

No less important is that the Jewish people though persecuted and slaughtered has never lost its will to live as a separate entity and its capacity to overcome superior power.

Israel has proved this time and again. It has served as an example to many oppressed minorities. I myself, attending a conference with Black African churchmen in Kenya, heard the references to the Exodus and the actions of Israel as an inspiration. We in the Jewish delegation were looked upon as the living embodiment of this idea.

The world needs the Jews, because in a world where misery is great and where hatred seems to be growing and where compassion is diminishing, the Jewish people is committed to *Tikun Olam*. The Jews have been the inventors and the carriers of the Messianic vision that the world can be perfected and man is God's copartner in *Tikun Olam*. The phrase in the *Olenu* prayer recited thrice daily that we are obliged to perfect the world under the sovereignty of God is the Jewish credo.

The world needs people who are dedicated to the Messianic idea of perfecting man and society and who are willing to agitate and to labor to realize Kafka's paradox that the Messiah will come only after the Messiah has come.

But at the beginning and at the end, the great Jewish idea for which Jews have stood unyieldingly has been that God is one and that the idols must be brought down. We did bring down the ancient world of idolatry directly and through daughter religions. But we have seen them succeeded by other idols: the state, ideologies, materialism, moral relativism, and all the idolatries of thought and doctrine. This we have opposed by speech and action, by blood and sacrifice. The collapse of Russia which began with obdurate Jewish Refuseniks is one of the latest examples of our long and unyielding battle with idolatry.

The world needs Jews.

293

Jews need to learn that there is in the final analysis, to quote Ecclesiastes, there is no discharge in the war.

Let us then on these days of awe and decision recognize that we live in great days which call for great and creative decisions.

The choice that he has before him is exemplified in the story attributed to the Rebbe of Kotzk and retold by Peretz; a story of the goat, which was designed to reflect the Jewish people.

In a remote Russian village there was a goat which had exceptionally long horns. They were due to the fact that the goat fed upon the grass in a ruined synagogue which had been watered by the blood of poets, singers, visionaries, and martyrs. In the silence of the night when all the village was asleep the goat would come to the village square, stand upon its hind legs and hook its horns over the moon and ask when will the Messiah come. The moon not knowing the answers would refer the question to the planets, and the planets to the stars, and finally a voice from on high would say, the time is not yet. However, one day a Jew discovered that the goat had very long horns. He needed a snuffbox, so he took a piece of the horn and fashioned a very beautiful box. He showed it around the village and everyone asked where he had gotten so beautiful a box? He pointed to the goat and so everyone in the village went and took pieces of the horn and fashioned a snuff box and now every Jew in the village has a snuff box. But the goat is no longer capable of reaching the moon and inquiring of the Messiah. We do indeed have an open society and free choice. The choice before us is the snuff box or the Messiah. Which will we choose?

DAVID J. WOLPE

Time and Chance
Befall Us All

Sometimes an entire world view can be summed up in a simple state-ment. Teaching a class in which we discussed the book of Koheleth, I was struck by the following famous quotation from the book of Koheleth (9:11), time and chance happen to all.

Time and chance.

I think this is the motto for the *Yamim Noraim*, for Rosh Hashanah and Yom Kippur. For we are confronted this year, as every year, with these two different and deep sides of human loss.

What does Koheleth mean by "chance"? We can understand by looking at a prayer from this time of year. It is a peculiar prayer, strange

Rabbi David J. Wolpe received his B.A. from the University of Pennsylvania, his doctorate in Hebrew Literature from the University of Judaism, and his M.A. and ordination from the Jewish Theological Seminary. Rabbi Wolpe teaches at the Jewish Theological Seminary where he serves as assistant to the Chancellor. He also serves on the Editorial Board of the Conservative movement's Torah Commentary. This ac-claimed author has written for national publications and has appeared on national television programs.

and forbidding, and we want to ignore it. Listen to the words of the *Unetaneh Tokef.*

On Rosh Hashanah it is written, and on Yom Kippur it is sealed; Who shall live and who shall die? Who by fire and who by water? Who by sword and who by beast? Who by famine and who by thirst? Who by strangling and who by stoning?

Time and chance. Here it is talking not about time, but about chance. *Pegah.* "For time and death will happen to them all." *Ki ait va'fegah yikre et kulam* (Koheleth 9:11). About the possibility of sudden catastrophe, the chance that something unknown, unexpected, unforeseen will suddenly tear our lives apart.

Perhaps the list seems remote. But imagine how frightening this prayer would be, how fearful a litany, if instead of being written in the language of the middle ages, if we translated it into our terms, and we said, "Who by cancer, and who by heart attack? Who by car accident and who by airplane crash? Who by hunger and who by heartbreak?"

The message is now clear and frightening; that to each of us, to all of us, to any of us, at any moment, a sudden calamity can occur, the moment that breaks and batters us; the instant that renders us helpless; one of those awful moments to which the reaction always is, "I didn't believe that it could happen to me." It is more common than we like to think. Suddenly, there is a tear in existence, as abrupt and as shattering as the gloomy diagnosis of a doctor, or the foreboding sound of a phone waking you up at 3:00 A.M. It rings. We answer. And nothing is ever the same.

But that is not the only kind of loss or of death. It is not only chance about which Koheleth teaches us, he teaches us about time. There is also the slow corrosive effect of loss and pain. Time takes a toll, exacts a price.

We all feel the slow, increasing lines that time draws deeper and deeper on our faces and the faces of those we love. People we thought of as perpetually young, friends, actors, musicians are now old. We are surprised. Even though we know intellectually that clocks don't move backwards, when we see the sweep of the second hand turn to minutes and days and weeks and years, and lifetimes, it always amazes us. Wasn't it just yesterday? How quickly it passed! In the preceding year, each of us, I am sure, has seen both sides of Koheleth's wise and frightening words. We have seen *pegah*, "chance," the single, horrible instant that leaves life in tatters, the pivot upon which the future turns.

We have also seen *et*, "time," the slow, painful process of dissolution, of decline and decay. Perhaps it is the decline of an individual or the pained strains of a marriage being pulled apart, even the slow disappearance from our lives of an activity, a hobby, or an idea that was once so important—that once fascinated us and filled us up, that once spoke to us. Now, its magic has corroded, and time has carried it off, out of our lives.

Time and chance.

We think of that now because this is the instant to understand and appreciate the message of the season. For this is the time, above all others, to recognize, to feel in our hearts, that there is very little time.

This is the time to recognize Koheleth's lesson; to live before we are robbed of life, slowly or swiftly, by weakness or by tragedy.

This is the time to recognize that there can be no delay in living. We all delay it—after school, after job, after children, then we will live. Time and chance happen to all. Every day of life is as precious as every other. We all prepared, and we never lived. Stop preparing. This is it. Each day of life is as precious as any other, no matter what the age: two, ten, thirty, fifty, eighty. This is life. We are living. We tell college students that it is not "real" life.

But intensity or duration have nothing to do with reality. Every bit of life is real, and it won't get repeated.

"Whatever it is in your power to do, do it with all your might," teaches Koheleth (9:10). It depends upon you, and we do not last forever. But in order to truly do that, you must understand the end of Koheleth's phrase *Yikre et Kulam*, "To everyone."

Not only to you, but to that person upon whom you depend; not only to you, but to that tower of strength. Each of us is as subject to loss as any other. No one is immune. So we cannot stake our existence on someone or something outside of ourselves. No matter how wonderful your relationship or how important your mission, we must never live solely for someone or something else. Ezekiel (2:1): "Son of man, stand on your feet that I may speak to you." If you cannot stand on your own two feet, even God cannot speak to you face to face. Do not live your life on the back of another. There is no human back so strong, so secure that it cannot break.

Yet, even the great feel the need to make a godlike protector out of human beings. Gorki said of Tolstoy, "I am not bereft in this world as long as that old man is alive." He pegged his existence on someone else. Jefferson, as he was dying, said, "At least Adams is still alive." Adams died the same day. You cannot live off others. That is not love. Love comes from a sturdy soul, not from an emptiness that needs the strength of another to fill it up. For no one else's strength is always certain. No one else's protection can last forever.

The first and most painful lesson of Rosh Hashanah and Yom Kippur is both to love and care for others and to know that everything passes away. The *Unetaneh Tokef,* the prayer we read before, goes on to say, "We are like a fragile vessel, like the grass that withers, the flower that fades, the shadow that passes, the cloud dispersed in the sky, the dream that flies away."

Do not live life as if it were forever. Do not delay that marvelous task you have in mind, thinking that your powers will always be here. Do not forego the word of encouragement or love because it can be spoken tomorrow. Do not turn away from what you need and can give, because there will be time.

Ki et vafegah yikre et kulam. "And they will steal the moment from you, and it will be lost, gone forever.

Our tradition teaches in a unique way the mixture of love and strength we all seek. There is a marvelous story in the Talmud, at the very end of the tractate *Sotah,* which stands in contrast to the stories of Gorki and Jefferson, who both pinned their hopes on others.

After the destruction of the Temple and the death of the scholars of the Torah, the devastated authors of the Mishnah, having seen their pious colleagues murdered before their eyes, composed the following dejected lament.

When Rabbi Meir died, there were no more storytellers.
Once Ben Azzai died, there were no more true students of Torah.
When Rabbi Hanina ben Dosa died, there were no more men of action.
With the death of Rabbi Jose Ketanta, there were no more men of piety.
When Rabbi Johanan ben Zakkai died, there was no more wisdom.
And when Rebbe died, Rabbi Judah, the prince, died, it was the end of
    humility and fear of sin.
One by one, all the important qualities of the world seemed to pass away.

All the great spirits lived in the past. Everything was gone. All merit had perished. You can feel the devastation of the rabbis. Their world had shattered and lay in pieces at their feet. And so they could no longer believe they were as good, as important, as what had gone before. But the Talmud does not stop here. For Rabbi Joseph stood up. Rabbi Joseph stood up and said, "Do not teach that humility has ceased with the death of Rebbe; for I am here."

At first, it sounds arrogant. "Don't say humility is gone . . . for I am here." But Rabbi Joseph is saying something important and very courageous. Humility and virtue do not belong to the past or only to others. They have to be here, in the world. Life is too brief to renounce what we ourselves can do. We too can be wise and good and humble, we too can fear sin. We will not allow the past or even those we admire in the present to rob us of our own place and purpose and vision. Be like Rabbi Joseph. Do not make gods out of human beings. No one has even most of the answers: no boss, no spouse, no expert, no scholar, no radio psychologist, no therapist, no rabbi. In the end, nothing is sacred if you do not accept the sanctity of yourself.

The same God that made Moses made me, made you, and he made us for a brief time. So let us not depend upon others to do the work in this world. Let us not give our lives away. It is a profound tradition that begins the new year by reminding us of death. But it is only by acknowledging death that we understand the inestimable, the incalculable value of our own lives.

Only that is precious which passes away. Only that is priceless which will not last forever, and we will not last forever. By facing death, we are spurred to life. The year to come will bring death. That is the inescapable certainty that haunts us each Rosh Hashanah and Yom Kippur. Some whom many of us knew who were with us last year are no longer with us. We can be certain that next year too will bring its tragedies. The next year will bring *et* and *pega*, the gradual ebbing of our powers, and the sudden, unfair catastrophe of death. The question, which each of us must answer in the hidden chambers of our souls and our hearts is simply this: knowing that next year will bring death, will we fill our days with the force, the promise, and power of life?

Amen.

Index

Tragedy, God-human relationship
and, 182–188
Truman, Harry, 282–283
Turgenyev, Ivan Sergeyevich, 211

United Nations, 77–78, 173, 177
United States
Jewish identity, 285–294
morality, 141–142
oppression and, 281–284
Universality, community and
individual, 15–19

Villard, Oswald Garrison, 55
Vorspan, Al, 234

Wagner, Robert, 246
Warfare. *See also* Peace
Conservative Judaism, 41–42
faith and, 171–172, 251–258
Iwo Jima military cemetery
dedication, 47–49
technology and, 75
western civilization, 56–57
World War II, 67–70
Waxman, Mordecai, 285–294
Wealth. *See* Economic factors;
Social justice
Weitzman, Chaim, 283
Wellington, Duke of (Arthur
Wellesley), 72

Wertheimer, Jack, 86
Western civilization, warfare,
56–57. *See also* Civilization
Wiesel, Elie, 186, 187–188
Wilson, Woodrow, 68
Winfrey, Oprah, 28
Wise, Isaac Mayer, 196
Wise, Stephen, 196, 197, 200
Wolpe, David J., 295–299
Words, power of, 21–31
World War I, 131–132
World War II. *See also* Holocaust
anti-Semitism, 67–70
immigration, 246
Jewish soldiers in, 288

Xenophobia, politics and, 245

Yehudah, Shmuel, 145
Yetzer, meaning of, 139–140
Yom Kippur
lesson of, 81–83
prayer, 222–224
sermon, 151–158

Zangwill, Israel, 56, 58, 283
Zimmerman, Abraham, 94
Zionism
aliya, 99–107
education and, 254

About the Editor

Rabbi Sidney Greenberg is rabbi emeritus and founding rabbi of Temple Sinai in Dresher, Pennsylvania, where he served from 1942 until his retirement in 1996. He served as Chaplain in World War II and he is the author of many books including, *Words to Live By: Selected Writings of Sidney Greenberg*, *A Treasury of Thoughts on Jewish Prayer*, *In Every Generation: A Treasury of Inspiration for Passover and the Seder*, and *Say Yes to Life: A Book of Thoughts for Better Living*.